Questions That Work

Questions That Work

How to Ask Questions That Will Help You Succeed in Any Business Situation

Andrew Finlayson

AMACOM

American Management Association

New York • Atlanta • Boston • Chicago • Kansas City • San Francisco • Washington, D. C.

Brussels • Mexico City • Tokyo • Toronto

Special discounts on bulk quantities of AMACOM books are available to corporations, professional associations, and other organizations. For details, contact Special Sales Department, AMACOM, a division of American Management Association, 1601 Broadway, New York, NY 10019.
Tel.: 212-903-8316. Fax: 212-903-8083.
Web site: www.amacombooks.org

This publication is designed to provide accurate and authoritative information in regard to the subject matter covered. It is sold with the understanding that the publisher is not engaged in rendering legal, accounting, or other professional service. If legal advice or other expert assistance is required, the services of a competent professional person should be sought.

Library of Congress Cataloging-in-Publication Data

Finlayson, Andrew.
    Questions that work : how to ask questions that will help you succeed in any business situation / Andrew Finlayson.
        p.   cm.
    Includes index.
    ISBN 0-8144-7077-7
    1.   Organizational learning.   2.   Success in business.   I.   Title: Succeed in any business situation.   II.   Title.
    HD58.82 .F56   2001
    650.1—dc21

                                                            00-049578

Printing number

10 9 8 7 6

Contents

Part II: New Work, New Questions

Part III: Questions at Work

Part IV: Crisis Questions

CHAPTER 15: Questions That Work When: You Are Put on the Spot 249

Part V: Questions When on Your Own

CHAPTER 16: Questions That Work When: Starting Your Own Business 271

CHAPTER 17: Questions That Work When: You Are Educating Yourself 289

Part VI: Leaders and Questions

Acknowledgments

There have been many contributors to this book, far too many for me to name in this brief space. Having absorbed questions from or been inspired to ask questions by the hundreds of people interviewed during nearly twenty years of journalism, I find that a list of memorable personalities alone would fill a book.

Because I have turned over this book in my mind many years, it is also impossible to thank all the colleagues who helped me ask better questions. I owe an enormous debt to the staff at KTVU Channel Two, where I have spent the past ten years of my career. In particular, there are two associates I must mention. First is Kevin O'Brien, the general manager of KTVU. His focus on long-term success has been a daily demonstration of the power of questions. I also owe the largest possible debt to Fred Zehnder, the former news director of KTVU. There is no better teacher of journalism than this strong newsroom leader. Anyone who works with Fred learns the power of positive questions, questions that raise one's sights and never lowers one's spirits.

I also have the instructors and classroom colleagues at the Poynter Institute for Media Studies to thank. The institute describes itself as a school for journalism, but this unique resource is far more. It was while I was attending a leadership program at this school that several key ideas for this book came together. The reader will find a wide range of questions from the faculty throughout this book, a tribute to the open dialogue the institute encourages. To my editors at AMACOM, a special thanks to Ellen Kadin and Christina McLaughlin for bringing a first-time author through the complicated birth of this book.

Finally, a very special thanks to my wife, Arleen Bolton. Her experience as a journalist in CBS newsrooms in New York and in Washington,

D.C., and her personal wisdom and patience as a friend encouraged me while this project consumed countless hours. Life, I am learning, is not defined by what you do, but through those people you spend it with. I could hope for no better partner.

Introduction

One reads in order to ask questions.

—Franz Kafka

If an introduction is a conversation between the author and the reader, let me begin with two thoughts:

Those who acquire a questioning attitude will be successful.

Organizations that create a questioning culture will be successful.

Individuals and institutions must ask and encourage others to ask more questions. If you doubt the value of questions, let me argue that when careers collapse, it is often the result of a lack of insightful questioning. When corporations falter, it frequently is a lack of questioning that has brought about the crisis.

Fundamental changes in business are forcing everyone to acquire better questioning skills. Where once executives led tightly organized hierarchies in slowly evolving marketplaces, the pace of business is quickening, and, minute by minute, changes are occurring around the globe. Where once employees followed one career path, now each employee faces a bewildering number of choices. The times demand questioning agility, and the quality and attitude of the questions asked determines corporate and individual success. Leaders must question what their company does and how employees are doing. Individuals must investigate everything from health plans to retirement options.

If a company does not encourage questions, the future of the business will be in jeopardy. If you do not know which questions to ask in critical career and business decisions, your future will be in doubt. While business schools and countless books teach statistics, structures, and strategies of change, they offer precious little instruction or insights into the essential art of question asking. Compounding this, hidden agendas in many organizations mentally assassinate the curious, crushing attempts to create a true and open questioning culture.

The new realities of business demand that everyone sharpen the skills of acquiring information and making decisions.

With the right questions you can:

- Find the right job

- Negotiate the best pay

- Hire the right team

- Find the best negotiation position

- Turn ideas into innovations

- Make the right impression

- Change your organization

- Inspire alternative futures

In an unsentimental world, staying power is increasingly defined by questioning skills.

This volume, I hope, will be an inspiration and essential guide; it aims to be one of the most important volumes in your business library. Each day, you should be involved in at least one conversation or situation that will have you reaching for a suggested question you can ask. The questions in this book are detailed and seek information, give choices, suggest direction, and open new possibilities. The book provides a broad philosophical and a practical approach to asking the right questions in many key business situations. It is designed:

- For those who want to have a game plan for asking questions

- And for those who simply need an adviser at their fingertips to find the best series of questions to ask in many oft-repeated business situations

This book encourages a **positive questioning attitude, awareness, and action.** The positive focus is on questions that do not minimize others' ideas but enlarge and encourage them. The intent is to introduce questions that show interest and the excitement that grows out of the realization that there must be a better way. If you have a positive questioning **attitude** about you at all times, your inquiry can create an **awareness** of people's character and circumstances. In turn, their answers can give direction to your **actions.** Organizations obstruct artful inquiry despite clear evidence that the new realities of business demand that all managers sharpen their skills in acquiring information and making decisions. Flattened corporate structures and rapid communication forces everyone to make quick decisions about the organization and its future. The need for inquiry is all around us and will only grow as formal power continues to dissolve.

The Content

This book was born of a careful examination of the art of asking questions and years of collecting queries. Its goal is to raise your **I.Q.Q.**—intelligent questioning quotient. The volume starts with an overview of the power and art of questions, the obstacles to creating a questioning attitude and culture, and the different types of questions and then goes on to demonstrate how best to ask questions. This discussion is followed by a flow of questions that cover the extent of a career, from finding a job to concluding a lifelong career.

The design of *Questions That Work* advances beyond offering general advice to providing specific inquiries you can apply in your work. The book is organized with cross-reference points to help speed you to the right questions and to make this book as useful and flexible as possible. This pattern of organization quickly creates a chain of questions for almost every major business situation. The questions are designed to go from the general to the specific in a standard deductive approach. You can also take an inductive approach, starting with goals and creatively mixing and matching strategies and questions to achieve them. *Questions That Work* offers the distilled essence of many conversations, specific suggestions, and broad theories. In many cases, different experts offered essentially the same questions. Rather than list all of the contributions, these variations on one question are merged into one ideal, in recognition of a standard question. In organizing the questions, the highest-impact inquiries are generally the first listed.

At the end of specific sets of questions are unique suggestions by select experts on the topic being reviewed. These "Questions That Work" are designed to show how one person uses inquiry as a practical way to home in on needed information. Throughout the book we provide original questions from businesspeople and others; these are titled "Questions That Motivate." While the book is organized around questions you ask others, these are closing thoughts to ask yourself, questions capable of changing how you see yourself, your job, and your organization.

The Research

No theorist, consultant, or specialist in transformation of organizations, I am a journalist who produced the nationally syndicated business program "On the Money" and now serve as news director for KTVU Channel Two in the San Francisco Bay area. Journalism has given me the opportunity to travel the world asking thousands of questions as a reporter/producer and manager in a highly competitive business. Over the years, I have handled union negotiations, participated in industry meetings, and had responsibility for budgets in the many millions of dollars. Broadcast journalism is a hothouse culture where management problems and opportunities grow quickly.

In addition to drawing on my own experiences, *Questions That Work* is based on interviews conducted with a broad range of authors, industry experts, and academics. Over the past twenty years, I've produced interviews with many business leaders, walked the halls of some of the world's cutting-edge companies, and written about the high-tech developments that are shaping our world. It was through these firsthand reports that I first came to appreciate how successful individuals and companies, while different in many respects, almost universally recognized the value of questions and of creating a questioning culture.

Specific research for this book began more than five years ago. I have surveyed everyone from executives of multinational corporations to independent consultants. To broaden the perspective of this book, I have also invited journalists, doctors, and scientists from around the world to contribute what one person called "gnarled knowledge," the careful questions, insights, and wisdom born of firsthand experience.

These contributors encouraged and shaped *Questions That Work*. Almost universally, those surveyed agreed that successful businesses and businesspeople ask and encourage others to ask questions. This may be no surprise; who doesn't use questions? However, they also agreed that there are key differences in how people use questions and that there is a need to further explore the role questioning plays in the workplace. Even some of those who wondered whether most questioning workplace environments are negative agreed that positive questions are a powerful tool in fostering creativity and communication. The art of questions builds a bridge between idealism and realism.

In approaching many of the people I surveyed, I asked variations on one question: What is the value of questions in their own life? The goal was to explore the role of inquiry in their workplace, to identify the best query they ask others, and to determine whether they knew of other people I should be questioning. In many cases, the investigation led away from corporate hallways to entrepreneurs and individuals who consult, coach, and train, all pursuits where inquiry is essential. As with all open and positive questioning, there were no right or wrong answers to my questions; the research invited opinions contrary to this book's thesis.

I quickly came to realize that the topic of questioning in the workplace is charged with politics, negative memories, and a variety of emotions. A few of those contacted used home addresses for fear of probing eyes in the workplace, while others declined to give the name of their company. Yet others provided insights into the process of asking questions in their workplace but asked not to be identified. These fears define the restrictive nature of some organizations and confirm the value of this book as a guide for those who wish to transform negative questioning workplaces into positive ones.

My research also included a review of business books published over a five-year period. I found few books that actively acknowledge the need for a questioning mindset or culture and only a handful that gave any specific techniques for inquiry; rarely did any book index mention the topic of "questions" or "questioning." Despite the clear importance of "asking" in the workplace, research for *Questions That Work* turned up very little material on the topic that is accessible and applicable for the average businessperson.

One point needs to be addressed here. Several academics surveyed thought that *Questions That Work* poses an interesting thesis but wondered whether there is a way to accurately measure an organization's "questioning culture." I considered asking people to rank their questioning ability or to rate the questions in their workplace. Such a survey would give this book the sheen of hard science but, in truth, such an attempt at a scientific survey could not replace actually talking to people. I did randomly cast the net for interviews. Journalists know that simply asking one person to suggest others to contact increases the number of interviews, but they also know that they may end up with answers that are variations on one theme (people generally know others like themselves). For this reason, I sought out a wide range of geographic, socioeconomic, educational, political, and business perspectives. By spreading my research out over several years, I have been careful not to let any short-term trends (such as the birth of the Internet) distort my findings. After a review of the initial survey results, I concluded that there is no one test that can quantify a person's or an organization's questioning ability. It is like measuring leadership; the proof is in the pudding. The best I have been able to do is to arrive at a description of some of the characteristics of people with a questioning spirit and the organizations where positive questioning is more common. It is up to the organization and to each department, office, or individual to determine whether questioning is welcomed and honest answers are given in a particular workplace.

I acknowledge that if one were to ask business leaders to list their top ten challenges, probably not one would answer "a lack of good questions." They would raise issues such as fostering quality, improving communication, inspiring innovation, and identifying and developing new talent. Little wonder. We all want to:

- Be in a workplace where quality is a priority and quality work is rewarded.

- Be heard and hear quickly and clearly needed information.

- Be creative and champion new products and services.

- Be recognized for our potential and taught the skills needed to be more successful.

The invisible but necessary foundation for each of these issues is the quantity and quality of questions we ask and are asked. The volatility of our disjointed society overwhelms and frightens many of us. Inquiry is the most powerful tool we have to help us handle change, become more flexible, and find others who can help us. In the face of a flood of new information and technologies, clear questions focus us and are a vital tool in communicating in the future. For, while information is changing too fast for many of us to keep up, quality questions are eternal and will always be in demand. In chapter 1, I make the case for why individuals, leaders, and institutions need to ask positive questions and encourage others to do the same.

Part I

A Questioning Manifesto

The Essential Skill

Find the right questions. You don't invent the answers, you reveal the answers.

—JONAS SALK[1]

How does a leader know which direction to go?

A great leader maps a course with others, gathering ideas and opinions.

What is the secret to making a deal?

A great negotiator creates breakthroughs by being curious.

Why are some workers highly valued for creativity?

Rising stars discover new ways to solve old problems.

Top leaders, negotiators, and creators are often the men and women who master the art of asking questions. After fifteen years of producing television and radio interviews of many of America's top political and business leaders, I've observed that they all share a desire and an ability to find needed information. These leaders know that questions take many forms, that they can be as precise as a needle pinpointing an important fact or as blunt as a sledgehammer forging change in an organization's direction.

Many achievers early in their careers find that making the right impression depends on the quality of questions they ask. They understand that, no matter what the situation, questions guide our lives. In the business world, where information is the critical commodity, questions filter out noise while focusing on the essential. To use the vocabulary of the day, the most powerful search engines available are other people. No computer is needed to find life-changing answers—just the right question.

For businesses navigating today's rush of commerce, questions are the rudder that gives direction. To survive, businesses must create a positive questioning culture and turn away from strict command-and-control structure. Leadership that constantly looks at its business from a questioning point of view creates a questioning culture. Such inquiry is not a separate function but a part of all functions at all levels all the time. Organizations that attract skilled questioners find an asset of incalculable value that will never show up on a balance sheet.

Asking questions is one universal factor shared by all people at work at all times.

Asking positive questions that lead to action is what *Questions That Work* is all about.

The Case for Having Individuals Ask Positive Questions

It requires a very unusual mind to make an analysis of the obvious.

ALFRED NORTH WHITEHEAD[2]

Like air, questions surround us, an invisible but constant element in conversations we have every day. Anything so common is typically undervalued. The ease of question asking makes most questions seem of little consequence. We do not long consider, nor can we long remember, questions we ask (unless it is the day we ask our lover to marry). However, if you examine your questions, you will find a new way to look at your world and how you act upon its stage. Psychologists see the world through issues of the subconscious; Marxists see the world through the imbalances of capitalism. There is another revolutionary way to see the world and its many different transactions—as a series of questions and answers.

If you take apart your day, you will see that it contains hundreds of internal and external inquiries. Many involve decisions (Do I want this or that?) or evaluations (Is this better than that?), and some simply involve social courtesy (How are you?), but mapping your questions will create an outline of your day. Each question directs the action that follows it. As you look at the questions asked in the workplace, you begin to see the fundamental guiding force they represent. It is this revelation *and* the response of starting to ask the right questions that can dramatically improve your performance and satisfaction.

At first, focusing on your questioning abilities may unsettle you. You are your questions. They show what is important to you, reveal hidden agendas, and publicly illustrate your attitudes toward and insights into others. The questions we ask or *do not ask* tell more about us than we may at first want to know, but, as one journalism professor tells his students, if you can't ask yourself insightful questions, you've no right to ask them of anyone else. Listen carefully to the questions of others; they reveal character and define priorities as quickly and clearly as any other spoken words.

How quickly can you be convinced of the virtue of asking better questions? Here are three short arguments.

Questions Help You to Find Focus

In all affairs it's a healthy thing now and then to hang a question mark on the things you have long taken for granted.

BERTRAND RUSSELL

Questions are an act of the here and now. They force you to be part of the conversation, to make an immediate exchange of ideas, while sharpening your mind to focus on what is wanted. They are the devices we use to sift through each day's conversations, to catch up with what is going on, and to cut through the clutter. If your inquiries become more focused, more productive, so do you. Good questions are tools that provide clarity, direction, and resolution in a confusing world. They combat the slow fading that is forgetting. Consciously and unconsciously, questions represent your desire to bring order to your world.

One virtue of entrepreneurs is their clear focus, symbolized by their persistent inquiries aimed at growing their business. After walking the hallways with these business builders, I have observed that they constantly generate questions, often of themselves. In a time when we all need to act like entrepreneurs, we all need to use questions to prioritize. When pressed from below and needing to manage up, managers use positive questions to find out what their superiors have in mind and what their employees really need. Instead of a "to do" list, consider creating a "to ask" list, to see what questions you really need answers to.

Examining questions that need to be asked suggest what needs to be done.

More Choices, Greater Consequences

The important thing is not to stop questioning. Curiosity has its own reason for existing.

ALBERT EINSTEIN

The increasing complexity of society and the blurring of the boundaries between one's career and one's private life require the focus created by questioning. Once corporations offered a career path that employees followed until their retirement; corporate restructuring now forces thousands of employees to consider their next job. This changing landscape is now a part of everyone's work worlds, even at the most stable of organizations. In the past, companies offered one retirement option. Now most employees make complicated long-term investment decisions, and a wrong decision can have far greater consequences; if one chooses the wrong retirement option, one's "golden years" will be more than tarnished, and they can be stolen. Life *was* simpler ten years and even more so twenty years ago.

Charles Handy in *The Hungry Spirit* speaks of today's greater options (both those desired and those forced on us) when he says, "The real social revolution of the last thirty years, one we are still living through, is the switch from a life that is largely organized for us, once we have opted into it, to a world in which we are all forced to be in charge of our own destiny."[3] How many times have you regretted an action, wishing you had asked one more question? Learning how to ask the right questions may prove the theory that 20 percent of any effort creates 80 percent of the results. To neglect to ask the critical "20 percent questions" may leave you in a job you despise looking forward to a future you dread.

Often there is pressure to make decisions quickly. Overwhelmed by such pressure, we often choose to limit our knowledge, even while knowing impulsive behavior can lead to overconfidence or missteps. The danger today is that every decision is connected to another. Quick sets of questions can help us define decisions and discover what we might have overlooked.

The more choices you face, the more time questions can save you.

Examining the Decisions You Are Making

Not to know is bad; not to wish to know is worse.

                                                                    NIGERIAN PROVERB

More closely examining the inquiries we ask each day has one virtue: It forces us to examine the decisions being made. Imagine having a bank account of questions to ask each day at work. What are you spending that sum on? If it is all going on topics you despise, you'll understand why you dislike your job. Those who are uncomfortable or angry often show it by neglect, by ignoring and not asking questions. If you haven't asked any questions of others about your career path lately, you are show-ing, by this deficit, a dangerous self-satisfaction or a deadly lack of inter-est. If, looking at your daily work habits, you discover that few of the questions you are asking have any long-term consequences, whether about your latest project or about your organization, chances are you are not learning or creating life-changing relationships.

Questions, in short, allow us to redefine what we do and who we are. After years of working in high-pressure workplaces, I've noted that one of the first signs of burnout among workers is often a failure to show curiosity. Bored or tired, people turn off their questions. They stop seek-ing satisfaction at work, for asking questions and receiving meaningful answers is one path to satisfaction. If you can't get meaningful answers to your questions, that may be your best clue that it is time to look for a new opportunity. If you are not asking many questions, you might be comfortable (or pleasantly numb), but are you growing and learning? Are new opportunities passing you by?

Examining your questions requires you to *be aware of what you don't know*. This is difficult but essential to the art of learning and positive questioning. If you think you know *the* answer, you don't look for any other answers. Many of us spend our days jumping to wrong conclusions because we don't know any better than to ask. When a decision turns out to be wrong, we rarely examine what *we didn't ask* that might have protected us from the mistakes. Dig a little deeper, and you will find the underlying cause of many avoidable disappointments are those questions that were missing in action.

Questions pry open problems.

Questions Help You Become More Flexible

A prudent question is one-half of wisdom.

FRANCIS BACON

Questions move you forward and give direction, even when you don't have a map and have no final destination in mind. Those moving from job to job, career to career, need to accelerate their ability to learn. While books are invaluable, the nitty-gritty of learning occurs firsthand, up close and personal, where inquiry is essential. As the work world moves toward an increasing emphasis on short-term projects and problem-solving teams, question asking becomes a key skill for those who need to be flexible in a changing environment. This flexibility comes from three abilities nurtured by *Questions That Work.*

Ability to Respond under Pressure

We should not only master questions, but also act upon them, and act definitely.

WOODROW WILSON

You offer the world skill, knowledge, and desire. All these are useless unless applied to the situation you or your organization is facing. Your ability to respond to the world around you and to produce something of value is your talent, what you have to sell, and so your skills must be up to date. Questions are the way to acquire the twin qualities of resourcefulness and readiness. While resourceful people may not know the answer to a problem, they are ready to deal with any situation and confident of their ability to find a solution by asking the right questions. They are confident that their inquiries will identify what has changed in the situation and what requires their response.

The widespread availability of information makes facts cheap but understanding dear. We have entered what some call the "light revolution" because information and business now move at the speed of light. As one survey respondent, Gary Lockwood, put it, "Answers have a very short shelf life."[4] Questions can help us keep up with the changes, for, as Samuel Johnson wrote, "Knowledge is of two kinds. We know a subject ourselves, or we know where we can find information upon it." *Questions That Work* gives strategies for finding information needed in a wide range of situations. In many cases, questions are needed most in moments of adversity, when the true abilities of an employee come out. Questioning employees, when faced with a situation where acting quickly is important, ask themselves and others variations on this question: "What moves can we make?" When you look at those who are thriving in this new era of information and speed, you'll notice one common theme:

Grace under pressure is knowing what questions to ask.

Ability to Find Problem-Solving Insights

Good questions outrank easy answers.

PAUL SAMUELSON

The vast realm of problem-solving techniques defies description. However, most problem-solving techniques share a simple enough question-and-answer pattern; who, what, why, where, and when questions define the trouble, while follow-up questions cut the issue into small slices that can be digested more easily.

I am convinced much of the problem solving going on today has one fundamental flaw—the essential question (the problem statement) being considered is rarely given enough thought. Often the larger, more profound question about direction or desired long-term result is ignored, while a temporary crisis is dealt with. This neglect continues, so the same crisis recurs in a dozen different colors until someone finally decides to examine the underlying cause. When a possible solution is discovered, questions also enable you to negotiate successfully on what you've learned. While you may know what you want, it is only through careful positive questioning and acknowledging of answers that you can discover other parties' true needs and constraints. Even the implementation of many simple solutions requires negotiation. No solution works in isolation; you must always consider other questions and decisions.

Despite being rarely mentioned in job descriptions, most workers know that problem solving is a required skill at work. Big or small, problems are a constant. As I once was told, "You'll never be without problems; you can only hope for better ones." We all need a little art of the diagnostician in us. A diagnosis is, after all, an analysis of the cause of a problem. Chapter 3 and chapter 13 examine the ways that questions in a certain order and perspective can probe complex problems, even those that stretch out over years.

Questions are the catalyst you use to create a solution when you are shaking and stirring a problem.

Ability to Cope with Inconsistencies and Ambiguities

There is only one thing about which I'm certain, there is very little about which one can be certain.

SOMERSET MAUGHAM

By posing a question, one begins to sacrifice assumptions and admits ambiguity into the discussion. Starting a flow of questions and answers opens the door to contradictions. The positive questioner is secure enough to admit to being uncertain and open enough to embrace contrary opinions that might be the answer. It is a thought mirrored across the centuries by Francis Bacon: "If a man will begin with certainties, he shall end in doubts; but if he will be content to begin with doubts, he shall end in certainties." Embracing uncertainty and contradictory opinions requires you to operate across apparently disconnected planes of thought. You can use questions to find relationships between ideas that are neither sequential nor directly connected.

This open mode of thinking may well prove to be one of the essential attitudes of our time. Since so many problems defy simple solutions, creative problem solving is needed. When faced with a dilemma, you should, in fact, intentionally pose vague questions, for too much precision during inquiry can become a problem if it shuts off odd thoughts and off-the-wall ideas. Often the best questions occur when we don't know enough to ask exact questions. Ambiguity and inconsistency are hobgoblins in many workplaces, but, if no one panics, uncertainty can be an inspiration for creative inquiry. Those who are comfortable asking questions can operate in the vague environment where breakthroughs occur on the far edges of what is certain. The connection between creativity and curiosity is explored later in this chapter and in chapter 9.

Questions give you the ability to sail safely in a sea of uncertainty.

Questions Help You Force Action

The great end of life is not knowledge but action.

THOMAS HUXLEY

If asking questions can be a constant form of self-renewal, it is also an inspiration for action. Questions are a call for a response from someone. The answer we receive should propel us to some reaction. Good questions have a creating energy and, as such, inspire new opportunities. Not surprisingly, that's why some people are reluctant to pose thoughtful questions; they are afraid the answers will force them to rethink their current situation.

Questions rock the boat. An inscription on the walls of the Library of Congress honors this thought in gilt letters: "Words are a kind of action and action a kind of word." Questions are certainly a form of action. In the right hands, they are the primary tools to craft knowledge, define power, and forge equality. This is particularly true in today's information age. The future belongs to those businesses that add value to information, where company assets drive off in the evening commute.

The future of business lies in thought and communication. While human innovations speed the communication of ideas, one of the few tools all of us have to speed the creation and implementation of those ideas is the effective use of inquiry.

Over the ages and to this day, the positions that carry the most prestige are often those where questions of import are the key to action. Judges, doctors, and executives are valued by society for their knowledge and judgment. Their wisdom becomes clear in the questions they ask. Those who know how to ask the right questions at the right time, will, like flint to stone, spark opportunity.

Just proposing a question does not solve any problem. Collecting information is often used as a substitute for deciding what to do. The reason this often occurs is that we don't know what to ask. The right questions can snap the spiral of endlessly gathering information. If nothing else, the right questions can help put an end to all the meetings that end without decisions. Questions that attack problems are explored in chapter 13.

Planning questions ahead leads to action afterward.

Attacking the Unknown

I know well what I am fleeing from but not what I am in search of.
MICHEL DE MONTAIGNE

The subconscious fears the unknown giving birth to apprehension and anxiety. When such fears remove freedom of action, questions restore it by giving a sense of security by offering options and information. If positive questioning is the weapon to fight fear, why do so many people fail to use it? One reason is that, in a world filled with growing time demands and complexity, many people don't want to have another "learning" opportunity. They turn away new challenges or new responsibilities. Rather than know whether a merger is to occur, with the risk that their division might be eliminated, they accept whatever may happen. These are people who are comfortable or numb. For such passive participants, to continuously assimilate and organize new information is not only a drain on energy and time but also an unconscious struggle with their fear of the unknown.

On the other hand, curious souls, questioners, are like searchlights, flashing their questions all around themselves. Continuous inquiry lights up the dark around them. For those who fear the unknown, *Questions That*

Work gives you confidence to go into these unexplored areas. The difference between feeling excitement or anxiety can be confidence created by the quality of questions. The most enjoyable and effective questions come from an excitement about *learning,* not from the anxiety of *not knowing.* Those who believe they are asking meaningful questions become much more excited about asking them. In addition, questions leverage the information you have. You may not know the exact answer you are after, but chances are you know enough to ask intelligent questions. A little information can, with a question, turn into all you need to know.

The speed of change today is constantly creating new frontiers of uncertainty. We have to accept this. The world has seen countless revolutions and will continue to see them in the future and as technology constantly reinvents itself, the future becomes more difficult to predict. For these reasons, the past is not always an accurate guide to what lies ahead. Questions that create knowledge are examined in chapter 18.

Better questions yield better information.

Why Executives and Leaders Need to Ask Better Questions

Reason and judgment are the qualities of a leader.

TACITUS

I have found that there is a growing agreement that leaders are those who ask questions. The management gurus Tom Peters and Peter Drucker have shared two thoughts on this subject. Peters has said that leaders have to ask the right questions. Drucker has said that the leader of the past is a person who knows how to tell and that the leader of the future will be the person who knows how to ask. One survey respondent, Dr. Marilyn Hamilton, says that her doctoral research on learning and leadership in self-organizing systems (researching an online community experiment) has shown that leaders ask more questions than other participants.[5]

Certainly, the leaders of today need to learn much faster than those of a decade ago. Every successful manager needs to constantly be adding to his or her arsenal of ideas. Besides meeting their own individual learning needs, leaders have the additional responsibility to reach out beyond their own concerns to learn about and live the concerns of their team, division, or organization. Executives' roles are many: leader, manager, and facilitator.

How can the leader embody the idea of one representing many? It often comes down to asking questions. Yet most leaders have received little or no training in asking questions when they first step into the manager's role. While some organizations invest in teaching management basics and strategic planning, often new managers have only the skills they had the day before they took on the job. There is no cheat sheet for leadership. Given the implications of wrong decisions by leaders, it's surprising how little consideration is given to teaching the skills of questioning and information gathering to new managers.

Like any other management tool, inquiry can be abused by leaders who seek to tightly control, rather than to liberate. Too often, new managers see questions as a tool of surveillance and inquisition. This leads to negative question asking, setting up an endless cycle of defensive responses and distrust. Chapter 2 explores more of the obstacles that lie in the path of those who want to create a positive questioning culture.

To Become More Connected to the Organization
What do I know?

MICHEL DE MONTAIGNE

As business is a shared experience made up of the relationships between people, questions are an essential tool for making those connections count. Much of today's management is isolated, performed inside a bunker created by corporate culture and physically distant from the front-line workers and customers. Leaders who want to find out what is going on find they need to get out and find time to question their people. You might think of these questions as taking the pulse of a company. With regular checks, the leader can feel if the organization's heartbeat is strong and regular or fading fast. Just as doctors value the stethoscope because it brings them physically close to their patients, beginning an intimate conversation, executives will find that inquiry invites a dialogue with their employees. The very act of asking a concerned question changes the relationship between employer and employee, creating a more empathetic and egalitarian workplace. It gives the employee the chance to give his or her side of the story and the knowledge that his or her voice is being listened to. That meets a need greater than almost any other in the workplace—the need to be heard. Executives known for managing by walking around are making this connection. At Hewlett-Packard, this "open door" policy was key. David Packard said, it "was a policy in which any employee could call a higher officer in the company, or actually call Bill [Hewlett] and me if he wanted to and through that we always got a good reading on what was going on in the company."[6] It is a matter of becoming aware of what your company is doing and why. As was engraved at the temple of Apollo at Delphi, "know thyself."

When a leader asks meaningful questions, he or she is looking for both facts *and* feelings. This is perhaps one of the most difficult management tasks. An open and curious executive who asks questions welcomes threatening facts and negative emotions. Constant inquiry serves as a wake-up call, keeping managers from ignoring the feelings and perspectives of others. The problems facing any organization are not going to go away on their own, but the right questions can discover them before they become life threatening. As IBM's legendary CEO Thomas Watson Jr. once put it, "You don't hear things that are bad about your company unless you ask. It is easy to hear good tidings, but you have to scratch to get the bad news."[7]

An executive should (but often doesn't) know exactly what the company is responding to, what changes need to be made, and where resources would be best spent. Executives who ask questions only when they think they know the answer may well miss those questions that could reveal the hidden danger that days, weeks, or years later will become a corporate crisis. As a manager, if I don't ask questions and listen, I don't get bad news until it is really bad. It may sound like a paradox, but even though managers are rarely the first to see a problem, they have to be among the first to realize how serious a problem is, given the larger picture.

Asking people how things are going is only the beginning of making these connections. As the stress levels rise and the pace of work increases, the role of the leader as social worker grows. Executives are building not only an organization but a community where people know and trust one another. Questions bring out what drives people and what gives them satisfaction. Finding out about values and priorities and detecting differences of opinion takes time. This probing is all the more important when problems are deep below the surface. Questions discover pressures, rivalries, and buried animosities. While dissecting organizational social structures can be delicate work, it makes all the difference in improving relationships and helping make sure the corporate nervous system that passes along important messages is working. Like the nervous system of the human body, managers hope their organization will rapidly transfer important information via a seamless network. Conversational questions speed that transfer because verbal communications usually occur far more quickly than anything written down. Timely information in the right hands creates decision-making power.

The quicker the answer, the faster the organization.

To Create a Motivational Environment

An effective leader will . . . ask questions instead of giving direct orders.
DALE CARNEGIE[8]

Should a leader care about how employees spend their days, care to find out how they feel about their work? A cynical manager would answer yes, because happy workers are more productive workers. A caring manager would answer yes, because work offers all an opportunity to grow and together achieve great things.

Are companies supposed to achieve great things? As dominant social organizations of our day (and as the place where most of us spend eight or more hours a day), corporations are more influential in our lives than many older institutions in society. One would hope every job has dignity and that any group can work toward a greater good, no matter the service or product. This need to provide a larger vision has led many companies to create written statements of purpose. Is there a company where a mission statement is as powerful as leadership that simply encourages inquiries about the company's vision and values? No piece of paper can compare with the powerful social role a curious and questioning leader can create.

The leader has to speak up for standards, question how people can reach them, probe why failures occur, and motivate people to reach for their own solutions. This role of facilitator is one that requires positive questions that keep conversations or meetings on track without dominating the creation of ideas. It is essential to create a feeling among employees that they are to take responsibility for their actions and have ownership of their accomplishments. Questions help people learn how their small successes of today lead to the big victories tomorrow.

Bringing the art of positive question asking into a business is one of the most powerful tools for developing the potential of the leaders on all levels. For as any Sunday school teacher knows, if you give emerging leaders answers to issues, they will always need to be fed. If you teach them to question, they will never go hungry for knowledge.

Questions bring a certain vitality to any conversation. Positive questions motivate by leading to focus and flexibility. These qualities help individuals and institutions move with purpose, engendering the feeling that circumstances can change for the better and something is getting done. Managers can use inquiry like a coach to encourage players to find their best technique. Questions encourage another coachable quality, one that involves being willing to change, to be flexible. Like athletes, if your employees are inflexible and can't handle the stress of sudden change in direction and acceleration, they will get hurt.

There is no better weapon and shield against cynicism than questions. There are few better inspirations for intensity of effort than well-used inquiry. The challenge managers face daily is how to tinker with the questions in their mental tool box so that they use the right ones with each person, find the capabilities of each person, tap those talents, and then find how patterns of high performance can be sustained. No one knows what dormant abilities or energies lie in people until a leader encourages everyone to question standards and expectations. With today's emphasis on teamwork, questions are a motivational necessity, one we explore in later chapters. If you want to get people's juices flowing, get a relationship on the right track, or create a new dynamic in doing old work, there is one point to remember:

Asking is better than telling.

To Encourage the Search for New Questions

Ignorance never settles a question.

BENJAMIN DISRAELI

The concept of "out-of-the box thinking" is well worn. Let's retire it and instead better define the challenge as *the search for new questions*. Questions can stimulate the unorthodox thinking necessary to keep an organization growing and healthy. As one survey respondent aptly expressed it, leaders know they must use questions not just to generate *answers* but to reveal *what is possible*. Asking original questions will be a new concept for employees who for years have done only what they have been told to do.

They might not be comfortable exploring the purpose, the process, or the roles of other people in the company. To overcome employees' suspicion, leaders have to testify in favor of the necessity of questioning and the benefits offered and must create an environment that supports those who are interested in discovering new ideas. Leaders can then use questions to begin the critical process of setting objectives, creating goals, and giving direction. As Bruce Ganem, the J. Thomas Clark Professor of Entrepreneurship at Cornell University, put it, successful companies are constantly on the lookout for new opportunities, "since standing still inevitably means falling behind."[9] Robert Grady, managing director, The Carlyle Group, says that, instead of describing a business as having a questioning culture, he would say it has a flexible culture: "They sometimes realize that radical change is necessary for true greatness."[10] In my own company, there is no suggestion box, but we provide a question box, and anyone can submit questions for our most senior executive to answer publicly. In the search for new ideas, inquiry gives you an ever-changing tool.

Questions are the links in a never-ending chain of progress.

Why Organizations Need to Encourage Better Question Asking

Intelligence is quickness to apprehend.

ALFRED WHITEHEAD

Is respect for inquiring minds woven into the fabric of your organization? I've outlined the benefits to the individual and the necessity for leaders to study and apply positive questions. It follows, then, that all institutions, made up of many combinations of individuals, can share these advantages. If corporations are to be treated as the living organisms they are legally defined as, then each business has a psychological profile, a way it "thinks." Like an individual, to be successful it must acquire a questioning attitude. Many of the world's leading companies share this virtue, and some even organize around it. They recognize that questions are the pulses that push vital information throughout the corporate body. A failure to encourage questions is one of the clearest signs that a corporation is unbalanced. The management theorist Peter Senge has said that one key way he knows a management team is in trouble is that, over the course of a several-hours-long meeting, no questions are raised.

To Become a Learning Organization

The ability to learn faster than your competitors may be the only sustainable competitive advantage.

ARIE DE GEUS

Dr. Rey Carr, a peer-counseling authority who has helped teach young people how to ask each other questions, said his reaction to the idea of successful organizations having a questioning culture is that they really have a "learning culture."[11] Certainly, if you want to become more focused, more action oriented, and more flexible, your values must encourage learning. John Tessier, an executive strategist, says that leaders need to recognize that a "knowing" organization is prototypical of a failed organization. Such organizations believe that all the information needed is inside the organization already.[12] With more and more businesses based on ownership of intellectual property instead of the mortar and brick factory buildings, businesses need to have a strategy for acquiring specialized knowledge inside and outside the company. A fundamental resource issue today is brainpower. True, companies can always go out and hire those with the knowledge and the intellect to use it, but that neglects the potential value of the assets already with the organization, the minds of those working there. Positive questioning cultures recognize that everyone should be learning for a living, that constant inquiry educates, enlightens, and even inspires.

After all the research into the brain, with all the high-tech scans and studies of chemistry, medical science has few useful insights into how people learn. Going from the time of Aristotle to the classroom of today's business schools, it can be argued that the most efficient learning takes place in a direct question-and-answer style. The former IBM executive Sam Albert says that questions give you "knowledge you can't learn any other way."[13] For, while books, lectures, and direct observation are time-valued learning techniques, at the heart of the most concentrated learning is the questions we ask. The best inquiry is immediate, important, and influential because it matters to us. New concepts make clearer connections in our head when we ask questions and get direct answers. By asking questions, we are rethinking what we know, making it part of us. Often we ask questions to confirm, to give us confidence in our standing. This is why computers have failed to some degree as learning tools; they can drill formulas but cannot yet directly answer the often convoluted questions of the human mind. This is also why consultants and speakers brought into a workplace often fail to change the workplace culture. They present information, but if employees can't actively and extensively question the new concepts, they cannot clearly embrace it and make it their own.

Managers have many reasons for supporting questioning as a learning tool, including a personal one. Peter Senge argues that "as managers rise to senior positions, they confront issues more complex and diverse than their personal experience. Suddenly they need to tap insights from other people. They need to learn."[14] Managers are leading a new movement in business, what a survey by Robert Half International calls a move from "what can I earn" to "what can I learn."[15] No doubt many managers are self-starters when it comes to gathering information, for rising in any business requires one to become a lifelong learner. This passion for new insights needs to spread throughout a business; for as the authors Kenneth R. Hey and Peter D. Moore argue, "knowledge is information in context."[16] The alternative to questioning is the deadly certainty that "we already know it all," which is fatal to learning.

Encouraging inquiry opens the door to play, for curiosity is the connection between playing and learning. Arie De Geus, head of Planning for Royal Dutch/Shell, believes that play is the best way to learn.[17] When you play with a toy, there is no winning or losing; there is only fun and learning. When you are playful, you are open to questioning, because you feel no harm or danger from others' inquiry. This is one of the neglected values of sports, music, and arts in our schools. The play they encourage creates a safe atmosphere of questioning without boundaries. Playful learning is neglected in the workplace because so much of the traditional focus of learning is on the young. The vital issue of how organizations can encourage learning/question asking is explored in chapter 3.

Asking questions makes ideas your own.

To Encourage Cooperation

An idea is a feat of association.

ROBERT FROST

One misconception about questioning is that it is confrontational, win or lose. Such an interpretation depends on the atmosphere the two parties create, their history and personalities. Inquiry creates a level of broad understanding, one of the vital ingredients in cooperation. The business adviser and survey respondent Mike Montefusco says that companies achieve success because they have everybody "pulling on the same rope, in the same direction, at the same time."[18] For this reason, Montefusco urges individuals not to make key decisions "without considering the unique perspectives, experiences and abilities of others."[19] Well-crafted questions create that context, the expectation of sharing information. In this way, positive questions build relationships, instead of straining them. This idea of using questions to create cooperation may be a new one to you. Let's further define how the virtues of questions can foster cooperation.

All business relationships have more than one aspect. They can involve many levels of needs and wants. These can be fully explored only if both parties are open-minded and interested, in other words, open to questions and answers. Questions provide the gentle heat that melds different groups into one larger unit. Successful organizations understand that employees must have an awareness of the wider environment in which they operate. The very nature of a concerned and aware question can help any team leader work through and with others. After attending a number of exercises where groups of people were expected to come together quickly and work, I've found that the groups that "bonded" most efficiently were those whose leaders informally enforced a time (often during group dinners) where mutual question asking was possible in a low-stress environment. The simple process of casually interviewing others about where they are from and exploring their feelings about the project creates a flow of information that cements relationships. A team that is beginning to work together has to learn how to ask questions together. Imagine a group where inquiry is used simply to one-up other people or to put others down. Trust is the first victim of such an antagonistic environment. Hostility often shows itself in blocked communication that dams up the flow of information.

Without questions there is no true cooperation, only compliance.

To Inspire Creativity

Creative thinking may mean simply the realization that there's no particular virtue doing things the way they always have been done.

RUDOLF FLESCH

One of the most pressing goals for teamwork is growing a group's creativity. For, while we may think of creativity as the result of a single person's thoughts, creativity becomes more active and useful when it is a shared process. Positive questioning triggers the creative process, just as it inspires problem solving (the two often intersect). We all need to generate new and useful ideas every day, but very few of us have had training in creativity. That's not to say it can't be learned. There are any number of books, theories, and games you can try to inspire creativity. The best creativity concepts share "what if" questions and attitudes that together bring fresh connections and possibilities.

The heart of creativity is to question what is, leading to what could be. One training consultant, Margie Sweeny, says that questioning cultures are engaging in dialogue, "holding ideas out separate from themselves, brainstorming, suspending judgement."[20] It's been said that the process of creating is asking a thousand questions and being ready to have many of them go unanswered. If we look back in time, even over our own lives, bursts of creativity came about when questioning led to the creation of new ideas, new ways of looking at the world. Jerry Hirshberg, a car designer and author of *The Creative Priority*, argues that creative questions must precede creative answers. He says these questions are the ones that reframe problems, triggering a reconsideration of traditional attitudes. If you've ever been in the midst of a truly creative session with questioning minds, you know this can be a messy process, filled with speculation and confusion. Hirshberg alludes to this when he says, "A fine way to judge whether a situation is likely to provide original thinking is to assess the character of the questions arising. If they are erudite, firmly grounded, eloquent and well-considered, it is a good bet there will be no new ideas."[21]

While we may assume creativity is an unofficial, unmeasurable activity, it can be officially encouraged and defined by leaders who stimulate a questioning atmosphere. Combinations of people and problems can be brought together with the opportunity to ask about one another's points of view. Some creative groups support creativity by providing toys, games, and magazines, all with the idea that these diverse stimuli will trigger people to ask questions of themselves and others. Odd things can happen when you start to mix up products and services, capital and people, traditionally separate concepts that can be blended with the right questions. The authors Don Peppers and Martha Rogers argue, "Again and again, economists, business consultants, and other students of free market systems have concluded that the *ability* to innovate is more important to a firm's long-term survival and prosperity than any particular innovation."[22] In a world where many products and services are turning into commodities, all businesses need to question how they can be, as the TV consultant Mackie Morris once called it, "distinctively better."[23]

Finding a new big idea has become very complex. It's rarely an idea one person can exclusively express or take on alone. Encouraging inquiry will capture and connect good ideas to create a killer concept. A free exchange of ideas is no good unless the creative potential can be turned into creative performance. Inquiry that inspires new thinking is outlined in chapter 9.

Questions promote creative connections.

To Attract Better Employees

I not only use all the brains I have, but all I can borrow.

WOODROW WILSON

While few organizations argue against the value of creativity and a questioning mind, it is amazing how few search for these qualities in their employees. Instead, many simply recruit the A students, those best at taking tests but often not best at asking questions. There is perhaps only one link between scholastic achievement and question asking; feeling smart gives one the confidence to ask one's questions. Still, we all know of the bright grind who prospers in the classroom and in life by not questioning authority. Hiring bright but unquestioning employees creates a corporation of yes men and women. Those who ask powerful questions may not politically prosper among such conforming colleagues and will likely have to leave such an environment. That is a loss for the organization. Asking questions shows excitement and involvement, both of which lead to energy and commitment, two of the key qualities of good employees.

Questions often come from differences, and so it's important that managers look for and recruit people with different priorities and work styles. A diverse atmosphere open to the free flow of ideas will uncover hidden assets. Employees who are able to find out why they are being asked to do something can often find a better way to do it. If they feel free to be themselves by asking questions and not just going along, they will be happier and more focused. Creating this sort of environment depends on rewarding employees who do ask questions; otherwise, those with the courage and the confidence to question will move to organizations that welcome a positive questioning attitude. The reputation of a group can in large part be judged by its ability to attract quality employees. If a leader asks, "How do we make ourselves more desirable to the best employees available?" the answer should include "Create a questioning culture." You want employees who, if nothing else, will be loyal to the idea of doing quality work. To do quality work, you have to ask questions.

Quality employees ask questions.

To Become More Efficient

To find the exact answer, one must first ask the exact question.
S. TOBIN WEBSTER

If information is the fuel of a company, inquiry is the spark that turns that information into energy. The better the questions, the bigger the bang. Such explosive energy is needed for successful organizations to operate at top speed and efficiency. What makes a workplace efficient? Number crunching is often seen as the essence of efficiency. It is the way companies handle matters of complexity, analyzing feasibility, risk, and price, but above all the numbers, true efficiency is found through a questioning culture where "a company regularly seeks clarity around issues."[24] Creating a clear picture of what is happening to you and around you is the best way to focus on the key question, "How does our business make money?" When you use questions to look into that question, you can be far more efficient in managing your resources, including the invisible but priceless one of time. It is a question of encouraging the group to constantly "tweak the mission." The consultant and survey respondent Diana Whitney summed it up by saying that questions set an organization's agenda for action.[25]

What makes workers efficient? In the days of assembly lines, it was the speed of performing a repeated physical process. Today, efficiency requires quick learning, focused filtering of information, clear decision making, and the ability to anticipate problems, all while following through on a long list of goals. Each of those elements of efficiency requires questioning as a foundation. As organizations use more self-managed teams, information no longer moves from top down; instead, it flows in complicated lateral exchanges where informal inquiries direct information more effectively than traditional authority. To have such flexibility, an organization needs to treat information as life-giving fluid circulating around all the employees. Curious individuals must be encouraged to use questions to pump the blood of information throughout the group to keep it alive and growing.

Extensive sharing of information throughout an organization increases efficiency because more employees can respond to customer needs and handle any crisis. Prominent organizations are often distinguished by leadership that encourages the sharing of information. They also use questions to wash away the muddy language that swirls around so many conference rooms and blocks the flow of useful insights. Indeed, inquiry also serves to preserve the independent spirit so important in a time of change. To be efficient, an organization must be able to rapidly respond to the environment. The author Kevin Kelly warns that the more integrated an institution is, the harder it is to change because of the interdependent coordinated nature of the company.[26] Avoiding institutional gridlock is one reason for the popularity of experimenting with decentralization.

Managers often worry about how to distribute time among talking on the phone, attending meetings, reading, writing, and dictating. These daily duties distract from the larger issues that need to be tackled. As I've argued, looking at the big picture often has to do with asking meaningful questions. Long-term efficiency is often the product of constantly asking and reasking, "What's the best way to do it?"

A key example of the relationship between inquiry and efficiency is hiring new employees. Some might see an efficient hiring as one that quickly runs through a number of interviews to find an acceptable candidate. This confuses speed with long-term consequences. In reality, an efficient hiring often involves extensive interviewing of a number of candidates to identify the very best prospect. If this top candidate takes the job, stays with the organization, and actively contributes and grows in ability, he or she represents a truly efficient hiring.

Efficiency results when the right question is asked at the right place and time.

To Support Conflict Resolution

As a general rule, if you want to get at the truth—hear both sides and believe neither.

JOSH BILLINGS

No organization can run a steady course without periods of conflict. Questions can provide the compass to navigate through these inevitable storms and help leaders create a culture that can cope with confusion.

Many people associate question asking with conflict. Questions are often seen as a challenge; after all, they can present an opposing point of view. The mind, like a computer, seems to be deeply programmed to resist input that conflicts with existing data. When there are different approaches to an issue, the natural impulse of people is to protect their long-held beliefs, to engage in endless face-saving. The secret of positive questions is that they do not perpetuate this game and instead use the question-and-answer process to gently open minds.

One neglected measure of the health of an organization is how well it deals with differences amicably, without a breakdown. Questions can help defuse conflicts and any contest of wills before emotions are entangled and a battle begins. They can do so by helping people probe the other parties' underlying interests and not just their stated positions. For one of the best summaries of this concept, explore Roger Fisher and William Ury's book *Getting to Yes,* where these two experts in negotiating urge those engaged in negotiation jujitsu to use inquiry instead of statements. "Statements generate resistance, whereas questions generate answers. Questions allow the other side to get their points across and let you understand them. They pose challenges. Questions offer them no target to strike at, no position to attack. Questions do not criticize, they educate."[27]

Asking questions can turn conflict resolution into long-term conflict reduction.

. . . .

Questions That Motivate

Be outrageous. What do you really want?
                              Peter Fahrenkamp[28]

. . . .

Chapter 1 Conclusion

Ideas into Action

Leo Tolstoy's fable called *The Three Questions* tells of a king who decides to reward anyone who can teach him how to answer the three most important questions. He wants to know how to tell the right time for every deed, how to know who are the most essential people, and how to decide which pursuits are the most important. Many people give so many conflicting answers to these essential questions that the king is driven to seek the wisdom of an old man. The king slowly learns lessons all questioners should embrace. The king learns the most important time is *now*. The most important person is *the one you are with*. The most important pursuit is *to do good to that person*. A positive questioning culture recognizes that immediacy, that focus, and that caring quality.

Questioning and creating a questioning culture in the workplace can help you take back your soul. There are few philosophical approaches that can create such direct and immediate results in your life as adopting positive questions. Encouraging individual and institutional inquiry inspires constructive conversations while cultivating the twin virtues of attention and accuracy. Positive questions develop your judgment and allow you to better turn your experience, imagination, and ideas into effective action. The most important result is the creation of respect. The theme of this chapter is the importance of creating relationships where each party is empowered and where respectful questions and answers create powerful personal and professional interactions. In chapter 2, we look at the obstacles that stand in the way of all inquiry.

Why We Don't Ask Questions

If I only had the right question. . . . If I only had the right question. . . .

—ALBERT EINSTEIN[1]

Asking questions is easy; asking the right questions is hard. Peter Drucker once said that "the most common source of mistakes in management decisions is the emphasis on finding the right answer rather than the right question."[2] There is much to be said about how little time business executives put into considering questions to which they want answers. They skip over the most difficult part of inquiry, which is turning over in their mind what constitutes the big picture before identifying the critical insight they need. Asking any questions takes time, and articulating a positive question requires thought, two resources many managers have in short supply. There are other obstacles, some obvious and some subtle, to constructive queries. What follows are the most frequent hurdles to honest and open inquiry in the workplace and our personal lives. My definitions of these barriers come from firsthand observation and examination using questions such as:

- Who are you?

- What are your disappointments?

- How would you improve your question asking?

When people talk about the trouble they are having getting something done at work, they sometimes describe the effort as jumping through hoops. Those hoops are often obstacles to asking questions and getting answers. If organizations hire employees for no purpose but to be productive, and if productivity is so closely linked to inquiry, why do so many managers seem to try to keep their people obediently unquestioning? Yet showing curiosity is often seen in a negative light, and institutions of all sizes discourage questioning.

Fear of Being in Trouble

No man really becomes a fool until he stops asking questions.

Charles Steinmetz

When something goes wrong, a rain of queries can start to fall. Almost any problem is soon followed by a dozen questions about why, where, when, and how something went wrong. The association begins in people's minds:

> problems = questions

> failures = questions

In any workplace, you will be asked provoking and incriminating questions. Typically the probe will focus on figures and specific facts (costs, participants, and deadlines) where a manager can pin blame on someone. There is no "taking the fifth" in the office. We are all battle scarred by Inquisition-like examinations by teachers, relatives, or employers and have a reflexive resistance to being interrogated. Even a question by a spouse about a tie or dress can trigger insecurity (Why are you wearing that?). Such innocent-sounding questions imply all is not right. Ask anything and the other party is automatically on guard in case the concern behind your question personally involves them. The psychological pressure created by negative inquiry is simple; it often makes you feel that someone is trying to gain control over your life. Skilled questioners know they must be very careful; one barbed question can bloody an entire conversation. The art of positive questioning is to respect while you inspect, so that inquiries do not intimidate or manipulate.

Fear of Confrontation

When your argument has little or no substance, abuse your opponent.

Cicero

When you seek information, you risk ego-bruising confrontations. First, the other person may reject your query. We've all had managers who show their power by ignoring any question. Higher in rank, they do not have to acknowledge or answer you and, even more frustrating, they can dismiss questions as unimportant. These intimidating and unchallengable personalities are found in every workplace. Bosses often make it clear they share the sentiments of a character in the movie *Chinatown,* Evelyn Mulwray, who said, "I am far more interested in what I have to say than what you have to say." Managers and coworkers who can't ignore another person's inquiries can reject questions by staging fits of anger or blustering to dissuade others from further investigation. Such behavior can be automatic among managers who make rules for others, yet break rules themselves. Question killers can also stifle curiosity and openness with obtuse or bureaucratic answers.

Those who fear conflict discourage discussion. The resulting tension creates a corrosive effect, eating away under the apparently calm surface of any relationship. In many organizations, the tolerance for conflict drops as one goes higher in the structure. This climate of fear leads to the creation of yes men who bite their tongues rather than contradict the boss (and risk their big salaries and perks). The rank-and-file can often quiz others more freely than the senior v.p. All one has to do is remember the story of the emperor with no clothes to find a story of the power of the powerless to question.

Why Can't You Ask Your Boss a Question?

A wise man's question contains half the answer.

SOLOMON IBN GABIROL

Consider the last meeting you attended with senior executives in your workplace. Did anyone in a junior position seriously question the senior executive's opinions? The answer should be no surprise, given the intimidating tones of many senior managers and their unspoken expectation of good news. Such circumstances create managers with fixed-grin charm but an almost complete inability to cope with controversy. Too often managers' expectations of communication remind one of the propaganda put out in totalitarian states, which the writer Gerald Butt said has the intention of "distract(ing) the public from the real conditions and discourage debate, anything that might encourage criticism."[3] Propaganda is the opposite of questioning; the more propaganda one sees in the workplace, the less likely the workplace is to be open to inquiry.

These brutal and brutalizing pressures can also be created by supervisors who pepper their staff with negative questions.

Some managers see active questioning in the workplace as a threat to formality and an affront to the respect they feel they are due. There was once a report about Prince Charles that reminded me of some executives I've met. "Can we ask His Highness a question?" someone shouted. "No," hissed Peter, one of his three umbrella-wielding, pin-striped bodyguards. "The prince only addresses. He can never be addressed."[4] In almost every organization there is someone who seems to demand such respectful behavior that everyone must practically tiptoe around. Some of these managers simply want to reinforce their traditional role; others are interested in staying in power at any cost.

You will never rid the workplace of pecking orders. Those who make significant sacrifices to achieve status are not often interested in sharing it. There is, however, a difference between forcing respect by virtue of one's title or one's power to punish and earning respect by being a strong enough leader to share authority through participatory management. (Almost all managers think they practice participatory management, but, if they were to survey their employees, they would realize they often fall short of the mark.) Many managers wear what some at the Poynter Institute for Media Studies call the invisible cloak of authority. Unseen and unappreciated by the manager, this cloak can stifle questions from others. This aura of authority can be apparent even in reports that are impressively packaged or presented. Such written material can awe others so that they do not challenge or investigate.

Robert Helmreich, a professor of psychology at the University of Texas and director of the University of Texas Aerospace Crew Research Project, has an interesting insight into the questions asked between levels of management. In his review of recorded cockpit conversations between senior pilots and junior crew members, he found some in which the junior pilot might have prevented a plane crash. Professor Helmreich says that junior flight crew members do not quiz senior pilots' actions for one simple reason: "Juniors fear to question seniors because they fear reprisal or losing face."[5] Even a piece of paper can be seen as challenging. Checklists (a series of questions) that might challenge the authority of an experienced pilot can be ignored even when they check basic issues such as "Does the plane have full fuel tanks?" We can all relate to this situation. How often have we been silent with a question throbbing in our mind, never asking it for fear of contradicting a higher-up? Imagine a junior doctor who is afraid to question a mistake by the senior doctor operating on your heart, and all of a sudden the need to allow for inquiry in the workplace takes on a very urgent dimension.

One's success in avoiding excessive conflict while still asking necessary questions reflects the quality of one's relationships with superiors. How successful are you in asking for information or in providing answers to awkward questions from those above you? How far you can go in questioning superiors depends in large part on your present and perceived future value to the organization. This can be a troubling concept for some. It is simple: Where you are and where you are going in the organization tells you a lot about the success you will have asking questions and getting answers. Those seen as "experts," for example, can quiz higher-level managers because of their expertise; even long-term employees can sometimes question higher-level managers because of their years in the saddle. Those who are seen as on the rise are given greater latitude in their curiosity than those who are sinking. Simple psychology dictates this; we listen to and respond to those we think can help us now or those we think will be able to help us in the future. It may not seem that answering your question is a favor, but it most certainly can be in the eyes of those who have the information you need. The giving or withholding of favors (and answers) is how the levers of organizational power are controlled.

Can You Question a Group?
I cannot teach anybody anything, I can only make them think.

SOCRATES

Without delving into a psychological analysis of egos and the dynamics of groups, we can say that a question can be seen as an assault on an individual or the community. A powerful collective feeling or groupthink can occur without anyone specifically pointing to it. This groupthink self-censors and causes a subtle but constant fear. It is the fear of being cast out if one diverges too much from the group's overall direction. This fear can live in a union hall or a boardroom. The only way to eliminate it is for the questioner to have confidence in the value of the question and for there to be a shared expectation that challenging questions are to be regularly asked and helpfully answered.

Organizations that mentally assassinate questioners create a "to get along, go along" environment. Those in such controlling workplaces should ask themselves about levels of tolerance and why the group is not open to curiosity and conversation. It is an inquiry that will affect everyone at every level in the organization. Two questions that can be asked are: Do we really listen to our employees? and Do employees in an organization feel they are good listeners?

Fear of Seeming Intellectually Inferior

It is error only, and not truth, that shrinks from inquiry.

THOMAS PAINE

In your last meeting did anyone admit ignorance and ask others for help? The physical consequences of feeling intellectually inferior are few, but the psychological threats are many. The perception of most managers is that posing questions implies that they are ignorant, out of the loop, in need of help. Many executives seem to feel that the less they ask, the more they appear to know and thus the greater their perceived power. Conversations have a flow, and to swim against that flow with questions, admitting you don't know something, can be difficult. We might not know what the others are talking about, but we can assure ourselves we are in control of our part in a dialogue as long as we don't upset the flow. We are ready to show off what we know, not reveal our lack of knowledge. Not speaking up saves us embarrassment.

Why Are We Unwilling to Allow for Not Knowing?

There are things that are known, and things that are unknown. In between there are doors.

WILLIAM BLAKE

Children express curiosity freely and without restriction; indeed, the hope of many parents is that their children will grow up with no sense of limits. Once we are in school, natural curiosity is replaced by formal instruction. Questions are directed at us, and we are expected to know the answer. We start to believe every question has to have a correct answer. To appear in control, we start to act as if we always know the answer. There is a school of psychology that says this bluffing device is one we all use to automatically protect us from the pain of appearing uncertain. How do we keep this subconscious need to protect ourselves under conscious control so that we do not keep ourselves from learning?

One step forward is for businesses to change the way the employees are treated. If an organization subjects employees to cross-examinations or investigations that trap and bleed, inquiry that is designed to reveal the opposing side's weakness, why should anyone admit to not knowing? People have to be given room not just to work but to learn. Leaders have to accept uncertainty and encourage honest appraisals by each employee of the knowledge each has and what each needs to learn. As the business strategist and survey respondent John Tessier put it, organizations have to "encourage—no, demand—staff admit their errors and also be willing to accept new ideas and ways of doing things."[6]

Failure to Distinguish between Arguing and Asking

Discussion is an exchange of knowledge; argument an exchange of ignorance.
ROBERT QUILLEN

The business world tilts toward rewarding those who advocate a view, not those who inquire into issues. Managers are seen as forceful if they take a stand, argue for it, and win. Those managers who creatively lead a discussion are not seen as decisive as those who dictate direction. Other managers can cut a question off and demand quick action on their proposal. It is human nature to try to get others to see we are right. Those who have studied conversational patterns have found that approximately 90 percent of any confrontational conversation is advocacy, and only 10 percent is inquiry.[7] A question-poor conversation is a recipe for disaster.

We've all witnessed turf wars in which everyone has a position to argue but no one is acknowledging other viewpoints. The process turns into one of evasion and attack. This, in turn, can create the centrifugal forces of rage and resentment. Questions can play a powerful role in breaking through a person's well-entrenched monologue and can disrupt a repetitive point-counterpoint discussion that is nothing more than an exchange of the obvious. Some arguments are marked by the inability of some people to give a straight answer to a straight question. Questions can take the war out of our words. With inquiry, one can represent a personal opinion or concern as a question without being the lightning rod for others' criticism. By tactful inquiry, one can steer around the mental landmines in the other person's mind.

Ill-timed or badly presented queries ignite their share of arguments. Too often questions are like daggers, stuck in someone's ribs and twisted. The shock of a poorly worded question can trigger a "startle-escape" reaction in the other person. Attacking an issue and not the people around it is an elegant art. The workplace needs to balance the standard role of managers as active advocates for a position with the practice of the positive question. This balancing act requires learning to ask and listen *before* taking a position.

Fear of Information Overload

A conclusion is the place where you got tired thinking.

BLAISE PASCAL[8]

Sitting in an office surrounded by memos, voice mail, e-mail, phone, and fax, you can understand Gertrude Stein's remark, "Everybody gets so much information all day long that they lose their common sense." Call it information pollution; many managers spend their waking hours collecting, sorting, and analyzing vast amounts of material—entire days can be consumed just by correspondence. Many organizations now face the challenge of too much information. Asking additional questions would simply add to the avalanche. How do you act when faced with excess or ambiguous information? Do you lock up and go into your shell, or do you start questioning?

Growing layers of technology are eroding the art of questioning. It's been said that some high-tech experts think so little of actual conversation that they call it "facemail," in their minds an inefficient and inferior form of communication. We have the illusion of keeping in touch through technology. Ideally computers and communication devices free one to make the most productive use of time. The problem is that we can become isolated, substituting access to infinite information and constantly updated software for real conversation and true understanding.

It doesn't matter how much information you have if you can't retrieve it when you need it for decision making. That's where questions can help; they can give focus and save time. The value of inquiry as a filter is clear to anyone who has ever been involved in answering an unfocused complaint. The fragmenting force of technology means you have to be more careful with your time. Too much information can pile up, blocking your view of the essential task to be done.

Fatalism and the Death of Questions

Life is an unanswered question, but let's still believe in the dignity and importance of the question.

TENNESSEE WILLIAMS

There is a pervading sense of weariness, cynicism, and indifference when employees are not allowed to question or questioning does no good. The author Guy Claxton offers this thought: "If the passive acceptance of not-knowing overwhelms the active search for meaning and control, then one may fall into fatalism and dependency."[9] Such fatalism can come from employees drowning in work but is more commonly found where management has not addressed the "why bother" question. Even those who are swamped will keep paddling if they have a goal, a finish line they can see. Fatalistic employees narrow their view of the world to just keeping their job, and everything else becomes someone else's problems. Since the status quo is always the most familiar, they choose the least challenging and seemingly secure patterns. Positive questions are the best hope for bringing these workers back to that challenging, energizing, productive place between boredom (coma) and anxiety (heart attack).

. . . .

Questions That Motivate

Why?

Why Not?

So What?

Alex Pattakos[10]

. . . .

Chapter 2 Conclusion

Ideas into Action

If you are not allowed to ask meaningful and important questions in the workplace, you have been deprived of one of your most important rights. Not only is it a matter of personal freedom; it becomes a matter of self-preservation. In outlining the obstacles to and the dark side of question asking, it becomes clear that inquiry is a topic closely connected to the human condition. It involves deeply felt issues of status, risk taking, tolerance, consensus, and cooperation. While I advocate a questioning attitude and culture, I acknowledge it comes down to choice. It would be a tragedy if a policy of encouraging "questioning" became a straitjacket, with even those uncomfortable with it being forced to ask questions even when they did not feel the need to use them. If inquiry is mandated, it becomes part of a punitive practice, not a positive and progressive one. Young people subjected to abusive questioning quit mentally and spiritually and forever see questioners as echoes of half-forgotten schoolteachers.

If you want to see more positive questions in your life, you must recognize that it starts with you. Asking an honest question involves taking a risk—the risk of ridicule and rejection. Positive questioners recognize the unavoidable political nature of inquiry any time there is uncertainty or conflict. The irony is that improved communication can come only from starting some sort of ongoing conversation, the very contact discouraged by conflict. To eliminate this fear of conflict and failure, the questioner must have confidence in the value of the question and hope it will be in a helpful and honest way. If you understand that many people have negative memories of asking questions, you can reassure coworkers and all conversational partners that you want to hear what they are really thinking.

Encouraging a new freedom of questioning may meet with subtle and stubborn resistance in many organizations. By knowing the obstacles and objections to questioning, you calm the mind chatter that often prevents questions from being articulated. In chapter 3, we discuss the pragmatic ways organizations can not only overcome the obstacles described here but use questions as a platform to bring about a new form of workplace relationships.

The Questioning Culture

Creating a Workplace That Questions

Sometimes, the question is more important than the answer.

PLATO

In chapter 1, we discussed *why* organizations need to welcome questions and to create a questioning culture. Now we focus on *how* they can do it. We have to return to the very basics of communication if we are to create a positive questioning culture. Language is a primary expression of our thinking. Jeff De Cagna, an author and speaker on learning, says, "A question, which is a basic construct of language, is still an expression of our not fully formed thinking or a device employed to help another shape his or her thinking." For De Cagna, fostering a questioning culture is really creating a culture that values thinking.[1] Thinking requires being open to new ideas, and it requires a culture tolerant of dissent and diversity. It is a workplace that understands, as the saying goes, that machines make it possible, people make it happen. For people who do not question, who are not asked to think, become machines, as replaceable as any piece of equipment.

Thinking and tolerant . . . two ambitions and definitions of a positive questioning culture. This is not surprising, since the respondents to the survey for this book believed the most important question managers should ask their employees time and again to be "What do you think?" If only creating a questioning culture were as simple as asking just that one question. It is, instead, a never-ending process involving issues as diverse as definitions of humor and the impact of e-mail. What follows are points you can contrast and compare to your own workplace and life. This is the distilled essence of many discussions on what can be done to bring about a culture where positive question asking is honored, rewarded, and encouraged and question asking is defined as every employee's right and obligation.

As these arguments unfold, I ask you to consider a rich question Jeff

De Cagna suggested that applies to each of the points in this chapter. If organizations today were more Socratic (questioning) in nature, "would they do less but accomplish more?"[2]

Why? Answering the Big Question

Some men see things as they are and say, "Why?" I dream of things that never were, and say, "Why not?"

GEORGE BERNARD SHAW

I've witnessed many questioning cultures up close in years of reporting on high-tech industries, particularly those in Silicon Valley. Michael Goodman, director of the graduate program in corporate and organizational communication at Fairleigh Dickinson University, summed it up when he told me that hi-tech companies are "driven by discovery, and questions are their fuel."[3] These companies have the first key ingredient to creating a positive questioning culture. *They pass the "why" test . . . they know why they are asking questions.* The deadline is right in front of them, and the competition is right behind. In short, they have a purpose, a vision of what they want to be or do. Without this, inquiry can be sound and fury, signifying nothing. The more a company is set on doing things the same way, the more it seems to have lost track of why it is doing something. There is sometimes the feeling of going through the motions, putting in time, just keeping busy. Too often, these companies are staffed with employees who are unsure what they want but won't ask the questions to discover it. Leaders recognize this need for a shared community purpose and the need for a goal, and they use questions to reach for them. Questions for helping to define an organization's vision are presented in chapter 18.

Questioning companies often have a highly competitive, meritocratic society shaped in the spirit of the founding entrepreneurs. Arnold Cooper, a professor in the School of Management at Purdue University, told me entrepreneurs ask a lot of questions "and engage in a continuous process of self-education."[4] Entrepreneurs, by one description, "have the ability to cope with a professional life riddled by ambiguity—a consistent lack of clarity."[5] Entrepreneurs, better than anyone else in the business world, can answer the question "Why?" They, in turn, ask everyone questions to help them make that why a reality. Questioning cultures are found not just among start-ups. Any business that continuously asks itself why it is in business has started to lay the foundation for such a culture.

Leaders who want to create questioning culture need to begin by asking:

- Why are we in business?

- Are we willing to take responsibility for our business's life and create the experiences that we want?

Corporations and Change

The man who never alters his opinion is like standing water, and breeds reptiles of the mind.

WILLIAM BLAKE

When an organization knows why it exists and what it hopes to become, its questions turn to change, for the value of a questioning culture is making the "why" work in a changing world. In many organizations, people are trained to preserve order, continuity, and predictability. Down the line it goes, a row of status quo dominoes, from the chairman's office to the front-desk receptionist. In many workplaces, employees are also rewarded for avoiding confrontation, despite historical evidence that most transforming change comes from conflict. Such unstated philosophies of preserving the status quo fly in the face of the constant transformation taking place all around us. If a company wants to create a lasting competitive advantage, it needs to consider how the company's people, processes, purpose, and philosophy turn what would be otherwise uncontrolled change into an opportunity for growth. One professor tells his students to examine how change is handled in any organization they might join. Is change welcomed and examined with energy and enthusiasm?

When faced with change, many organizations form a committee in which someone junior is assigned to gather information and file a report. This codified response often leads to paralysis by analysis. It is as if the committees think change might pass them by if they can study it long enough. Creating a questioning culture not only encourages change, it helps to define the change process (question/answer repeat) and provides constant feedback of whether the change is going in the right direction, at the right speed, and with the right resources.

If a company wants to change, I can think of no better starting point than to ask questions. Employees trained in a positive questioning culture can look into the future, define desired outcomes, and force action. Employees will be quick to learn that questions are closely linked with positive change. Ask a good question, and you act on any change in your circumstance, rather than the change acting on you.

Leaders need to encourage everyone to ask one key question day after day: What has changed? This one question will spark further questions and lay the foundation for a thousand other questions.

Organizations that use inquiry to examine changes in advance can turn any anxiety into positive energy. Whenever change is proposed or forced by circumstances, the employees start asking questions. They want to know what the change will look and feel like. They are wondering if they are going to fit in or even survive the change. The management guru Peter Drucker explains that "resistance to change is grounded in ignorance and in fear of the unknown. Change has to be seen as opportunity by people—and then there will be no fear."[6] Command and control, macho-style management may not recognize the need to deal with the fears and frustrations of workers. Positive questions recognize and respect those feelings.

Leaders know people will be ready to change if they ask the right questions and create a positive sense of restlessness. Such unease is not always a liability; progress depends on it. A questioning culture embraces and seeks out the changes, making the changes its own. In questions words are not dead; they are alive.

When change is happening, leaders who encourage positive questions can anticipate being asked:

■ How are things going to change?

■ What will be the benefit of the change?

■ How will things be better?

Redefining the Role of Managers

Every sentence that I utter must be understood not as an affirmation, but as a question.

NIELS BOHR

As presented in chapter 2, the list of obstacles to asking questions is deep and disturbing. It is rare for any workplace to exhibit none of these problems. Human nature alone often explains why we don't show curiosity. Organizations, however, are supposed to collectively overcome individual weaknesses. The first place these weaknesses need to be addressed is among supervisors. A cynical workforce that lacks faith in its managers is not going to become a bubbling cauldron of ideas overnight simply because a manager or even a team of managers suggests employees start to ask questions. Leaders who want a questioning culture need to realize first that they have to look at the role of frontline supervisors throughout the organization. A manager who almost exclusively asks prodding, closed-end questions (Are you going to finish the report on time?) needs to understand that he has likely beaten his staff into becoming order takers. A manager who issues long memos and isn't available for questions has first to realize she has slowed the momentum by the brakes she applied.

Managers can be encouraged to explore and apply positive questioning abilities with one powerful incentive: Their worth and future success are directly linked to the number of people they can successfully supervise and lead, whether it is a thousand factory floor workers or a dozen scientists. Positive question asking is one of the most powerful tools managers have to increase their effectiveness and efficiency in working with their staff. Generating pure fear won't do it; big bonuses won't always do it. Considerate, positive questioning can. It is the only constructive tool (when linked with listening) that *every* manager, no matter what their budget or circumstances, can use to encourage the contributions of *every one* of their employees. Intelligent, curious employees can be the most challenging to manage, but they are any manager's best hope for long-term success.

There is no questioning switch you can flick in the back of a supervisor. Creating such a questioning mind-set requires time, teaching—and one other key ingredient. It is important to be consistent with questions. If the manager or leader is erratic in questioning, the culture will be fragmented and eventually fall apart.

At one well-known fabric manufacturer I surveyed, there appeared to be a consistent questioning culture. A lattice structure describes all employees as associates with no traditional managers. As one employee explained it to me, everyone is empowered to ask questions, perhaps because, as the owners of part of the company, each person has the reasons and will to ask questions. Since the organization in theory is open from the top leaders down, everyone can ask questions, including the hard ones. This is not to say that no one at this company or in any other questioning culture ever discourages inquiry. In any organization, one manager sets the tone for his office, welcoming and asking questions graciously, while in the next office or department, there exists a snake pit of resentment and disagreement. A questioning culture can be made up of just three or four people, but to survive and grow it must have a leader who supports it and participates in it.

Diffusion of Power

All human beings by nature desire to know.

ARISTOTLE

Many organizations are starting to recognize the different ways of distributing power across and deep into an organization. Autonomous teams are one illustration of how to increase power by dispersing it. The power rises up from the teams and individuals that do the work. The logic in favor of creating a questioning culture is simple. A manager who has several proactive (inquisitive) teams that use questions to solve problems and think of new ideas on their own is more powerful than a manager who has moribund groups that wait for directions and call for instructions regularly before they respond to changes. Distributing questioning power across the organization has other benefits. Inquiring employees speed expertise, energy, and effort directly to problems that appear. By independently practicing their inquiry skills, not only do employees gain valuable experience; they gain confidence. A leader who encourages inquiry by all employees is setting up an infinite number of practice arenas in which he can watch for promising leadership candidates.

Encouraging questions in the workplace can be seen as a threat or restraint on the power of managers (see the discussion in chapter 2 on challenging superiors). In reality, it restrains anyone who would abuse their authority. This is not to say many managers might have reasonable expectations of conflict if they encourage questions and, in effect, share some of their power. Encouraging creative dissent, as question asking does, can fracture fragile authority figures. Organizations need to consider establishing question-asking boundaries so that their teams will not clash or lose focus. It does little good if employees go off on tangents over which the group has little control.

Leaders of organizations who want to encourage more questioning have to recognize that many organizations have a hidden caste system. One division or department can be more powerful than the others, able to question but not easy to question. Even within a department, a caste system may exist. The positive questioning culture builds a self-managing organization where there is open debate and accountability. The ability to question means that there is a fundamentally different distribution of power than in command and control companies. Like citizens in a democracy, employees in a questioning culture have to learn some democratic rules—how to compromise, how to bargain, how to take turns. A questioning culture is not a people's republic but a recognition that power hoarded is power wasted. A questioning culture spreads authority and energy to employees, benefiting the organization and its customers.

Leaders who want to share power need to ask:

- Is there anything on your mind?

- Where are the bottlenecks in our company?

Teamwork, Networking, and Questions

Live your questions now, and perhaps even without knowing it, you will live along some distant day into your answers.

RAINER MARIA RILKE

The way the world works today is all about working together. Questions are a critical part of networking and teamwork. The business consultant Suzanne Vaughan described a questioning culture this way: "We are much more powerful together than we are alone . . . if we can just learn to use that tool [questioning] it will make us all look better!"[7] A positive questioning culture creates, supports, and depends on teamwork and networking. Today's teams often have to work together on complex issues where not everything is neatly packaged for them. Finding solutions often depends on drawing on resources and support throughout the organization. If members of a team lack passion for the business at hand and for each other, the team rapidly comes apart. By giving teams the power to question, managers help satisfy employees' thirst for responsibility and ownership. Taken together, a team plus a purpose creates a questioning hothouse, where new ideas grow. Creating teams and networks (formal or informal in the workplace) gives people the connections to find the right person to question. To use the vernacular of the computer industry, building teams gives people the right routing points for their requests. Networks can extend in so many directions that they are hard to categorize. Silicon Valley is one, a giant human network that crosses all professional and business boundaries. William Miller, a CEO emeritus of SRI International, said that William Hewlett, cofounder of Hewlett-Packard, once said that "three things were different here [in Silicon Valley]. First, he said, it's okay to change your job. Second, it's okay to fail. And third, it's okay to talk to competitors."[8] This is the reason that universities from the East Coast are opening extensions in the Silicon Valley—to learn about the West Coast (questioning) style of entrepreneurship.[9] They want to observe and absorb this open network and the questions flowing through it.

Leaders who want to use teamwork and networks to support questioning need to ask:

- ■ What is the level of knowledge in the group?

- ■ What information needs emphasis?

Informality Welcomes Inquiry

You can tell whether a man is clever by his answers. You can tell whether a man is wise by his questions.

NAGUIB MAHFOUZ

Positive questioning cultures are always moving toward informality. The details may vary from department to department, but, because it encourages conversations, the questioning culture encourages the creation of less formal groups. Meetings are full of give-and-take. Questions are asked of everyone. The informality promotes the ability to have continuing exchanges, questions asked in the hallways and lunchroom. At more formal institutions, managers act as if employees aren't working if they are casually talking. In a questioning culture, the hallway, the water cooler, and lunchroom are as important as the boardroom. Requests are made not via memo but more often in person, using the chemistry created with the informal request "Can you help me?"

Many questioning cultures are populated by people who (even if they don't have it on their cars) embrace the bumper sticker philosophy of "Question Authority." They don't see their bosses as parents they can trust. They see their employers as business partners who need to be questioned closely. These are people more motivated by the power of personal commitment than by the power of authority created by titles and organizational charts. Some corporations have made this challenging of authority official policy. One major company even published one business principle that says "Listen, Ask, and Speak Up."

Informal inquiry takes many forms. Those who want to ask original questions must not be rule bound and official. They cannot live with a police-state mentality of intimidation and control. They need to talk freely and openly, sometimes wandering around searching for an answer. Leaders must recognize that learning is sometimes vague in purpose and that there is no perfect, final answer. Because a questioning culture does not treat knowledge as property, something to buy and own exclusively, it encourages the exchange of information to share the benefit of each other's experience.

Stress is a great killer of informality. The clothing designer Mossimo Gianulli encouraged those who were stressed out to knock a golf ball around on company property, provided a company gym, and invited employee's children to visit the office, something he said made his workplace "very fun and young." Mossimo, as he is known to the world, kept a can of Playdough around because "if you are having a really bad day, take a whiff of [it] and it will remind you of your childhood."[10] Children and childhood memories—both remind us to loosen up to ask questions.

Informality creates a place where you can question yesterday, today, and tomorrow. Leaders who want to encourage informality and questions need to ask:

■ When does a feeling of formality keep us from communicating freely?

Questions That Motivate

How do you know (measure) if you are successful?
Pat Lencioni[11]

Chapter 3 Conclusion

Ideas into Action

If you proceed deliberately and with forethought, you can bring a questioning attitude to your professional life and workplace. The unasked questions in our lives are often those of direction. Do you want to move in the direction of better communication, appreciation of knowledge, and use of questions to foster teamwork and change management? There is no static position; an organization is either moving in the direction of a questioning culture or is moving away from it. In a time of information economies, the demand is for more questions and more frequent questioning. We are entering a time when knowledge is what is increasingly produced and consumed.

The virtue of acquiring a questioning attitude is multifaceted; it clears a person's judgment, opens the capacity for reasoning, and sharpens the intelligence. When T. H. Huxley wrote of the liberal education, he said it created a person "full of life and fire, but whose passions are trained to come to heel by a vigorous will, the servant of a tender conscience; who has learned to love all beauty, whether of Nature or of art, to hate all vileness, and to respect others as himself."[12] It is a virtue that grows with us, for as we mature, we have the wisdom of the years. The Greeks said the unexamined life is not worth living, and in questioning we find a discipline that helps us find the values that make life worth living. Like any other discipline, its worth is in the results it created day to day and year after year. Inquiry creates the personal and professional confidence to find what you need on your terms.

In the end questioning is about a passion for learning. I am reminded of Tom Peters's idea, related in his book *Liberation Management* about the childhood of the Nobel Prize–winning physicist Isidor Isaac Rabi. Rabi's mother used to greet him after school by asking, "Did you ask any good questions today, Isaac."[13] Questioning creates a world of perpetual learning. The questioning attitude can addict you like a drug, a healthy habit to experiencing the world around you.

In chapter 4, we look at acquiring a positive questioning attitude.

Learning a Skill

To be or not to be that is the question. Whether it is nobler in the mind to suffer the slings and arrows of outrageous fortune, or take up arms against a sea of troubles, and by opposing them, end them.

WILLIAM SHAKESPEARE, *HAMLET*

As with any skill, you can learn questioning by chance experience or by organized study. Those who focus on studying any discipline master a broader range of skills more quickly and find greater opportunities. Ask yourself this: who taught you how to ask questions? You might answer, no one. Unless you went to law school or studied philosophy, chances are you learned how to ask questions from the examples of parents and friends. This might be all the expertise you need if you want to be like your parents or friends. When you look around, you realize everyone has questioning patterns of varying degrees of effectiveness. How can you ask better questions?

You need to study the art and the artists if you want to be more positive, precise and persuasive in your questions. The key is to consciously observe how those you respect conduct themselves:

- Are they graceful when meeting new people? Chances are they impressed you with their sincere way of showing interest in the other person, an attitude created by the positive questions they asked.

- Do they get things done? Chances are they use positive questions to zero in on the matter at hand.

- Are they known for taking quick action on issues? Chances are they have the right information to make a thoughtful decision, insights created by the positive questions they asked.

- Are they at ease with themselves when facing new situations? Chances are even if they know little about the challenge they are facing, they are comfortable with how they will approach it. They know the positive questions they will ask, and they are comfortable taking action.

As you focus your attention on those you regard with favor, what often impresses you is their insight and grace in asking questions.

Spend one day tracking the many questions you ask. You will find that many are posed so easily and with so little thought that they are almost instantly forgotten. A closer examination provides new insights. Did any inquiry lead to miscommunication? A badly worded or an incomplete question is confusing. Did you get the information you needed? Simply demanding a response without an exchange of information can lead to a dead end. On reflection, did any exchange seem rude? Abrupt questions can offend.

Think of the questions you were asked during the same day. Some you answered without hesitation. Others you resisted. Which questions seemed not to threaten but to invite a conversation? Which led to a conclusion you otherwise might have missed or provoked a useful debate of an issue? You will find that important questions remain unasked because they imply that the questioner does not know something he thinks he should. In the business world, many fear a simple or "stupid" question can haunt someone's reputation for years. Yet the most fundamental questions are often the most important ones. Never be shy about posing simple questions, for they are the stuff that can change the direction of corporations. The management writer Tom Peters has evoked this, saying, "Mostly, it's the dumb elementary questions, followed up by a dozen even more elementary questions, that yield pay dirt."[1]

If you keep a list of occasions where you had to ask questions but the outcome was not what you expected, you can discuss those questions later with a mentor or coworker. Ask how the person would have handled the situation and what questions she might have asked. One value of having a mentor is that you have someone to model your professional questioning behavior on. You will still need to develop your own style of questioning, an authentic and comfortable presentation.

Imagine that you could improve the quality of the questions you asked by 10 percent. Would that result in 10 percent more useful information? Would it save you 10 percent of your workday in time? Could it lead to a 10 percent raise in salary at the end of the year?

Where Did the Art Go?

Always the beautiful answer who asks a more beautiful question.

EE CUMMINGS

Conversation and the art of questioning were once practiced in a less hurried, less media-intensive time. More time spent talking face to face created more opportunities for honing questions and for developing the social savvy to evaluate responses. The very nature of our lives today discourages conversation. The novelist Paul Theroux once talked about New York as being "so cellular, so like an asylum, an island of vertical compartments" that it isolates people.[2] One wonders whether our homes are becoming, as Charles Handy called it, "a privatized prison."[3] A generation is being raised in a cocoon of high-tech gadgetry. According to William Damon, a professor of education at Stanford University, "Two-thirds of [adolescents] have their own TVs, a lot of them have phones, 30 to 50 percent of them have computers in their rooms and can go online, so they don't need to go out."[4] Since so many people surround themselves with machines, it is no wonder questioning skills have suffered. People can find inspiration and ideas on television but can't ask questions or receive answers. The emerging technologies create a form of freedom through anonymity but represents the passing of polite society and a world that depended on conversations to transmit information.

If you are going to be a positive questioner, you need to anticipate answers in some ways, to be sure you are focused and don't ask awkward questions. Questions can be an unusually vivid form of language. Nothing can set someone more on the defensive than a question seen as prying or too pointed. By thinking ahead, you can make sure that your inquiry is sensitive and focused and that it leads to the information you need. A positive question is like a gift to the person being queried. It offers a chance for genuine and lasting communication, a vital link between what was and what can be.

We all know that the tone of a question (vocal) and the gestures (visual) that accompany it can turn a friendly question into a threat. Many businesspeople use the tone of questions to control and intimidate. The best questions are conversational yet direct, leading naturally to more questions. They create a neutral zone where the two sides can converse. Simple questions can be enormously powerful and efficient. If we could imagine we had a limited number of words (or imagine the limit of the other person's attention span), we would be far better at asking meaningful questions. Here is a high-tech analogy: After the end of the Cold War, some American companies hired Russian software engineers. It turned out the Russians were better at writing compact software than were Americans. It was a skill the Russians had had to learn because their computers were relatively underpowered and contained less memory than their U.S. counterparts. The coding was elegant and direct and did more with less. The engineers had to think about their purpose before committing precious resources to it.

Those who can quickly come up with logical yet positive questions are able to mine all their conversations for valuable informational nuggets. These questioners know that, whatever their job today, they will face new challenges tomorrow. The more information they have at their fingertips, the better able they will be to respond. Listening carefully to answers, the positive questioner finds the thin thread of the conversation that she needs to gently tug on to get vital information. Often these questioners are simply filing away the name of the person and their interests for future reference. They may not retain all the information, but they will at least keep the contact for future questions.

Successful people know a universe of people they can ask for help. The world is far too complex for you to always know the right expert to ask for information. The key lies in keeping an active connection with people who have many contacts through whom you can route your inquiries. You, in turn, should offer your expertise and experts to others who call on you. This has been called networking. In another time it would have been known as having friends. Whatever you call it, the benefit is simple. The more qualified people you can ask questions of, the more input you have when making decisions.

We cannot always know the answers, but we can always know how to get the answers.

The Questioning Attitude

Think like a man of action, act like a man of thought.

HENRI BERGSON

Question-asking skills will do you no good without a positive questioning attitude. It is the perspective of exploring (positive) not exploiting (negative), of cooperation (positive) not of confrontation (negative), of empathy (positive) not of apathy (negative).

Such a consciousness of positive possibilities reminds us that we "think" using questions. If you doubt this internal dialogue, reflect on what happens when we are asked a question. We begin to automatically think for an answer, even if we never verbalize it. We ask questions while reading, asking ourselves whether a statement is true. We ask questions even while witnessing others' actions; we wonder what will happen next. Advertising uses this effect. It poses questions to us all the time that we can't resist answering.

T. S. Eliot once asked, Where is the knowledge that we have lost in the information? Questions stimulate higher-level thinking, regardless of the level of knowledge one begins with. The authors Neil Postman and Charles Weingartner define the reason that question asking is so important in schools and life:

> Consider . . . where "knowledge" comes from. . . . Knowledge is produced in response to questions. And new knowledge results from asking of new questions; quite often new questions about old questions. Here is the point: Once you have learned how to ask questions—relevant and appropriate substantial questions—you have learned how to learn and no one can keep you from learning whatever you want or need to know.[5]

One academic's study found that the more comfortable students became with questioning, the more confident and independent the students became, with the teacher assuming the role of facilitator.[6] It is important to remember that inquiry is often a form of information bargaining. All communication involves a need, and we communicate that need by selecting words and hope the other party interprets those words (I would like to know . . .) as we meant them. Questioning does not take place in a vacuum; at the very least, past events influence the interaction between the parties.

The communication skills trainer Dennis Rivers says that developing this "thought tool" is a matter of trying to find not just the right question but also the style of questioning that brings the most fruitful responses.[7] You have to learn to mix up ideas and to let patterns emerge in your mind. This is how we make decisions subconsciously all day long. We gather clues and evidence, always questioning what we need to know. It is the pursuit of clarity, as opposed to simplicity. With questions, you are taking a look into people; it is the most complex critical thinking skill and the most elaborate troubleshooting you will ever attempt each day.

Once you have the necessary focus and attitude, questions articulate themselves.

....

Questions That Motivate

If you weren't in this business, would you choose to get into it now?

Jack Welch[8]

....

Chapter 4 Conclusion

Ideas into Action

Questioning skills are rarely discussed and little understood. The intent of a questioning culture and attitude is not just to ask more questions, but to ask better questions. Your increase in proficiency will become clear when the replies you obtain are consistently superior to those you received before. With better questions, you can discover whose facts are being used and how they are being used. To your benefit, your analysis will also discover ways that perceptions are more important than facts in many decisions.

The type of question you will use will vary from situation to situation, moment to moment. The point of the process is not to gather data, it is to reach an understanding. I am reminded of a profile I once produced on the wine maker Robert Mondavi. He talked about the ways that making wine is "like raising a family, a family can have one child and the next is completely different." Mondavi talked about how wine makers have to ask questions about every variable of light, water, and soil. I was inspired because, at age 82, he still didn't rest. He said: "I'm learning so much right now, and the more I travel every time I learn wherever I go."[9] Life should be a powerful and direct story of positive questioning and learning.

When you learn to question and develop the instinct of inquiry that all of us have, you sharpen a skill that can never be taken away. Questions follow from the first one asked, helping you anticipate and adjust. By gathering raw information and honest feedback, you will realize you are not defenseless but will see where and when you should invest your time, your effort, and your heart.

Forming questions is useless if we fail to ask them. In chapter 5, I offer a specific set of seven steps to take you from idea to action.

Raising Your I.Q.Q.

The true test of intelligence is not how much we know how to do, but how we behave when we don't know what to do.

JOHN HOLT[1]

In this chapter we introduce a different description of intelligence. It is the Intelligent Questioning Quotient, or I.Q.Q. Like many forms of intelligence, it represents the ability to identify ideas and connect concepts. I.Q.Q. is a description of intelligence that supports the many other forms. If there are right and left brains and a variety of intelligences, they are all supported by unconscious questioning and the need for answers. While there has long been a debate about whether you can increase your standard I.Q., I believe there is a way to raise your Intelligent Questioning Quotient with a straightforward, seven-step assessment process. Through this process, you can discover the different aspects that are part of any inquiry. Identifying each of these aspects is the process of learning how to question effectively.

Assessment—Seven Steps to Better Questions

Our life always expresses the result of our dominant thoughts.

SØREN KIERKEGAARD

Questions are a process of discovery. This description makes asking questions sound like the adventure it can be, an exploration into the unknown. Someone has observed that an insightful question is one of the most challenging acts of creativity possible. An original and useful question is born of an active and open mind, a process involving many levels of thought and experience.

One way to judge the competency of another is by the questions the person asks. You can, for example, judge a teacher by the quality of the questions he asks his students. Doctors, therapists, lawyers, and journalists all use questions as a fundamental technique. In researching these different careers, I found there is rarely any "class" for questioning. A review of course work for these professions turned up some instruction in cross-examination technique for lawyers that focused on questioning skills. Other professionals, it appears, learn the art of inquiry through real-world applications. Unfortunately, there is no map, mechanical formula, or shortcut to acquiring questioning skills. There is, however, a specific sequence you can use, an interdisciplinary, seven-step process of accessing awareness, ability, atmosphere, attitude, answer, appreciation, and action.

All questioning involves an unconscious self-assessment and an assessment of the questioning situation. What do I know? What do I want to do? What we think of as habit or instinct when we ask questions is this instant, internal, two-step assessment. It is reflexive. We think in questions so fleeting they barely register in the mind before we say them. Because of this rapidity, it is difficult to articulate the thoughts that lie behind questions. These seven steps break this process down so that questions can be more productive.

Awareness—What Do You Really Want to Know?

The first step in asking any question is a needs assessment. As you start to think of a question, you need to know what you need to know. You can be looking for:

- Context—What do I not understand?

- Contact—Who can help me?

- Facts—What is the reality?

- Opinions—What do you feel?

- Options—What can be done?

- Consent—Can I? Will you?

As Stephen Stuntz, a survey respondent, puts it, "The most important question to be asking is why are you doing something. The second most important is how do you want to be treated."[2] An awareness assessment asks what you want to know but also the reaction and the relationship you want to create. In a positive questioning culture, questions start with a commitment to honesty by both parties seeking to discover a truth.

You will discover the world has one big divide, between those who value feelings first and those who deal largely in facts and figures. You need to decide whether you are requesting feelings or facts. You need to decide how much you really need to know and whether there is anything you should insist on knowing. Since questions and answers go both ways, you also need to decide how much information you are willing to give out.

This examination of inquiry should focus you on what is the most important question you will ask. This is what should be called the position question. It lies at the heart of what you are investigating or acting on and is the question that, when answered, will change a relationship. The position question often has the shortest answer—yes or no, buy or sell, you are hired or fired. If you cannot decide which is the position question on your list, imagine you could ask only one question of the other person. What would it be?

Focusing on awareness of what you need to know creates three advantages: It gets your attention, confirms what you already know, and sets your goal. Positive questioners keep "to ask lists" instead of just "to do lists."

You need to begin by asking yourself these position questions:

- What do I really need to know?

- When do I need to know it?

- How can I focus my questions on the right information at the right time?

Once you know your purpose, you are ready to move on to the next step.

Ability—Who Has the Expertise and Authority to Answer Your Questions?

Before you ask a question, you should find out whether you are addressing the right person and whether the person has the time to help you. Basic etiquette requires this, since you are building a relationship, however brief, with that person. Telling someone you think she can help is the first step to setting the atmosphere. Being able to help gives others a sense of importance. Most people, when asked a question, want to answer, unless they are hurried, don't know, or have an ulterior motive. Positive questioners know they will have better success if they can find a subject of interest to the other person. Typically, this involves asking someone's advice in an area where the person has some expertise or exploring a problem both share.

Your self-assessment should have you exploring a mental list of everyone you know who might know the answer to your question. Those you have a past relationship with will likely go the extra distance to return your call or e-mail. Ask yourself, "Who is accomplished in handling the issue or problem I face?" These are the people you keep in your files for quick consultation. These are also the people you may consider your mentors.

It is best to start any inquiry by clearly identifying who you are and what you want. This immediately lets the other person know you are being up front. If you have a referral to that person, use it right away to see whether it will get you any extended courtesy. If you don't know the other party's name, ask. Being able to use the person's name allows you to ask for direct assistance and dissolves the anonymity that kills courtesy. To make the relationship more formal, use the person's last name and title, in effect attaching the person's complete identity to the ability to answer.

Your first inquiries immediately "qualify" the person you are talking to. If you are soliciting the wrong person, the responses to your first set of questions will stop you from wasting any other queries. You are searching for the voice of authority. The questions contained in the rest of this book show how to check credentials and experience to see whether the other party really is the right one to help you.

To identify those with the ability to answer your questions, ask these position questions:

- Who knows the answer?

 - Who has mastery of this topic?

- Who is willing to answer?

Atmosphere—When and Where Should You Ask Your Questions?

Questioners want to create an atmosphere quickly where they can have the seemingly conflicting feeling of structure and spontaneity. Structure is necessary to ask questions in some order that makes sense, but spontaneity is needed to allow for unexpected answers that give new questioning directions.

Creating the right questioning atmosphere means adapting your presentation to the situation and the other's personality. The first issue is timing. No question will be answered if it is asked at the wrong time. If you are setting up a meeting to gather information, anticipate the other people's schedule and estimate the time you need to ask the questions you'll have. To save time, successful questioners often describe their need for information in advance. We have all met with suppliers or coworkers who seem to be unprepared for our questions. If you can circulate an agenda in advance, even an informal outline of what is needed, the session will be far more productive.

You need to assess the audience your questions will be addressed to. You need to evaluate your style, both verbal and nonverbal, to make sure you are speaking the audience's language and to see whether you are paying attention to the reaction (both verbal and nonverbal) when you talk. You often receive what you reflect, so your signs of interest in the other party's reply should inspire the other party to be interested in your questions. Such authentic gestures have no cost in time or money. They are the signs of a positive questioner who knows that a small emotional investment pays big information dividends.

Creating the right atmosphere requires that you physically respond to the other person's answers. The gestures made in conversation can tell your audience more about your questioning attitude than your words say. As if on stage, you have to be aware of your audience, even if it is an audience of one. Your energy level should stay up from start to finish. Gentle eye contact at the start of a session, eyebrows sometimes raised to suggest reasonable curiosity, leaning forward to draw the other person's comments, even occasional note taking, if done sincerely, confirm to the other party you are interested in her responses. A firm tone with varied inflection, combined with smooth gestures, creates confidence and suggests your questions have weight.

People sometimes assume that "professionals" should be cool and aloof when questioning others. It takes an almost musical ear and a keen sense of rhythm to be in harmony with the other person's inner q-and-a beat. Once you put the other party at ease, continue to observe his reaction to your questions, to observe if he feels exploited or unsure. If the other party's eyebrows are constantly upraised and his arms are closed across his chest, you need to answer the questions he is asking with his body. Inquiry often stimulates emotions and can easily trigger anger. If you want to be known as a compassionate soul, you have to learn to ask and listen with empathy, no matter what the answer or attitude you receive.

Being careful not to mock your listener, you can mirror the presentation style he is most comfortable with. Matching the other person's tone and pace of speech can increase your success in requesting information.

Creating a welcoming and open environment doesn't mean letting down your guard. The best reporters often bring a healthy skepticism, not cynicism, to their interviews, a trait many businesspeople also acquire. The journalist David Shaw had a useful definition on this topic: "A skeptic is wary and dubious; he asks a lot of questions. He says, 'I don't think that's true; I'm going to check it out.' A cynic is convinced he already has all the answers."[3] Cynics interrogate others; they are looking for the lie. Such a prosecutorial tone is best reserved for the courtroom, not the workplace.

The physical surroundings often determine the type of questioning. At a party or any other informal get-together, nothing sours a mood more than an aggressive tack of questioning. No one wants to be put on the spot when trying to relax. These occasions can be perfect, however, for some of the most productive inquiry anyone can hope for; they permit some of the most unanticipated, yet revealing, information to come to light. Keep a supply of questions that inspire conversations and put people at ease if you want to reach out to future contacts. Some of these questions are outlined later in chapter 15, section 6, Mixing with a Roomful of Strangers. Golf's popularity among businesspeople in large part comes from the social atmosphere it provides for informal give-and-take. Those who head out to the golf course with a business associate should have not only their clubs but a series of questions to informally guide the conversation.

The role played by spoken questions in communication is critical. Some of the most important words you've ever spoken have been in the form of questions, for we use questions to relay our most complex concerns. The more complex, abstract, or sensitive the message, the more we talk about it, rather than write it. Trouble often begins when questions are written down for another to respond to. Often they are committed to paper to put someone else on the spot. Reassure those being approached that you are ready to hear what they have to say. In a positive questioning culture, there is a sense of respectful collecting of opinions.

To see if the atmosphere is right for questioning ask:

- Do I have a list of questions I need to ask?

- What is the appropriate time to ask this question?

  - Does this question have to be asked now?

    - Does it ever have to be asked?

THE FIRST QUESTION: "IS THIS A GOOD TIME TO TALK?"

Knowing how to get people to talk is a powerful skill. The timing of your question is one key to successful inquiry. If you can find the right time, when someone is most inclined to help you, the information needed is that much closer. By asking the question "Is this a good time to talk?" or "Do you mind if I ask you a question?" you are doing more than showing you are considerate. If the other person agrees the time is right or says that she doesn't mind answering your question, she has just made a commitment to hear you out. If you do not ask for permission (or a variation on seeking consent), you risk being interrupted halfway through your first query if she decides she doesn't really want to answer you. One survey respondent, Robert Knowlton, argues that you need to seek "permission to proceed in any endeavor" because "as soon as someone gives you authorization to go further [permission], they are open to ideas, to suggestions, to possibilities."[4] Managers often neglect to time the questions they ask. After all, if someone reports to them, should they not always be on their toes ready to respond? The hidden virtue of asking whether it is a good time for the other party to talk is that you find out what demands she is facing. If she is facing pressing commitments, she will be distracted from your inquiry. By asking whether the time is right to talk, you avoid being known as someone who steals the time of fellow employees. By asking about the demands facing the person, you immediately set the right mood, letting her know you are sympathetic to her point of view. Being sympathetic, you help take the war out of your words. If your first questions acknowledge both parties' concerns, you calm the other person's hidden fears and set the stage for future agreement.

Attitude—How Should You Phrase and Present Your Questions?

Arnold Wytenburg, a business consultant, says questioners know the issue is "not asking the right questions as much as asking the questions right."[5] Asking a question "right," means working with the other party, not against it. You cannot change another's character and personality, so why work against them with your inquiry? Some might consider fitting your question to the other party's personality a form of manipulation or deceit, but in the real world doing so shows tact, political savvy, a sense of diplomacy. Questions should not be continually posed as a challenge to the other person. Instead, inquiry can be framed in different ways as a request: "Can you help me through this process so that we both benefit?" When asking for something, it often helps to explain why you need it. Questions can offer exchanges: "I'll do this if you'll answer that . . . is that acceptable?" At the very least, you need to give some information in return.

The exchange of questions and answers triggers complex internal processes in the minds of both parties. Questions are a powerful stimulus that can trigger equally powerful reactions. While I believe it is the content of your questions more than their order that will determine your success, thinking ahead makes every question count. Mapping out questions in advance helps you head in the right direction to get where you want to go as quickly as possible.

To decide how to phrase and present your questions, you can write them down and mark those that are most important. Writing down questions in advance doubles the amount of time you can use to listen to the person's answer. You eliminate the worry about missing an important topic and the distraction of thinking of the next question while listening to the end of the respondent's answer. The final thought is often the most important part of the answer. It may help to write small notes with the questions so that you can rearrange them in the best order to create a flow of information as you create the final list.

The flow of inquiry should begin with brief and to-the-point questions, preferably with an upbeat tone. The first requests should be easy to answer. You can always ask an opinion on something noncontroversial such as the weather or other informal topics to encourage people to easily open up. Do not, however, assume a false sense of familiarity with the other party. Positive questioners genuinely identify a common experience or desire that adds energy to the conversation. Realize that answering question after question can be a fairly dull process, like listening to someone reading a list, so vary the length, tone, and pace of your questions. Invite their questions. Beware of making the other person's ear tire.

You don't want to waste time getting answers to secondary questions until you can answer the most basic ones. Use the funnel technique, beginning with broad, open questions and rapidly narrowing the inquiry. When you receive a controversial answer, take the advice of Dale Carnegie: "If you disagree with them you may be tempted to interrupt. But don't. It is dangerous."[6] You have to listen even if you don't want to hear what the other side is saying. Understand first and judge later. Carefully lead up to a tough question so that it doesn't just spring from thin air. It is no secret that interviewers should save tough questions for last, since pointed questions can stop conversations. An awkward or indelicately posed question threatens trust, even if both sides wish to cooperate. If someone feels the questions are too direct and are an attempt to lay blame or set a trap, he will close down. Mick Yates, company group chairman at Johnson & Johnson Asia Pacific, says it helps to keep the questions future focused, "not seeking to assign blame."[7] Suspicion takes an expansive, sharing attitude and shrinks it down to silence. As anyone who has raised a teenager knows, asking questions of an unwilling respondent is an exercise in futility.

To learn how to better present questions, let people ask you questions. Listen to what they ask. Listen to how they ask it.

Good questioners in any business bring the talents of a dedicated reporter to their queries. They genuinely are interested in the answers and know that, without an overall focus, any line of inquiry can fall flat. Good questioners turn their conversational partners into the only people in the room that matter. They find a way to establish a relationship with the person they are talking to, a sense of shared purpose and a degree of trust. The goal is to give the person who is answering the questions a sense of value from the exchange. The best journalists create an odd sense of instant confidentiality even if the answer will be shared with millions. Great reporters base their next question on what was just said, so they stay with the interviewee's line of thought. The TV journalist Ted Koppel says that the key to his insightful follow-up "is that I listen. Most people don't. Something interesting comes along and—whoosh! It goes right past them."[8] The importance of listening to create the right questioning environment is underestimated by many. If someone is whipsawed from one question to another with no sign that what he just said was received, he will soon feel he is being abused. If the questioner acknowledges the point just made and expands on it with another query, uses it as the bridge to the next question on another topic, the person being interviewed will feel that he has participated in a conversation, not a cross examination.

The positive questioner doesn't ask unless he or she is open and aware, encouraging and responsive, ready to hear the answer. In a positive questioning culture, there is a sense that, no matter what the challenge, everyone can approach problems with a spirit of success.

You need to ask these position questions:

- Do I have the time and energy to really listen to the answers to my questions?

- Who else should be asking this question?

- How can I refine my questions given what I now know?

THE SECOND QUESTION: "CAN YOU HELP ME . . . OR . . . THE REASON I ASK IS . . ."

Successful questions and answers require cooperation and trust. You can encourage these feelings by asking for help and by telling the other person why you are asking something. Genuine questions come from a need to learn something. The other person is your teacher, helping you to find information. Most people, even those not invested in your success, generally want to share their experiences or opinions.

Questions are one of the best tools for getting people involved in any project. You can appeal to a person's higher instincts by asking for assistance. Even coworkers with too many projects, when approached in quieter moments, will generally be happy to try to help you out. Positive questions can show concern, an awareness of what is troubling both parties. The simplest way to start this cooperative process is by asking, "Can you help me solve this problem?" and by following up with "The reason I ask is . . ."

By explaining your inquiry, you avoid having your questions seen as an inquisition. You also prevent the other person from jumping to conclusions. Present the reason you are asking the question, and you may find that the other person opens up and is more willing to make a commitment to her answer. Qualifying questions can often allay the other person's fears of being put on the spot. This elaboration before asking a question takes a little more time, but it often helps the other person answer the question more completely. Having a clear purpose in questioning helps your cause and your reputation.

Answer—Did You Get What You Needed?

How do you know if your questions have worked gracefully and forcefully for you? You know if you walk away with the information you need and the other person is happy to have helped you. Consistent success in receiving answers is the result of carefully choosing questions and tracking the results of your choices. Asking the right questions does not automatically result in receiving the right answers.

Thomas Faragher, a consultant, warns that, too often, "people do not listen AFTER they ask a question." He says he's played the customer in several role plays in sales-training situations and, while "I have tried to give hints to what my wants, needs, hot buttons, etc., are, many are just completely ignored—even when I have repeated the hints."[9]

We ask a question, hear an answer different from what we believe, and switch gears from listening to preparing responses that dissect or put down the answer. That move shifts us from the reflective mode, focused on understanding the other, to a debating mode. To really listen, you have to focus on what you are hearing, not just on what you'll be arguing. Aggression often has its roots in a failed connection.

Asking better questions is one of the best ways to become a better listener. Insightful inquiry is an important way to show you are tracking the conversation at hand. You can with a few questions show you care about the other person's opinions and problems. Learning how to listen, to use listening as a verb, begins with an evaluation of talk versus listening time. All questions and no listening is a recipe for disaster. After any question you have to give a generous portion of silence. Pause for at least three to four seconds after asking each question and after receiving each answer. This gives the conversation air and allows for a conversational style, rather than a machine-gun-style interrogation. Asking questions one-fourth of the time and listening the rest of the time puts your questions and, more important, your interruptions on a diet. Listening is wanting to hear, the active capturing of ideas. You hope when you ask a question that people will listen to you as aggressively as they give answers. There is a quickening of the heartbeat when you are really listening to someone. That energy can make you enthusiastic, but you have to make sure it doesn't lead to snap reactions and the drawing of hasty conclusions. When listening to answers, you don't have to agree with them. If necessary, you might say your silence just means you are thinking about what the person is saying and does not represent agreement or disagreement.

A good way to check whether you are being a good listener is to summarize what someone just told you by saying, "If I heard you correctly, you are saying . . ."

Listen to the entire answer. Everyone knows it is rude to interrupt, particularly if you've asked the question that prompted the other person to speak. Almost all of us, when asked a complicated question, react with a false start as we organize our thoughts and confirm in our own mind the answer we are about to give. If you find the other person simply has trouble answering any questions, you need to better focus what you are asking for, guiding the person's replies as honestly as you can. You may need to take a step back to the prior question or offer to rephrase or repeat the question.

You need to listen not only for what you wanted to know but also what you didn't expect. This is the paradox of being aware of what you don't know. Good questioners are aware of and attack their own assumptions. Oddly enough, you also have to listen for what is not said. You have to peer through the muddy language many use to obscure their thoughts. You might get a story or a joke instead of direct reply. What should you do if you don't get an answer? Dr. Mike Turner says his favorite response when someone has just said "I don't know" is to ask "But if you did know, what would the answer be?" He says it's surprising how often this evokes an answer.[10] You may have to rephrase your questions several times to get answers to important questions. Beware the respondent who says, in reply to your question, "That's a very interesting question," for in that not too subtle flattery can be hidden an avoidance of your inquiry.

The most important part of listening is to look for words with emphasis, the key words or phrases that define what the other person is trying to tell you. If you are taking notes and hear someone stressing or repeating a phrase or a thought, take the time to underline it in your notes. Listen with your eyes. Watching the speaker indicates interest and catches the emphasis she can give to her words by physical appearance. Eye contact tells the other party "I'm here with you" and asks a question for you: "Can you tell me more?"

While it is important to listen to someone's emotional emphasis, don't allow emotion to be the only answer. Feelings are neither right nor wrong; they simply exist. Another obstacle to useful answers is vague recommendations. Remember the old adage that there is no greater distance than that between advice and help. People often give advice that benefits them, not you.

You can't demand the answer you want. You have to ask for the truth as the other party sees it. Honest answers can be bruising. Positive questioning is a matter of seeking the causes of rejection, finding the deeper problem, and sometimes pulling back the curtain on hidden agendas. Your investigations should focus on seeing whether the obstacles are really as substantial as some would make them appear. One question rarely solves a problem, but a set of questions following these seven steps can provide a breakthrough.

Sometimes you may not understand an answer. People will generally cut you some slack if they know you're trying to grasp their meaning. Show your commitment to listening and they will often explain. Remember that you train the people around you how to respond to your questions. If you are consistent and clear in your patterns of questions, those you regularly question will be able to answer more quickly and more clearly.

If you are not sure of the answers you are getting, you have to reconsider the source and filter the responses using your own judgment. Recognize that making up your mind can be fatiguing. Sometimes you have to be brave enough to go against recommendations and precedent. It may help to think of the facts you gather as nails, useful for constructing your thoughts along with your hammer of experience.

A final part of listening for answers is going beyond facts by asking for opinions and commitment. By doing so you will quickly find out if the other people agree with your conclusions. You can say at the end of a meeting, "Are we all agreed that this is the best course of action or solution?" Or "Does anyone have another opinion on what we should do?" Too often this question goes unasked by those arguing for a position because they are too worried about inviting dissent. The positive questioner invites others to state their case so that both parties can deal with the objections that otherwise would sabotage future agreement. Too often meetings end without a direction because no one has asked whether the group is set for one course of action.

If you ask for opinions and get none, you might say that one objection might be such and such (an objection you have anticipated and have an answer to).

Why put all this effort into listening? Not only does active, focused listening capture answers; it saves time and reduces errors in communication. It challenges the illusion of understanding so many walk away with after asking only a few questions.

You need to ask yourself the position questions:

- How specific were the answers I received?

- How accurate were the answers?

- How verifiable are the answers?

- Can I transfer this information to something else I do?

- Did I cover my list of questions?

- What questions are still unanswered?

THE THIRD QUESTION: "WHAT IS YOUR OPINION?" (OR, "WHAT DO YOU THINK WE SHOULD DO?")

After you define what you need help with, you earn the respect of others by asking for their opinion. An opinion goes beyond fact; it is a statement of position both now and in the future. While facts generally remain the same, opinions shift and may need to be checked several times during a conversation. When you seek an opinion, you are honor bound to pay attention and to respect it by not immediately countering it. As you explore opinions, you are cutting close to people's identity and therefore should probe with respect. Any manager knows he can make a demand for information, but the most valuable response to a question can be an honest opinion. You want to seek people's specific objections, whether you're speaking to the client who is not ready to buy or the employee you want to try a new task. By soliciting opinions, you go beyond *what* the person is thinking to *how* he is thinking.

You also have to brace yourself for the difference between people's public and private opinions. Most coworkers will be blunt behind office doors but will moderate their position for public consumption. If you are in a meeting and ask a question, you might find that everyone hedges his or her bets. One-on-one, people will express opinions express more clearly. When you ask for an opinion, you are bound to the conditions in which someone tells it to you. If it is offered in confidence; you have to resolve to keep it to yourself.

When you solicit another's opinions, it is important to make sure you understand why someone feels the way she does. If you accept an incomplete answer, you are playing a dangerous game because the other person will assume you do understand her feeling. The bottom line? You need to continue with questions until the other person provides the reason for her position. When soliciting opinions or comments, you need to beware of criticisms that are groundless, find the supporting information or evidence. If you do not hear it, ask for it. Look for facts, not just feelings. Unsupported opinions are one of the deadliest forms of workplace discontent and misinformation because they live independent of reality.

"What is your opinion?" and the sister question "How do you feel?" are essential questions to ask over and over. Often, someone will say something will not work because of one or more obstacles. This is a reservation, not necessarily a contrary opinion. The person may still agree with your general position but see a cause for concern. It is important to follow up by asking whether there is general agreement, rather than accepting a specific detail. At the very least, you can ask whether you can put the concern to a closer examination later or in another meeting so that the general opinion can serve as a shared platform for moving forward.

Appreciation—How Do You Form a Relationship?

Listening with empathy when asking questions is one of the most profound social graces. Being interested in another person and spending the most valuable currency you have, your time, on them is a gift to the other person. Skilled questioners can make even thirty seconds special by the unique focus they can bring to bear on the other, appreciating what the person has to say in a matter of moments. Once you make the commitment to asking questions of someone, you have to show appreciation for the answers. A tactful questioner does this even if he doesn't like or is not receiving the answers he needs. He knows there may be a time in the future when he will need that person and the information she can provide.

A businessperson should never forget the power of a good conversation. Conversation depends on the art of asking questions.

Appreciation and respect for the other person requires you to acknowledge the other person's perspective and pressures. If she has objections to your line of questioning, you have to try to understand these and customize your inquiry so that you do not continue to trigger the same response. If you hear the other person start to ramble, bring her back to the point of your last question or move on to the next. One useful technique is to comment on something the person has said that you honestly agree with (acknowledging that they have a legitimate point of view) and then move to the topic at hand: "Yes, that is a problem, but how are we going to resolve it?" or "Your coworker may be failing to meet deadlines, but what can we do to help?"

Positive questioners know they cannot argue their way to knowledge; they have to listen to learn. The careful listener who recognizes and appreciates another person's point of view finds a wealth of information she can use as she focuses on what she wants to see accomplished. Showing appreciation and understanding inside questions is an essential skill (e.g., "You've given me good information; can you give me a little more background on this situation?" or "If I understand you, we can't do the job because you're missing a part. If I can get that part to you by tomorrow, am I correct in understanding you'll finish the job on time?").

Many managers rose to where they are because they talk better than they listen. If you ask questions and actually listen to answers in a meaningful way, you may shock your coworkers. A manager who has never solicited input and all of a sudden is all ears should expect some resistance. Begin slowly, and show you really are listening to what colleagues are saying. When you go back later and ask for more information, you will see how your coworkers will change. They want to be heard and to know that their point of view has penetrated. Once they realize you actually appreciate their perspective, they will offer you greater insights, more honest opinions.

If you still are unconvinced of the importance of appreciation, you need to imagine a conversation where the other party asks you a question. You give what is a reasonable factual statement or opinion, but the other party ignores you or says "so what." You can be completely crushed. In a variation on this, someone says, "You didn't answer my question." You probably tried to answer the question and now resent the questioner's stupidity or stubbornness.

Gentle and constant appreciation has another virtue. With it, you can encourage questions and answers from shy people. The reward for getting these quiet types to participate is that in their silence they are often thinking about information you need to know.

Often appreciation has to extend to a form of payment for the information you need. You need to make sure before you get into such an exchange that you can follow through with your end of the deal. If you think you will have to "pay" for information, know the price tag in advance.

Before you thank someone for his answers, consider asking two more questions: "Have I missed anything?" and "Is there anything else you think I need to know?" Do not count on the person's having a good answer to these. Most of the time the respondent will say that all points have been covered. The value of this type of closing question is that occasionally you'll be told something vital you might have otherwise overlooked. You can also ask whether there is anyone else you should talk to on this point. People often say no but again occasionally come up with a suggestion that is a real time saver.

Appreciation of questions and answers is the enjoyment of the quirky human irrationality and spirit. In a positive questioning culture, an open and accepting atmosphere is created by the questioner who embraces the answers he gets no matter what they are.

Ask yourself these position questions:

■ What questions generated the most useful response?

■ Did I understand their answers?

■ Did I thank people for their answers?

■ Did I give them a reason to help me in the future?

Action—What Are You Going to Do with the Answer?

Asking questions is a pointless and frustrating experience if nothing is done with the information gathered. Those who endlessly ask questions are often just seeking to delay a decision. If you are investigating a problem, you must seek answers that create a course of action or lead to a solution. Hamlet still lives in many workplaces, endlessly asking

"To be or not to be?" Bruce Woolpert, president of Granite Rock Company, a business that has been honored with a Malcolm Baldridge National Quality Award, cautions against letting questions take precedence over action. He says that businesses need to have a passion or persistence in the things they do. Woolpert believes that a drive to set goals and move quickly to implement changes is more important than having a questioning character. His theory is that if a company does make a change and it turns out to be wrong, there is time to implement something else.[11]

Successful questioning results from knowing what to ask to create the information needed so that you can act in a timely fashion or from knowing what to ask to create a reaction in others so that they will respond to your concerns. Positive questioners recognize the power of persuasion hidden in a positive and focused question. It is a call to action, a question mark that demands resolution. I have said that questions are a form of action. They can be the small sparks that set off an explosion. Questions should have consequences.

If your questions have no results, no direct link to the future action, you have wasted two people's time. For most of us, inquiry that cannot be connected to action is best left for another day. If a meeting ends and no conclusive results have been achieved, any questions that have been asked are expressions of frustration. This is why those running a meeting should form the agenda around questions that must be addressed.

In a professional setting, one clear spur to action (and one way to demonstrate that you are listening) is to take notes. The human mind can hold only so much, and everyone knows the absolute limit for accurate recall is often about thirty seconds. What is forgotten can scarcely be acted on. If you take careful notes, the questions you ask will not be wasted. You should, of course, try not to allow note taking to distract you from the flow of questions. If you must, ask people for a pause so that you can write down what they said. This pause can give you a chance not only to capture their thoughts but to think of the next question you want to ask. Consider your notes a "third ear," a way to listen later to the questions you asked and to the answers you received.

In a positive questioning culture, you create a consistency by doing what you say and saying what you mean. This means turning ideas into action.

The position questions that create action are:

- Did I ask the right questions so that I can act?

- Are we a go or no-go on this issue/action/choice?

- What question needs to be asked so that I can move forward?

Questions That Motivate

Are we winning, and if not, how can we totally change the rules of the game?

Mick Yates[12]

Chapter 5 Conclusion

Ideas into Action

Questions are an act of self-interest. Someone has something you want or need, and inquiry is the way you get it. Using the seven-step assessment described in this chapter will improve your ability to acquire vital information. It develops an invisible talent that will lift you above the rest of the crowd and their blunt, meandering, and sometimes antagonistic questions. The only way to improve your questions using these seven steps is through repetition. By practicing them, you form habits that will serve you well the rest of your life. You may have already mastered some of these steps, but there is always one you can improve on. Working on them in the order suggested (awareness, ability, atmosphere, attitude, answer, appreciation, and action) will prevent you from asking questions that are at cross-purposes with your action goal and make your hits more frequent than your misses.

As with any other skill, the better you master the basics of questioning, the faster you will be able to adapt to any situation you face. These seven steps demonstrate that inquiry is not only a science but also an art, and mastery of these fundamentals can lead to creative leaps of thought. The best questioners see their q-and-a with another person as a tool for building a relationship. In the final analysis, a good question is its own justification.

A Word on the Organization of This Book

The chapters that make up this book are divided into a logical sequence of events or related activities. Depending on where you are in your workplace or career, you may wish to read later chapters if they fit your current situation, then revisit the earlier chapters if they should become relevant later on. Subchapter headings present the questioning topic; these are followed by a brief introduction describing the assessment needed when questioning, a suggestion of whom to question, and the order of questions you would most likely follow.

Almost every lead question has a follow-up question or point. I encourage you to put them in your own voice and pick out those focused on what you need to know. If you have your own favorite questions, you can use each category of queries as a checklist to prepare for what you need to know about the issue at hand. At the end of each subsection are suggested connections within the book where you can go next to resolve the issue at hand. At the end of each chapter is a review of how to put these ideas into action, for questions do not matter unless they are asked. To create your own question list, start with one of the more than one hundred topics in *Questions That Work* and then use the seven-step I.Q.Q. process to:

- Think of what you want to know and then focus your questions accordingly. Refine your questions as you learn more about a topic.

- Make an overall list of questions before you go into any new venture or have to make a decision.

- Think of those who may have the information you need (if you know of no one, your personal questioning network needs to grow).

- Define the atmosphere needed to ask your questions successfully.

- Pay attention to your list so that you don't get off on a tangent that doesn't serve you or the person you are questioning.

- Highlight any question not answered (such questions may indicate evasion or a missing piece of information).

- Review which questions generated the most useful information (as in the rest of life, 20 percent of the effort often creates 80 percent of the result).

- ■ Always ask whether there is something else you should know or someone else you should talk to.

- ■ Thank those who help you. Information is rarely free; it is purchased with your reputation, your time, and your intellect.

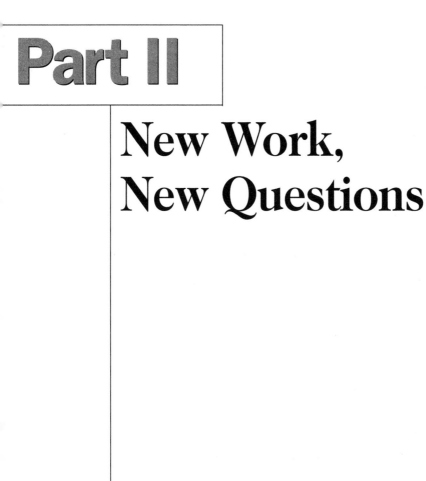

Part II

New Work, New Questions

QUESTIONS THAT WORK WHEN:
Looking for a Job

Do you have any questions for my answers?

HENRY KISSINGER

6/1 Looking for a Job

Assessment

You have to keep asking about the future. Chances are you will not retire at the job you have now. It is always wise to begin looking for the next job while with your current employer. This is when you have the most leverage in a search (and, correspondingly, the most confidence asking questions). It may seem that I am suggesting too many questions. The reality of your next job decision is that you do not just pick a job; you pick a boss. Discovering the qualities of a boss requires an extra level of inquiry.

Questions, Questions

Whatever the company you are applying to, you will want the job to offer you adequate authority, the funding necessary to do the job, the needed productive capacity, enough time to do the job, the right people to help you, and management commitment to your success. I believe you should also seek a questioning culture where your spirit for inquiry and independent thinking will be appreciated. You are seeking a strategic partner in your success.

If you restrict your knowledge about a potential employer to the company's general reputation, you'll be missing one of the richest sources of information, the employees of the company itself. Those workers provide the real-world, in-the-trenches view of the workplace. In a world where you can choose between established companies, start-ups, or venturing out on your own, such questions are critical to picking the path that best suits you.

Whatever the questions you consider using, practicing them ahead of time pays off.

6/2 Starting the Job Search

Assessment

Friends and associates are the vital connection to your next job. Not only will friends have insights into what you do well, they are also the most likely to answer your questions. It is speculated that some 75 percent of jobs are found through referrals, or through the use of questions to discover jobs yet to be advertised. If you once hired a headhunter or helped one with a project, now is the time to see whether you can question her about future opportunities.

Network questioning begins with those closest to you and spreads out from there.

ASK YOUR ALUMNI ASSOCIATION OR PAST PROFESSORS:

- Do you have anyone who works in the field I am interested in that I could contact?

ASK FRIENDS OR AN ALUMNUS:

- Where would you look for a job now?
  - What leads do you have?
- What job would you recommend for someone like me?
- Whom should I be talking to?
  - Can you share the names of those in the profession I am interested in getting into?
- What are the areas of growth?
  - Which areas are slowing down?
- What technology is changing the job; what skills do I need to know?
  - How quickly can I get those skills?
- How much could I make?

■ What kind of competition will I face?

■ What is the buzz about the company?

  ■ Are former employees glad to tell people to work there?

■ What should my resume include to help me get an interview?

6/3 Needing an Informational Interview

Assessment

Informational interviewing is particularly critical when you think of changing careers. You may have false assumptions and a grass-is-always-greener view of someone else's job. A set of informational interviews can save you from very expensive mistakes. Begin with questions focused on the person you are interviewing; then move on to questions about the position or career you are considering.

ASK THE INTERVIEWEE:

■ What is the best part of your job?

  ■ What satisfies you in your work?

■ What have been the big turning points in your career?

  ■ What are the exceptions to the rules that helped you succeed?

■ How do you plan your day?

  ■ What is the part of your job you wish you didn't have to do?

■ What has been your biggest failure?

  ■ What holds people back from succeeding?

■ What do you still want to do in your career?

■ Would you repeat your career over again if you had the choice?

  ■ What is the greatest obstacle to success you face?

■ Why do you think most people leave your field?

  ■ What problems are facing the business I am interested in?

■ What are the jobs available to someone trying to break into this field?

  ■ Can you give me an idea of the salary range for someone with my experience?

■ What would the ideal background be of someone who would be hired?

  ■ If I decided to make a career change, how would you suggest I make it?

■ What is the formal education of the top candidate like?

  ■ How important is education compared to ability?

■ What advice would you give someone trying to break into this business?

  ■ Do you know of any openings in this business?

■ Whom else should I talk to about finding a job?

  ■ Whom are the specific people I might contact about job openings?

■ What do you think of my resume?

  ■ What changes do you think I should make?

■ What is a job interview like at a company I might apply to?

  ■ What is the best way to prepare for an interview?

■ Which groups do you think I should talk to for more information?

  ■ What professional organizations do you belong to?

■ Can I have your business card?

  ■ Can I have the correct spelling of your name?

If you stumble across an actual job opportunity during an informational interview, keep the focus of the immediate opportunity of gathering information *just as you promised.* You can ask about scheduling a second opportunity to talk about the opening.

6/4 Needing to Use References

Assessment

You should prepare your references. If you provide your references with a quick set of questions you can be sure they are prepared for any callers.

If your references are called, chances are they will be asked a standard set of questions they can easily answer. You need to confirm that they know your date of hire, title, reporting relationship, and salary history and whether you are eligible to be hired again.

ASK REFERENCES:

■ Is it all right that I give out your name and contact number as a reference?

  ■ If you are contacted, can you let me know how it went?

■ Will you write a letter of recommendation?

  ■ Do you have any concerns I need to address?

6/5 Preparing for an Interview

Assessment

Your careful thought and preparation for an interview should include preparing a set of questions. This advance research will clearly distinguish you from other applicants. Here's how to test the water without jumping in.

ASK THOSE IN THE SAME INDUSTRY/CONSULTANTS/ FORMER EMPLOYEES:

■ What is the reputation of the company I'm considering?

  ■ Do you know anyone who has or is working there?

■ What are the business's long-term prospects?

  ■ Is it rapidly growing?

■ What is the annual growth rate?

  ■ What is its sales revenue?

■ Is it gaining or losing market share?

  ■ Are bills not being paid?

■ What is this company's turnover rate?

- Is it a hire-and-fire organization?
- Is it laying off people?
  - Has it started a hiring freeze or early retirement program?
- How big is the organization?
  - What are the best niches in the company?
- Will it give me responsibility?
  - Will it allow me to advance?
- What is its corporate culture?
  - What is its mission statement?
- Where is it headquartered?
  - Who owns it?
- How secure is its funding?
  - Who is backing it?
- What are the company's key products or services?
  - Who are its major competitors?
- Do you have any insights into how it does interviews?
  - Who is in the interview loop?

ASK CUSTOMERS:

- How satisfied are you with the company's product or service?
  - Why did you pick the company?
- What are the company's strengths and weaknesses?
  - Do you think the company will grow?
- What competitor of theirs would you consider using?
  - What would get you to switch?

ASK THE COMPANY:

- Can you send me a copy of the job description?

- Can you send me an annual report?

- Is there a company newsletter or other literature I can look at?

6/6 Responding to a Recruiter or Headhunter

Assessment

Headhunters find people for jobs, not jobs for people. Bear that in mind when you feel flattered by the call from someone with a tantalizing job they want to fill. The recruiter is working for someone else. This makes your questions all the more important. Jay Ferneborg, vice president of the recruiting firm Ferneborg & Associates, argues that you need to first determine the motivation of the recruiter. If it is a "retained firm," it is hired by a company seeking the best individual for the job, says Ferneborg. Contingent recruiters are looking for people willing to let them represent them in a job search.[1] If you are interested in the job, here is an opportunity to find out how much you are really worth in the marketplace. Politely questioning a headhunter can create a new information connection for you. One recruiting expert suggested that the most important question that a manager can ask a recruiter is, "What can I do to help you?" If a manager is unemployed, he may have few resources to draw on. This is why these relationships are best nurtured when the manager is employed.

Respect the recruiter's time (it is a key resource not to be squandered), and avoid asking for career advice (such as what the recruiter thinks of your resume and how the job market is doing.) You can generally ask as many questions as you are asked. Focused questions show you are a careful and considerate executive. Your interviewing will ferret out jobs that sound seductive but have the wrong location, the wrong responsibility, and the wrong money. A candidate for a job gives headhunters a lot of information; she deserves replies to her questions. When answering questions, be careful not to give away confidential information.

Top executives are not alone in talking to recruiters. Each fall college campuses see a growing number of recruiters as businesses compete for the right people. Who are these recruiters looking for? Those who know what needs to be done and how to do it. Those who ask positive, perceptive questions in an interview will demonstrate those twin virtues.

ASK THE HEADHUNTER OR RECRUITER:

- What is your relationship with the company; are your retained or a contingent recruiter?[2]

- How did you hear about me?

- Do you have a specific assignment?

- What is the timeline you are looking at?[3]

  - How long do you have to work on filling this position?

- Can we talk about my background to see if it is relevant to your search?[4]

- What can you tell me about the client?

Be wary of exchanging information about your company that could get you into trouble.

ABOUT THE JOB:

- How long has the position been open?

  - Why has it been vacant so long?

- Why are they looking for someone outside their own company?

- What is the job description?

  - What are the responsibilities of this position?

  - What specific problem needs to be solved by this person?

- Is this a new position?

  - What happened to the person who previously had it?

- What is the salary range they are considering paying for this position?

  - How much am I worth?

■ What is the benefit package?

■ Are there stock options?

■ What is the job title?

■ To whom would I be reporting?

■ What characteristics do you think he or she most values in an employee?

■ What is the preferred working style at this company?

■ What is the location of the job?

■ Would this involve relocation?[5]

■ What is the structure of the company?

■ Is it highly centralized or not?

■ Is it growing?

■ What are its long-term, medium-term, and short-term goals?

■ Can you send me a catalogue, price list, or annual report from the company?

EXPERTISE:

■ How many placements have you successfully completed?

■ How often have you worked filling similar positions like this one?

■ Which companies have you worked for?

■ Whom else have you placed at this company?

■ How did they do?

■ Which professional organizations do you belong to?

■ Where does your company have offices?

■ Can you send me information on your firm before we talk?

■ Can you give me the names of anyone I've worked with that you've placed?

FOLLOW-UP:

■ What will be the next step?

   ■ What will be the screening process?

   ■ When and where will there be interviews?

   ■ Will I have to provide references?

      ■ Will I be asked to sign a reference-checking authorization?

■ Who will call me before my resume is sent to the client?

■ Are you a member of the Association of Executive Search Consultants?

   ■ Do you abide by its code of ethics?

Be careful with your resume; it may be sent to other prospective employers without your knowledge.

BEFORE A BIG INTERVIEW:

■ Has there been any change since the last time you talked to me?

   ■ Is there anything I should know before I go into the interview?

■ What will the interview process be like?

   ■ How long did the other interviews last?

■ Will it be a group interview or one on one?

   ■ Who else is in this loop?

■ What kinds of questions are usually asked?

You may also want to ask many of the questions presented in section 6/5, Questions That Work When Preparing for an Interview to check out the company before you interview. If you are not interested in the job, you might ask the recruiter if he would like names of people who might be interested. The recruiter might remember your help when another job comes along. Even if you are not interested in the position, by exchanging information you can ask about the salary range in your field, a very valuable insight.

6/7 Arranging an Interview

Assessment

You may want to see potential employers even if you are not interested in their current openings. By meeting and questioning the prospective employer, you begin to form a relationship that can lead to opportunities in the future. You must be available to talk to potential employers rather than just send resumes, since a resume is a static document. By talking to potential employers, you can judge the effectiveness of your letter and resume. Take the example of one young woman who applied for jobs at more than one hundred newspapers. The budding reporter didn't hear from anyone. Why? Her investigation showed that she had misspelled "sincerely" at the bottom of each letter. To get a job, there needs to be a flow of information between you and an employer. Your positive questions create relationships.

ASK THE POTENTIAL EMPLOYER:

- I'm in town next week for two days; which of those days could you meet me on?

- When are you least busy?

- May I see you for just one half-hour?

IF THE EMPLOYER SAYS NO:

- When is a good time to call back?

- Can you suggest a time?

- When might you have an opening?

- Who else in the company [if it is a large one] might be hiring?

- Do you know of others in your industry who are hiring?

- Can I use your name when calling them?

- Can I give you my name and number in case you think of someone who might be hiring?

ASK THE SECRETARY OR ADMINISTRATIVE ASSISTANT:

■ How is Mr. or Ms. _____ [name] properly pronounced?

■ What are the directions to your business?

  ■ Where is the best place to park?

■ What is the order of people being interviewed?

  ■ Can I have one of the last interview slots?

If you are responding to a post office box ad, check to make sure you know who placed it so that you are not applying to your company.

6/8 Being Interviewed

Assessment

The first interview is often simply an attempt to get a second interview. Anticipate a series of interviews for any important position. For a popular job, there will be dozens or even hundreds of applicants, and you will need to rise to the final cut. Interviews are a two-way process. You should have eight to ten questions ready to ask the employer, with one rule of thumb: Ask one question for every two the interviewer does. The interviewer will be asking you questions that should relate to your ability to do the job and to whether you will fit the company style.

By asking questions and listening carefully, you show focused competence. By questioning the interviewer, you create a personal relationship with someone who has probably interviewed dozens or hundreds of people. Your questions make you a little different in the other person's eyes by offering a little challenge. In survey after survey, those who hire place good verbal abilities at the top of the list, no matter what the position.

Look around the office; see whether there is anything that suggests a personal interest you can use to honestly show your curiosity.

Use your questions to find the hidden job, the critical tasks you can help the organization accomplish. Inquiry designed to discover why the job exists will give you an idea of the problems you are supposed to solve. Informed questions subtly allow you to advertise ways that you will produce results that matter. Just by asking about underlying issues, you show how you anticipate problems and listen carefully. In some way or another, everyone is hired as a problem solver.

Don't focus exclusively on whether the job offer is perfect; instead, ask what you need to do to be offered the position. If you get the offer, you can use the information you've gathered to negotiate the job you desire. Your questions also give you critical insights you'll need when it comes time to discuss the salary. If you are an older candidate and are worried that the organization is seeking only young guns, informed inquiry sets you apart by demonstrating depth of experience and active curiosity. Carefully crafted questions encourage the employer to think of you as a top candidate, since all managers look for candidates they can clearly communicate with.

Questions serve one last purpose in the interview process. They return some measure of control over the interview process to you. If you worry about appearing anxious or upset during the interview, having one or two questions you are confident about asking can calm your nerves. Confident questions serve you well by alluding to other options available to you. They also help you handle the moment when an offer can be made, especially if you might be given an "exploding offer," one where you are given limited time to consider whether to accept the job before it is withdrawn. Positive questions will assure the employer that you are interested, if only you can have time to consider their offer.

If you are meeting for a lunch or dinner interview, ask the host about where he or she would like you to sit. Many recruiters consider the meal the ultimate stress test because there are so many opportunities for mistakes.

ASK THE INTERVIEWER:

■ Is this a new position?

■ Was the previous person who held this job promoted to a new position?

This is an elegant variation on the question "What happened to the last person who had this job?" By phrasing it this way you avoid suggesting that the person before you was fired. You are also trying to see whether the company is growing and where the position's career track may lead. If necessary, you can also ask what the previous two people in this position did.

■ How does this job relate to the rest of the company?

■ How does it contribute to meeting the company's goals?

■ What was the last major project the person who had this position worked on?

  ■ Why is this position important?

■ What are the company's objectives?

  ■ What challenges does the company face?

■ Are there any upcoming changes in this business that will change the nature of this job?

  ■ Is there going to be or has there been a company reorganization?

■ What background are you looking for?

  ■ What are the qualifications of the ideal candidate?

■ What makes people succeed here?

  ■ How would you advise someone new here to start off right?

■ If I work hard and succeed here, where could my efforts lead to in a year? Two years?

■ How will the managers I report to help me meet my goals?

■ Will I work alone, or will I work with a team?

  ■ Can I meet the coworkers?

■ Who would be my supervisor? Would you be my immediate supervisor?

  ■ Can I meet him or her?

■ Who would be my coworkers?

  ■ Can I meet them?

■ How will my performance over the first few months be measured?

  ■ Who will measure it, and what success levels do I need to reach in the first six months, year, two years?

■ Is there any travel required? How much?

■ Is there a detailed position description, or is there a written job description?

■ What was this job like yesterday? (This is to get a typical descrip-tion. If you ask what a typical day is like, you'll probably be told there is no typical day. You might ask about a typical week.)

■ Who will give me an orientation program?

   ■ Is there a training program for new hires?

■ What are some of the ways I can continue to learn new skills?

   ■ Is there any in-house training or provision for tuition payment for out-side study?

■ Are there any training opportunities in the future?

   ■ What are the requirements to be considered for it?

■ What do people like best about this company?

   ■ What is unique about this company?

■ How long have you been with the company?

■ What tools will I be given to work with (like a laptop computer)?

■ Can I talk to the person I'll be replacing?

■ When would you want me to start?

   ■ When would I have to start?

IF YOU ARE APPLYING FOR A MANAGER'S POSITION:

■ What is the biggest challenge I will face?

   ■ What are the personality issues regarding the people I would be supervising?

■ What should be my goals for the first month?

   ■ What is the most important responsibility?

■ Whom will I be working with?

   ■ What kind of working relationship will I have with others?

■ What support staff would I have?

- Can I meet some of the people I would be supervising?

- Which decisions can I make on my own, and which ones do I need approval for?

- What is the budget I will have to work with?

AT THE END OF THE INTERVIEW:

(You want to see what will be the next step and show you enjoyed the interview. If you are still interested, these questions should help you to ask, "What should we do next?")

- Where do we go from here?

- What is the timetable for finding someone for this job?

- What date do you need someone by?

- When will the company be making a decision?

- Will there be another round of interviews?

- Can we schedule that meeting now?

- What parts of the job should I be thinking about until we talk again?

- When is a good time to call back; can you suggest a good time?

- Do you mind if I call in a week if I don't hear from you?

- What can I do in the meantime to help you decide I'm the right person?

- Can I get the spellings of _____ please? I met these other people today, and I'd like to be able to thank them.

Before walking out the door, look for hidden objections by asking whether the other person has any concerns about your ability to do the job. You might feel that this is just asking for trouble and finishing on a less than positive note, but it offers you a final chance to make your case. The fundamental question you would like to ask is, "How can I prove to you that I am the best person for the job?"

Once you're clear of the interviewer's office, the second round begins. Review the questions she asked you and see whether you need to clarify any of your answers. If you've asked the right questions, she knows you want the job, know about the organization, and have demonstrated how you can help it succeed. Ideally, questions create an ongoing flow of information between you and the company and show you are someone it can work with smoothly.

Don't ask about pay until a firm job offer is made. The rule of thumb is he who mentions money first loses.

See sections 6/11, Questions That Work When Negotiating Salary and Benefits and 12/3, Questions That Work When Asking for a Raise for insights into exploring an organization's pay philosophy.

Help, I'm Stumped

Some interviewers will aim to stump you. There are questions that help if you are uncertain how to answer, particularly those "yes" or "no" close-ended questions that limit your ability to respond. Prepare to ask clarification questions when a curveball comes your way.

ANY QUESTION WHERE YOU ARE NOT CLEAR ON THE INTENT:

■ What type of information are you specifically looking for?

FOR EXAMPLE, WHEN ASKED HOW YOU WOULD HANDLE A CRISIS:

■ It depends on what type of a crisis. Can you give me an example of a recent one your company has faced that I would be asked to help resolve?

IF ASKED QUESTIONS SUCH AS "WHAT ARE THE BEST SKILLS YOU CAN BRING TO OUR BUSINESS?"

■ What area is most important to the company?

WHEN JUST GENERICALLY CONFUSED:

■ Could you help me with your question?

WHEN ASKED A RUDE OR ILLEGAL QUESTION:

■ I'm sorry; how does that directly relate to the job I'm being asked to apply for?

IF YOU FEEL THE INTERVIEW HASN'T MADE A CONNECTION:

■ Which areas of interest or importance haven't I covered?

■ Are there any questions left in your mind?

■ I feel that I would make a real contribution, don't you?

IF ASKED ABOUT SALARY:

■ Ask what the company normally pays someone in that position.
  You can ask what the interviewer thinks is fair given your experience. If the pay is not acceptable, see whether you can table that
  issue until other issues have been resolved. If you can make it to
  the next round, you might be talking to someone with the authority
  to raise the amount. Prospective employees often don't negotiate
  the right salary because they lack information. Survey colleagues,
  recruiters, and even competitors to determine what the fair market
  rate is. See section 6/11, Questions That Work When Negotiating
  Salary and Benefits for discussion of questions for salary and
  benefits.

*Do not ask several questions about just one topic. It may not be an issue
the interviewer wants to spend time on and may make you look fixated on that
concern.*

You will face two types of questions: general and job specific. One
theory is there are only about twenty basic questions asked at interviews.
For a philosophy behind job interview questions to consider, see section
11/2, Questions That Work When Doing Interviews.

6/9 Being Turned Down for a Job

Assessment

You'll want to ask one question: "Why didn't I get the job?" Be careful.
How you ask it may open or close future opportunities. There is always
the chance you could still find work with the organization in the future.
You might have been in a shootout with several people competing for a
job. If the company's first choice can't do the job, you might be second
on the list.

ASK THE PERSON WHO INTERVIEWED YOU:

■ Do you mind if I ask why I wasn't chosen?

   ■ Are there any specific skills or abilities I need to have to be considered in the future?

■ Is it possible I might be considered for another interview?

   ■ I really want to work at your company; is there a possibility I could have a trial position?

IF THE JOB WAS OFFERED INTERNALLY AND YOU'VE BEEN TURNED DOWN FOR A PROMOTION:

■ How can I improve?

   ■ What expertise do I need?

■ How can I get enough experience to advance?

   ■ What degrees or credentials should I pursue?

■ Which departments should I develop relationships with?

   ■ Is there a profit center I can manage?

■ Who makes the selection of who gets the job the next time?

Being passed over is never an easy matter. If you feel stuck in one slot in your organization, your ability to get information on the reasons takes on a keen importance. Questions get you thinking in new directions and increase interactions with others that bring new opportunities. See section 11/10, Questions That Work When Doing Performance Appraisals and Setting Goals; section 12/1, Questions That Work When Asking Your Boss to Give You Feedback; and section 12/4, Questions That Work When Asking for a Promotion.

6/10 Being Offered a Job

Assessment

Before you celebrate the offer, find out more about the boss you will soon report to and ask for the job offer in writing. You have to negotiate for everything at every step of the way. Once you have a job offer, the negotiations begin again and won't end until the day you quit. In particular, you will want to understand:

■ How will my performance be evaluated?

■ What are the opportunities for future promotions and raises?

If you are offered a job but still have a possibility at another company, ask the second company "Can you give me a sense of where I stand?"
What follows are difficult questions but questions that bring about the best returns of any queries you may ever ask at work.

6/11 Negotiating Salary and Benefits

Assessment

Your positive questions indicate the paycheck is just one part of the compensation you are looking for. All areas of compensation are important. This is especially true today, where benefits have become more complicated and choosing the wrong benefits has more serious consequences. This is an area where previous questions about the job should pay handsome dividends. The opening of negotiations is a time when everything is askable. Guaranteed severance packages, sign-on bonuses, stock options, grants, and performance bonuses—all are on the table. Today you need to investigate a company just as an investor would analyze it before investing.
One rule of thumb is that changing jobs should bring a 10 to 20 percent boost in salary.

IF YOU ARE ASKED WHAT SALARY YOU WOULD LIKE, ASK THE INTERVIEWER:

■ Can I have more details on the overall compensation package?

  ■ Do I need to give a salary range?

■ Salary is only part of my consideration; can we talk about the benefits?

  ■ What are the benefits that this position includes?

■ Can we talk about the job for a minute?

  ■ Those duties seem to cover many of my areas of expertise; how
    can we structure the salary to cover them?

IF BONUSES ARE IN QUESTION:

■ How are they determined?

■ When will they be paid?

■ How will they be paid?

IF THE SALARY RANGE IS DISAPPOINTING:

■ Is there any flexibility in the compensation package?

  ■ Could we move forward my first salary review?

    ■ Can we do a performance review in sixty days so that I may be
      considered for a salary review?

■ Could you consider these benefits in addition to what you currently
  offer? (You can then give a list of benefits you would like to negotiate.
  This is discussed further later in this chapter.)

■ Can we upgrade the title?

  ■ If you can upgrade my title, would the salary you've proposed put
    me in the lower bracket of that position salarywise but give me
    more room to grow?

■ Is there a signing bonus we could negotiate?

  ■ What work tools can you offer?

  ■ Can I have a laptop computer (or other equipment)?

IF YOU MEET WITH RESISTANCE:

■ If I can't look out for my interests, how well can I look after the
  company's?

NOW ABOUT YOUR MEDICAL PLAN:

■ Can we shorten the period before coverage begins?

■ What is the coverage for catastrophic illness?

■ What medical services are not covered or are covered with restrictions?

  ■ What restrictions apply to pre-existing illnesses?

■ What dental coverage is there?

■ What is the maternity/paternity leave policy?

■ What is the sick leave policy?

■ Can I receive annual medical exams at no cost?

■ Does your plan cover domestic partners?

NOW ABOUT YOUR INSURANCE PLANS:

■ What supplemental life insurance can I purchase?

■ What is the long-term disability plan?

■ Is there a maximum payment or restriction under that disability plan?

NOW ABOUT A PIECE OF THE ACTION/SAVINGS PLANS:

■ What opportunities are there for stock grants?

■ Would this job be considered eligible for stock options?

■ Is there a profit-sharing plan?

  ■ How am I judged for it?

■ Do you have incentive savings plans such as 401K?

  ■ When would I become fully vested in the 401K?

■ What is the retirement plan?

NOW ABOUT YOUR VACATION AND SCHEDULE POLICY:

■ How flexible is the company about flextime?

　■ How do I go about requesting it?

■ Can we discuss additional time off?

　■ Since I'm still not satisfied with the progress we've made on the salary issue, can we look to improving my annual vacation allotment?

■ Can I sell back vacation time at the end of the year?

　■ Are there any restrictions on vacations (e.g., being allowed to take only one week at a time)?

■ What is the policy on personal days?

NOW ABOUT PERKS:

■ What is the policy on use of a company car?

■ What access do I have to a cellular phone or pager?

　■ Do you offer employees laptop or personal computers to use at home?

■ Will you be able to help with club or association membership fees?

　■ What help can you offer with professional association fees?

■ Is there any program to help with tuition reimbursement for ongoing college work?

　■ What training programs can I participate to improve my skill level?

■ What help do you offer with child care?

■ Is there a company program to help with college expenses for children of employees?

■ What can I have in the way of an allowance for improved office furnishings?

- There are numerous trade publications I believe will help me in my work; what is the policy on subscriptions?

- Since I'll be representing the company in public, is there a clothing allowance?

IF YOU ARE MOVING OR IF YOU MAY HAVE TO RELOCATE IN THE FUTURE AT THE COMPANY'S REQUEST:

- What can we do about the cost of living difference between the two areas?

- If I have to relocate for the company, what is the policy on moving expenses?

- Is there any assistance with home loans?

- Do you help spouses find new work?

NOW ABOUT TRAVEL AND ENTERTAINMENT FOR THE COMPANY:

- What is the expense account for this position?

- Does the company sometimes pay for travel for a spouse?

- Do you offer a van pool or any help with commuting expenses?

- What about parking expenses?

- Who gets to use the frequent flyer miles?

If you need to negotiate larger or more complicated issues, see section 8/10, Questions That Work When Beginning the Negotiations or section 12/3, Questions That Work When Asking for a Raise.

6/12 If It May Not Work Out

Assessment

Leaving any job is a delicate issue. Asking about leaving a company before you join it is like asking for a parachute before getting on a plane. The employer may feel nothing should go wrong and wonder why you are asking for a way out. You could say it's a fundamental issue that needs to be addressed, like looking for the exit signs when sitting down in a theater. If you are thinking of leaving an organization after gaining ten years of seniority, you don't want to take a new job and be fired shortly, only to get two weeks' severance pay.

ASK THE PERSON HIRING YOU:

■ What is the standard severance package? (You could say, "I've given up a lot from my old employer to come here. I'm glad to do it given the excellent opportunity, but can my agreement to work here include some recognition of the years I've invested?")

If you are worried about being fired, see section 14/1, Questions That Work When You Are Worried about Your Company's Future. If you are leaving your company, see section 6/14, Questions That Work When Leaving Your Current Job.

6/13 Being Asked to Sign an Employee Contract

Assessment

Employment contracts typically come up in discussions about positions high up in any organization. Contracts can range enormously in complexity, which is why you need to consult an attorney. While the language in any competently constructed contract answers many questions, further inquiry helps you understand the reasoning behind contract proposals. While it may never have occurred to you to talk with an attorney at this stage of your career, think of how many people wish they had talked to one when they were hired, rather than waiting until they were fired. Employment agreements can work to everyone's advantage if both parties know the ground rules for the business relationship.

ASK THE COMPANY REPRESENTATIVE (AND YOUR ATTORNEY):

■ Does the contract include language that will make sure I have the tools and authority to do my job?

■ What is the duration?

■ How does it spell out the salary and benefits?

■ What are the rules on the bonuses?

■ Are they related to company, department, or individual performance?

■ What are the grounds for dismissal?

■ What would I get in a severance package?

■ Does it include a noncompete clause?

■ Can we limit the area or type of companies?

6/14 Leaving Your Current Job

Assessment

You will want to leave your job on good terms, but be careful of the exit interview the organization may want to conduct. Any criticisms offered in good faith may prevent you from ever coming back to the company; you may be burning the bridges you may have to walk back over.

ASK YOUR CURRENT MANAGER:

■ What work do you need me to finish?

■ What would you say about my work at this time?

■ Are there any policies about resigning that I should know about?

ASK YOUR CURRENT EMPLOYER:

■ Can I leave my savings in your 401K if I leave this job?

■ If I have to take the money, who can help me fill out the appropriate forms to transfer the money directly to a new custodian?

■ Do I have any money left in any flexible spending accounts?

Questions That Motivate

Are you as satisfied with your career (work) as you hope your children will one day be with theirs?

Where do you think your children are learning what it means to have satisfying, fulfilling work?

Do you suppose they will follow your desires for them;
will they follow the example you show them?

What do you suppose your parents wished for you?

Gerry Sexton[6]

Chapter 6 Conclusion

Ideas into Action

Life is a series of questions. Looking for a job involves coping with ambiguity, requiring the best questioning abilities. If there is ever a time to follow the Socratic prescription to examine our own beliefs, to be aware of them, to evaluate them, it is when we are seeking a new job or career. In the end, no matter what the position or paycheck, nothing substitutes for job satisfaction. Choosing a company means choosing a way of life. Good organizations are places you can ask questions and receive meaningful answers. Those who find a positive questioning culture find a place of learning and growth. On-the-job education is what will keep your career and earning potential moving forward.

The difference between looking for a job and searching for a career is how much information you gather. As you approach and interview employers, listen carefully to what is asked of you. Those questions tell a great deal of what you want to know about how the organization sees and works with employees. The interview, with a two-way exchange, is the first indicator of the type of learning environment the company offers. If you log the questions asked during an interview, a close review will tell you what is important in the job you are applying for.

Questions can change your future. Asking the right ones can make the difference between landing an offer and losing a job, between having equity and not. Questioning skills add another dimension to you, making you an appealing, well-rounded candidate. If nothing else, by surveying others about their work, you subtly let them know you may be looking for a change. In chapter 7, we look at how to use questions to prosper in a changing workplace.

QUESTIONS THAT WORK WHEN:
Taking on a New Job or Career Change

Chance favors the prepared mind.

LOUIS PASTEUR

If the only constant is change, why do so many workers think success is doing the same work the same way, day after day? The marketplace of the world is rapidly changing its priorities, and the only way to keep up is with careful inquiry. You need to keep on questioning the very basics of what you are doing. In many workplaces, what was critical the day before is quickly forgotten in the face of a new crisis. As you change jobs, questions are the best tool to help you move into the future. Those new on the job are the subject of speculation and, in some tightly knit workplaces, seen as threatening outsiders. Positive questioning develops the helpful relationships that will alert you to problems. Asking questions shows that you are ready to learn, that you appreciate the expertise of those you work with, and that you are ready to contribute.

If there is a change in ownership of your company or you have a new supervisor, you effectively have a new job. Beware; many new managers are so busy, they won't ask to see whether you know their priorities. You can discover their concerns only by focusing your inquiry and keeping your eyes and ears open. If a supervisor does not give you clear objectives, you have to set them yourself by asking questions. Inquiry can be key to getting your supervisor to sign off on your personal goals, to back your efforts, and to appreciate your accomplishments. There is usually little profit in working extra hours on a project your boss or management deems not a priority.

Your workplace should be a place where you are told not only what to do but why to do it. Asking questions encourages the give-and-take that creates meaning.

7/1 Your First Day on the Job

Assessment

New employees possess a gift many long-time employees wish they had: Everything is new and everything is askable. If there is a formal job orientation, there will be plenty of information to absorb, including a history of the company, the corporate culture, what your duties will be, any dress code, and benefits. Even if there is an orientation, you need to use questions to take you more deeply into the organization and into the mind of your supervisor. If your direct supervisor hired you, chances are you have some grasp of his operating style. Because you asked focused and positive questions during your interviews, you know the company's general goals and challenges. Still, it never hurts to be sure of where the boss wants your energy and attention to go.

You shape your relationship with your manager by asking questions. You can use them to take on more responsibility and to attack what is bothering your boss. One philosophy of career success is to ask what makes your supervisor look good. This concept is simple, whatever is important to the boss should be important to you.

ASK THE PERSONNEL OFFICE/HUMAN RESOURCES PERSON:

- Can I have a tour?

  - Is there someone who can show me around and answer some basic questions?

- Can I have any employee manuals and material that describe benefits?

- Who are all the people to whom I will be reporting?

- As I prove myself, what are the opportunities for advancement?

  - How can I get enough experience to advance?

ASK YOUR BOSS:

First-Round Questions

Because I want to quickly get started on (the office's, the organization's, your) priority issue:

- How will I be introduced, and when?

  - Can I help give a summary of my skills and background to help introduce myself?

- Can I preview the announcement?

  - What's the best way to establish my credibility?

- What can I do to help?

  - What are your goals or missions?

    - Are there any special projects I can work on?

- By what date do you need my first task finished?

  - What other deadlines should I be aware of?

- What authority do I have?

  - Whom are the people I should report to?

- What other departments will I be working with?

- Whom can I call when I have a question?

- What equipment will I have to use?

Second-Round Questions

- When will my performance appraisals be done?

  - Should we set some goals for me to aim towards?

- What's the best communication style here?

  - Should I write memos, call meetings, or be more informal?

- Whom should I copy on a memo?

  - Is there a distribution list I should know about?

    - Whose name should go first on my memos?

- Would you like progress reports?

  - How often would you like them?

  - Would you like them verbally or written?

- Whom are some of the important clients I'll be dealing with?

  - With whom in the office and outside should I form relationships with?

- What times should I avoid scheduling vacations?

- What is the policy toward accepting gifts if a client gives me one?

Third-Round Questions

- How can I add extra value to what we do?

- What research do we have on our customers?

  - What is their age, sex, and economic status?

- How are new ideas for products or services evaluated?

- What professional groups or associations should I be a part of?

  - Will the company pay the cost of membership?

ASK COWORKERS, AFTER YOU GET TO KNOW THEM:

- What did the last person who had this job do right?

  - What did she do wrong?

- Who gets the promotions, and why?

  - What does it take to advance here?

- How can I get enough experience to advance?

  - Should I work in or with other departments?

7/2 Taking on the Duties of a Manager

Assessment

There are few experiences more daunting than becoming a first-time manager. A colleague said instead of feeling grown up when promoted to manager, he felt like a kid. New managers can have a child's insecurities and feel that a lot of question marks surround them. Dan Thompson of Edge Training Systems, a survey respondent, warns that new supervisors typically act as though they must "know all the answers."[1]

New managers are often under extreme pressure to take action on a pressing problem or crisis. Questions will determine the success of their plan of action. Many new managers struggle because they do not understand what is expected of them or because they have no shared goals with their immediate supervisor.

As you take charge, use questions to show what you are interested in accomplishing. Make it clear your inquiries do not indicate uncertainty; instead, point out how they show what information needs to be gathered and acted on. Your first questions show you are committed to making choices with your colleagues' help. Ask questions that get to the heart of the problems you know your coworkers face, those clearly related to the work at hand. You need to quickly get to know the players and learn the history of the group you are taking over. I've heard some new managers ask employees "Why shouldn't your job be eliminated?" Such a question is blunt, businesslike, and sure to create paranoia.

First impressions are often shaped by another's queries, and you can expect your employees will be quick to form impressions of you. This first impression all depends on what you ask and how you ask it. What complicates life as a manager is that each time you take a step up in the number of people you supervise, you will find you cannot ask as many questions of each individual. The friendly, hands-on questioning of twenty employees often fails when the number swells to two hundred or two thousand. Your inquiry skills must expand as your supervising demands grow.

ASK YOUR SUPERVISOR:

■ What do you want to see from me?

■ What changes will I be expected to make?

   ■ Will I have free rein to cut staff or areas that are not productive?

■ Are there any problems I need to deal with right away?

   ■ What is the reputation of the department?

■ Can I have a copy of the current budget?

   ■ What is the budget timeline?

■ Do you have a staffing chart?

- Who reports to me?

  - Whom am I responsible for?

- What are the salaries and job functions of the staff?

  - What past personnel problems have we had?

  - What has been the employee turnover?

- What's the work pace you think I should be aiming for?

  - What is the daily routine I should establish?

- How much time will I have to brainstorm about the changes I would like to make?

- Would you like to see a plan for what I intend to do?

  - Will I be able to ask for a bigger budget to address these challenges?

  - Will I be able to hire consultants when needed?

- What new products or services are in the pipeline?

  - What market research is taking place?

- Do you expect this department to grow in the future?

- Whom will I have to work with on a regular basis?

  - What alliances do I need to form to make this work?

ASK THE PERSON WHO HELD THE JOB:

- Do you mind if I ask a few questions?

  - Whom are the key people I will report to?

  - What are the top priorities?

  - Are there any sensitive political issues I need to watch for?

ASK YOUR EMPLOYEES:

- Can you make a presentation on your major project?

- Where are the bottlenecks?

- What exactly do you do?

- How long does it take you to do parts of your job?

- What deadlines are realistic?

- What are three things you would do to make the company succeed?

  - What do you need to do your job more effectively?

- What new assignments, skills, or opportunities would you like to have?

If you are facing a conflict right away, see section 15/1, Questions That Work When Facing a Conflict, or section 15/2, Questions That Work When Communication Is the Problem.

7/3 Reporting to a New Boss

Assessment

You need to discover a new supervisor's game plan as soon as possible. Managers quickly judge who is going to help them succeed in their new role and those who are an obstacle to be removed. Avoid surprising a new boss with any unpleasant development or problem. Any unhappy news will be magnified in the mind of a new supervisor who is often insecure in his role or overwhelmed by details. Be sparing in your initial inquiry, and respect their workload. For your own protection, if your previous boss was dismissed, you need to explore why it happened. What mistake did he or she make that you need to avoid repeating?

ASK THOSE WHO HAVE WORKED FOR THIS BOSS BEFORE:

- Is she formal or informal?

- What is the background of this person?

  - How did she get to this position?

- What style of communication does this person prefer?

  - Verbal or written?

  - How does she like responses to her questions?

  - How does this boss like to be told bad news?

- What are her priorities?

- What is her career agenda?
- Who succeeds in this person's department?

ASK YOUR NEW BOSS:

- Is there anything I can do to help speed your plans along?
  - What is your approach to _____?
- Is there anything I can do to help make your job easier?
- Do you need any information to help understand the situation or the people in place?
- What are the challenges you see us facing in the future?
  - What would you like to see happen in the future?
- What changes do you see happening?
- How am I doing?

Listen carefully to the answer to this last question. While you may not get a promise of continued employment, be careful if your question is deflected or ignored.

If you think the new boss means changes in your job, see section 14/1, Questions That Work When Worried about Your Company's Future. If you would like more guidance, see section 12/1, Questions That Work When Asking Your Boss to Give You Feedback.

Questions That Motivate

Why are you really here?

Amy Taylor[2]

Chapter 7 Conclusion

Ideas into Action

Questions are the most inexpensive and most readily available tool for any worker who needs to anticipate and manage personal and professional change. When you are new on the job, being inquisitive helps you quickly determine the organization's goals and helps make sure you don't violate any sacred values. Your question marks move you through and help you explore the new work world. Questions serve as icebreakers, creating a sense of belonging, and help you become a catalyst for positive change.

The measure of a job is not found in the salary; it is the culture of an organization, how it feels to work there, that determines whether many workers feel fulfilled and whether they stay or go. In the workplace, we desire respect and a feeling of accomplishment often found in a positive questioning culture. As you progress through your career, it is useful to have a mentor or a close associate regularly question you about your goals so that you continually grow.

Inquiry helps employees discover and focus on the most important priorities, while helping new managers determine whether they are getting the results they hoped for. While it is critical to consult with and survey your staff about what is happening in your department, be careful of becoming too dependent on the advice of your staff. Use questions to focus on what your intuition tells you are the problems facing you. Ask skillful, sensible, and sensitive questions, and you'll establish your credentials as a diplomat and a doer.

In chapter 8, we present the questions that can determine the success of any business in a changing world and that serve you well when selling and negotiating.

Part III

Questions at Work

QUESTIONS THAT WORK WHEN:
Selling and Negotiating

A timid question will always receive a confident answer.

LORD DARLING

Every day we find ourselves selling something. Even those who never call a client are selling their abilities and point of view. Since every organization has customers (if nothing else, internal customers), leaders should examine the questions the business should be asking, from the customer's point of view. These questions include the following:

■ Why do customers need our product or service?

■ How can we organize our business around the customer?

■ What do our customers need from us to help them serve their customers?

This line of inquiry is a hard-core reality check. For those who feel such questions are exclusively the work of market researchers, the truth is that understanding the customer, getting into his or her head, is everyone's job. It takes a wide variety of viewpoints to come up with the nonstandard questions needed to discover the hidden needs of customers. Only when all employees of an organization feel they should ask questions can the company carry out a continuous dialogue to see how the customer uses its products or services. As a company asks questions, it decides what it will become. The information about the customer's needs and priorities is out there; you have to go and get it.

Selling is solving a problem. So says Ron Popeil, the Ronco pitchman for such products as Mr. Microphone and the Pocket Fisherman. When asked about his secret to success, he described his job as "point[ing] out some of the serious problems you really don't focus on." Until Popeil came along, millions didn't know that life is empty without a folding fishing pole that fits in a glove compartment, but such an appeal has

115

helped sell a billion dollars' worth of merchandise, products even Popeil admits customers may not have wanted. "I'm selling items to the public they had no intention of buying in the first place."[1]

There is a saying that "You don't have to sell; you just have to get them to buy." Focused questions show understanding of your customer's business and what they need to succeed. Every customer worries almost exclusively about his or her welfare tomorrow. Customers buy when they are satisfied that your company will save them money or help them make money. You need to keep quizzing even the most familiar customers, since the situation of any customer is never static. As you are given information, you need to give information in return. Customers value and pay more for services that provide useful information.

8/1 Understanding the Customer

Assessment

Who understands your customer better than you? Is it a competitor? Those who learn more about your core customers are on the path to providing superior service and outstanding value. Don't *expect* sales success if you don't *inspect* what is going on with customers. Use questions to put yourself in your customer's shoes, to focus on the customer's problems, and to explore what the consumer does and does not do with your product or service. David Palmer, a partner with the Customer Manufacturing Group, asks a key marketing question: "What is the customer buying?" Palmer says, "The right answer is that he or she is always buying a lot more than what you are selling." He argues that most companies don't truly understand everything their customers are "buying."[2] They may be buying a reputation, convenience, trend, nostalgia, or a color. In many ways, the question is not just *whether* your customers use your product or service but *how* they use it.

Don't assume; be a little naive when asking why people buy from you.

As Bruce Woolpert, president of Granite Rock Company, noted, the advent of the computer has made it possible for businesses to track and analyze an enormous amount of information. Companies can now do customer surveys, focus groups, and "trial runs" of new products more easily. Woolpert says this testing is now a much-used form of asking questions.[3] Not only can learning about customers help you sell today; asking staff, suppliers, and customers creates an early warning system that tells where your company is falling behind in today's crowded marketplace. Get to know your front-line employees and through them you get to know your customers.

Walter Dean, of the Pew Center for Civic Journalism, asks a question to gauge how broadcasters see their viewers: "Do you see [customers] as furniture to move around or Joe 6-pack or as fellow citizen residents with real problems and the desire to find solutions?"[4] How does your business see your customers?

ASK YOUR STAFF:

■ Who are our most important customers?[5]

  ■ Are we giving them enough attention?[6]

■ Are your clients happy?[7]

■ Why do they buy from or hire us?

■ What are they looking for?

  ■ What do they really want?[8]

  ■ What are they buying?

■ What can we do to make it easier for our customers?

  ■ How can we most easily exceed their wildest expectations?[9]

■ What do you think the customers value the most about this product?[10]

■ What do they think they need?

  ■ What are their unmet, unspoken needs?[11]

■ How is our product or service used?

  ■ What do you think it does for them?

    ■ Does it improve their life?

      ■ How could it?

      ■ When it is used, what seasonality is there to demand?

  ■ Where is it used, what geographic demand is there?

■ Where do people shop for or find our product or service?

- What advantages does our product or service have?

  - What benefits set it apart?

    - Are those benefits compelling?

      - How could they be made compelling?

- Is our product or service convenient?

- How could it be more convenient?

  - Is it comfortable?

    - How could it be more comfortable?

  - What status does it give?

    - Could it give more status?

  - Is it more stylish?

  - Is it of a better quality?

  - Is it cheaper?

  - Is it safer?

  - Is it more reliable?

    - Is it more durable?

- If your brother or sister were the customer, what would they want in this experience?

  - Are customers contacted after the sale to see about their satisfaction?

ABOUT COMPETITORS:

- How is the competition hurting us?

- Do we closely monitor the competition?

  - Where does our competition sell its products?

  - Has the competition's market share been growing or shrinking?

  - What are their strategies?

  - How are their products different from ours?

- What are the sales and earnings trends that have caused this concern?

- What changes have taken place in the market?

- Is the overall market shrinking or growing?

ABOUT THE FUTURE:

- What can we do to get our fair share of the market?

  - What are the barriers we are facing on making sales?

- What are the opportunities in the marketplace?

  - Which new areas should we expand into?

- What customer service or product can we offer that others can't easily duplicate?

- What are the long-term and short-term goals?

  - What is the five-year trend for the sales volume and profitability of this product or service?

ASK CUSTOMER SERVICE EMPLOYEES:

- Who are your customers?

  - What are your customer's expectations?

- Do we organize our efforts around customer needs?

  - Why not?

- Do we treat different customers differently?

  - Do we create a learning relationship with your customers?

- Do we keep our customers?

  - Why not?

- What customers or clients are never satisfied?

  - Are any late on paying their bills?

  - Do any expect too much service?

  - Do any take too much time?

■ How do you evaluate the competition?

  ■ Is there a noncompetitive business trying to reach the same customer that we can work with?

ABOUT A SPECIFIC CUSTOMER:

■ Does the order represent the beginning of a long-term relationship?

  ■ Can the customer lead us to new customers?

Experience your own customer service. Call and ask questions.

If you need to problem solve for a client, see section 13/1, Questions That Work When Investigating a Problem. If you need to think about how customers use products, see section 9/4, Questions That Work When Brainstorming about a Product.

Questions That Work

Jonna Contacos, a vice president with HR Consultants, says that if an organization is truly customer service focused, a series of mandatory questions should be asked. These include:

1. Can you describe an employee's role in the company-customer relationship?

2. Can you tell me about a time when it was very difficult to carry out this role?

3. Be specific; how did you resolve this situation?[12]

8/2 You Are a Retailer or Customer Service Staff

Assessment

Customers expect salespeople to know about the product and to know about related products. Salespeople who are good questioners and listeners are those who try to find out what product or service would best fill the customers' needs. Customers want to know that their buying decision was based partly on their own input. This depends on the quality of the questions the salesperson asks. Good inquiry is not fast and cheap; fast and cheap inquiry is not good.

ASK THE CUSTOMER:

- What do you like?

  - What don't you like?

- When do you think you will be buying?

  - How much time do you have to shop?

  - Where else will you be shopping?

- How can we improve our service?

  - How do you feel about shopping here? How do you feel about our service?

  - In which aisle are you spending most of your time? Which service do you use most?

- Why did you start shopping here? Why did you start using our services?

- What do you think of our assortment or range of services?

  - What do you think of our quality?

  - How convenient is our service or location?

- Would you recommend us to a friend?

ASK FORMER CUSTOMERS:

- Why don't you buy with us anymore?

  - What can we do to bring you back?

8/3 Finding the Customers or the Right Person to Pitch To

Assessment

It doesn't matter how good your pitch is if you are selling a product, service, or idea to the wrong person. Your first questions should qualify the buyer and get the commitment to go to the next level. This first contact is often exclusively a process of gentle interviewing that leads to the opportunity to present more detailed information in the future. This is the moment when questions serve as the hook. Some call it the curiosity script, a pitch built around questions designed to create an itch only your proposal, product, or service can scratch. It can sometimes take several new messages or sets of questions to get your proposed opportunity across. Those messages, often delivered by your salesforce, are often the only contact the customer has with your business. These messages have to stress a central selling point, the benefit of your product, service, or idea. This message often takes the form of a question your product or idea answers.

Brief and professional questions—who, what, why, where, when, and how—can inspire the other party to wonder about your proposal. When you have only a matter of four or five seconds to get the person's attention, questions can engage the person in your proposal from your very first sentence. It is often a matter of asking a question to which the other party would like to answer with an enthusiastic yes. Ruth Owades, founder of the national flower delivery company Calyx and Corolla, had a simple concept—flowers should go direct from the field to consumers. As a result, she wanted to sell her concept to an overnight delivery service that would serve as her partner. Owades said, "My idea was a bunch of notes on yellow pieces of paper where I was scribbling my notes and Fed Ex was a nine billion dollar corporation . . . so getting to the right people was a big challenge because, after all, they get a lot of ideas from crazy entrepreneurs all the time."[13] Her presentation asked Federal Express if it would like to have a big new source of overnight business. The answer was "yes."

You need to avoid deciding how much influence you think someone has until you are certain where the person stands in the sales process. Questions may reveal hidden pockets of authority and influence that you might otherwise never suspect. Through inquiry you can discover new people who might be interested in your proposal. Mark Smith, a survey respondent, has novel questions to find sales leads. He asks, "Who can you think of that deserves to be treated the way that I've taken care of you?" and "Who can you think of that would find these ideas of value?"[14]

Your questions create customers' curiosity. Their questions create their commitment.

ASK THOSE WHO KNOW WHOM YOU ARE APPROACHING:

■ Who has the authority to decide?

■ What is the best way to approach this person?

- Does she prefer to be called or should I write up my proposal?

- When is the best time to approach her?

- Does she have any commitments that tie her up at this time?

8/4 Making the Sale and Pitching the Project

Assessment

Customers and managers are often not clear on what they want. They may not understand what their problem really is. Questions focus the customer on what is currently bothering him, opening the door for you to solve the problem with your product, service, or project. Much has been made of the use of questions in sales, the new "consultative selling" compared to the old "have I got a deal for you" technique. Selling through inquiry is not new. Dale Carnegie summed it all up years ago: "Asking questions not only makes an order more palatable; it often stimulates the creativity of the persons whom you ask. People are more likely to accept an order if they have had a part in the decision that caused the order to be issued."[15]

The telecommunications and Internet revolution increasingly puts customers in charge of the buying process today. Michael Lee, a real estate broker, says that today salespeople must "become more like consultants than order takers. We must provide information to see who can meet the customer's needs."[16] Open-ended questions encourage conversation. I once had a million-dollar decision to make about the leasing of a piece of equipment and services, and I heard a number of different pitches. What staggered me was that almost all the salespeople had only one real question for me: "How much can you afford?" They never bothered to find out my needs or the challenges facing my business. Just be careful not to become interrogator, someone who asks endless questions that offer no apparent benefit to the customer. Too many questions make customers uncomfortable; they can start to worry their answers will be used against them. In particular, be careful not to request confidential or sensitive company information. You should never ask questions that imply criticism of the customer's past choices or a company's direction. You want to be seen as the partner, not the intellectual superior or critic of the person.

Anyone pitching a product, service, or idea has to realize that the customer has a world of conflicting data to consider. She is searching for the sure thing.

ASK THE CUSTOMER:

■ How can I best serve you?

■ What new services or products would you like?

■ How are you doing _____?

  ■ What applications do you have?

  ■ Would you like to see a demonstration?

■ Where are you now in relation to your company's goals?

■ What would you like to see improved?

TO DISCOVER THE CUSTOMER'S AMBITIONS:

■ How would you like to . . . ?

■ What are your goals?

  ■ How do you want to get there?

  ■ What barriers stand between you and your goals?

■ What can we do to help your business succeed?

  ■ What do you want to accomplish?

TO DISCOVER PROBLEMS:

■ Other customers of ours have had difficulty with . . . , has this been a problem for you?

  ■ Are you concerned about that?

■ What do you attribute that to?

■ Are you satisfied with . . . ?

  ■ Is your current level of . . . acceptable to you?

■ Any idea what's causing your problem?

  ■ What factors bring about that problem?

■ How much time is lost?

- How much money is lost?

  - How much overtime does it cost?

  - How much business is lost?

  - What is the impact on your customers?

- How does that affect . . . ?

  - Does that lead to . . . ?

- If you don't solve that problem, what might happen?

  - What other problems does that create for you?

TO DISCOVER WHETHER YOUR PRODUCT OR SERVICE COULD HELP:

- Suppose you could . . . ; what would that enable you to do?

  - How would that help?

- Would . . . have any advantages?

  - How much would you save if?

- Could our product or service increase the amount of work completed?

- What research have you done to prepare for this project?

  - How will you decide what product or service will be right for you?

TO DISCOVER POSSIBLE CHANGES:

- Are you making any changes in your business?

  - Do you have any plans for expansion?

- What changes would you make with your current system?

  - How would you like it to operate?

    - How many times a week?

    - What is your normal schedule?

      - How will it change in the future?

BEFORE GIVING A CUSTOMER A FORMAL PROPOSAL:

- What questions do we need to answer?

- What details do you need?

- How will you evaluate the proposal?

BEFORE LEAVING THE CUSTOMER:

- Was my presentation helpful?

  - What was most helpful?

    - What did you like best?

      - What did you like least?

- How can I improve?

- Is there anything else we can do for you?

  - Would you like more information?

- Do you know of anyone else who might need what we offer?

  - Can I have an introduction to the next person?

BEFORE GIVING CREDIT, ASK YOUR TEAM TO FIND OUT:

- What is their credit rating?

- What kind of a company is it, a partnership or a corporation?

- How long has it been in business?

  - Who are the partners or owners?

- Which bank do they do business with?

  - What loans are outstanding?

It is not unusual to be asked to write up a sales proposal. This paper tests your questioning skills, since it should be designed to answer the client's concerns. A well-thought-out proposal is the result of the two parties agreeing on the questions that must be answered. The proposal writer who carefully interviews the client will find the resulting proposal rises far above the level of those submitted by the competition by clearly outlining the solution and expenses.

If you need to creatively rethink your proposal, see section 9/2, Questions That Work When Inspiring Creativity, or section 9/4, Questions That Work When Brainstorming about a Product.

Questions that Work

Michael Lee, the host of a national radio business show, focuses his selling questions on one word, "problem." He asks these questions to explore the customer's problems as the first part of an effective sales pitch.

1. What problem, if any, do you need to solve?

2. When do you need to solve the problem?

3. Do we have a product or service that can help you solve that problem?

4. Are we the best company to solve the problem? If not, who is?[17]

8/5 Trying to Close a Deal

Assessment

Not asking for the order can be seen as a sign of weakness. Ask all potential customers to agree, buy, and commit. Confirming the order is such an important part of any deal that it pays to rehearse these particular questions. It helps to remember that everyone has others who are questioning his decisions. To subdue the other party's concerns if he hesitates to sign, use questions to discover the risks he is worried about and help him overcome the doubts of others inside the organization. Almost everyone operates under the oversight of some committee or another department, and you need to answer the questions of those invisible persons. By asking specific questions about who these people are throughout the sales process, you avoid the other party's using unhappy but vague higher authority figures as the reason he won't buy.

Questions help you make sure you do not underprice your service or product by helping you learn what the market and the other side considers reasonable.

ASK THE CUSTOMER:

- If we make you an offer that does . . . and at a reasonable cost, will you say yes?

  - Is there any reason why you can't buy today?

- If you get this discount, do we have a deal?

- Can you make a commitment now?

  - If not now, when can you move forward?

- Can we get the paperwork started?

- Can I meet with the person who can make the decision?

If you need to have a follow-up meeting, see section 10/3, Questions That Work When You Are Asked to Attend a Meeting. If you need to prepare for negotiations, see section 8/9, Questions That Work When Learning about Your Customer's Position.

8/6 Having Trouble Making the Sale or Pitching Your Idea

Assessment

When a good prospect falls through or a proposal meets resistance, you need to explore why it didn't work out and what can be done differently in the future. Just as this book is a collection of questions, you should keep a collection of objections. The first objection is often not the real problem. The other party may have objections it doesn't want to reveal, such as a lack of budget or a lack of power. The danger of inelegant questioning is that it forces people to repeat their objections. The more often people repeat a position, the more it hardens. It becomes a matter of pride not to give in. Those who sell, even if it is simply selling a point of view, need to be polite and patient. You discover patterns of behavior you can unravel only with questions. Rejection is frustrating, but inquiry offers an infinite capacity for renewal.

Questions discover the hidden objections why people won't commit.

ASK THE CUSTOMER OR CLIENT:

- Is what I'm saying making sense?

  - Are you getting the information you need to make a decision?

■ What is giving you trouble . . . ?

  ■ Would it help you if . . . ?

■ Do you have any questions?

  ■ Can you help me understand why is there still some uncertainty?

■ Are you unhappy with something about our product?

  ■ Is there some objection that I just don't understand?

    ■ Would you like to talk about it now or should we just move on?

■ Why do you consider my idea to risky given the possible payoff?

■ You seem impatient; how much time can we take to address your concerns?

  ■ Can you delay the decision?

    ■ Can I have time to review your request?

IF YOU ARE TURNED DOWN:

■ Can we speak again when the circumstances change?

■ What would make you reconsider?

■ Would you review our proposal again considering this new information?

If you need to review what went right or wrong with your proposal, see section 10/14, Questions That Work When Reviewing a Project or Event.

8/7 Negotiating

Assessment

Negotiations are about discovering the needs and limitations of the other party. The more the other person talks, the more you learn. With this information, you can control the initiative and point the discussion in the direction you would like to go. Offers and counteroffers are a series of inquiries, even if they are not stated as such. As you focus on the finer points of negotiating, you will increasingly appreciate the value of questions. G. Richard Shell, director of the Wharton Executive Negotiation Workshop, confirms this with a study he reviewed on labor and contract negotiations. The study found that skillful negotiators ask twice the number of questions as the average negotiator.[18]

How is negotiating different from problem solving? Problem solving defines a concern and the options and often takes place between those who share the same point of view. Negotiations can do the same but are focused on defining the value of and the priority of issues where the parties have deep differences. In both, information is exchanged, but in negotiations you do not reveal all your information. Skilled negotiators know they need to carefully consider their inquiries so that they do not inadvertently reveal information they wish to withhold. Many negotiations are a deal making that revolves around two questions: "What do I need to know?" and "What does the other side need to know?"

If you need to form a negotiating team, see section 10/9, Questions That Work When Forming a Team.

8/8 Learning about Your Position

Assessment

In most cases you are not negotiating just for yourself. Questioners need to fully understand the priorities and alternatives facing the group they represent before entering negotiations. To be able to represent the group's concerns, you need to define their needs. There are few workplace frustrations worse than aggressively negotiating a position and then being told by superiors to suddenly change the terms. As the author Mark MacCormack urged, "collect—aggressively solicit—their opinions on the deal and allow these to shape your idea or presentation: 'We were wondering such-and-such'; 'Would it be better to emphasize this or that?'; 'We'd like to know your feelings on the following.'"[19]

ASK YOUR TEAM:

- What is the deal we want?

  - What is our need for price/delivery/terms?

  - What are our time issues?

    - What is our deadline?

- What precedent has been set by similar past negotiations?

■ What's the best outcome?

  ■ What is our walk-away point?

■ How will the other side evaluate our offer?

  ■ How can we present our offer in positive terms?

■ What are our best arguments?

  ■ Who are our allies?

■ What are some of the simpler issues we think can be resolved—shall we begin with them first?

■ Is this a one-time deal, or is this the future?

■ What will happen if the other side doesn't pay us or doesn't deliver?

If you are disagreeing about the items to negotiate on, see section 15/4, Questions That Work When Disagreeing with Another. If you need creative solutions, see section 9/1, Questions That Work When Creating the Right Environment.

8/9 Learning about Your Customer's Position

Assessment

Those who regularly practice positive questioning are more comfortable and skilled when looking into the other side's position. They know that the first few questions set the tone for the rest of the negotiation. They carefully approach the other side with questions they can easily answer and never make their first question the most crucial. The first responses indicate whether there will be a cooperative or adversarial situation. The first inquiries on both sides educate all involved as to the form of the negotiation and to the type of questions that will be used. If possible, you want to use open-ended questions. Such questioning allows you to constructively "play dumb," giving you more options than would stating hard and fast facts or locking yourself into a specific position to begin with. You want the other side to give you as much information and as many feelings as possible for you to analyze. With these feelings and facts you can determine who is in charge on the other side. You can't effectively negotiate unless you know who the real decision maker is.

ASK YOUR TEAM:

- How well do we know the other side?
  - Whom do we get along with and trust on the other side?
- What is the personality of the person we'll be negotiating with?
  - Does she like to haggle or cut straight to the chase?
- Who are the other people involved in making this decision?
  - What time pressures are they under?
  - What is their workload?
  - What is the limit of their authority?
  - Are they on commission?
    - When do they need to make the sale?
- What does the other side want?
  - What would their list of their needs include?
  - What is their walk-away point?
    - What else do we need to know to understand their position inside and out?
- What are the best arguments the other side has?
- Who supports the other side?
- Have we asked for a proposal?
  - What are the key numbers from which we can negotiate?
- What has the other side agreed to in a previous similar situation?
- Do we need a third-party negotiator?
- Do we have any shared interests?

8/10 Beginning the Negotiations

Assessment

Emotions are part of every negotiation. Even the driest business topics involve egos and anxieties. Since many people find that the head never hears till the heart has listened, negotiations can't proceed until some emotions are vented. It is important to recognize the importance of feelings, especially when you are selling. The opposite of desire is fear. Asking questions shows you are reasonable and open to the other side's concerns. If someone is particularly emotional, it may help to explain why you are asking a question. While the person may never see you as an ally, such positive questioning makes you less of an enemy. You have to neither accept nor reject their feelings; just recognize them.

Anticipate a lack of patience during the long back-and-forth of many negotiations. Temper these feelings by pointing out that your queries show you appreciate what the other side has done, that you are attempting to understand its concerns, and that you are aiming for a fair conclusion. Being this sensitive does not mean you can't make a large initial demand. The unspoken rules of negotiation require that you ask for more than you think you will get. Those who think they can skip this step are wrong. An aggressive opening proposal might be accepted and, if not, it creates the essential room to negotiate down. The large initial demand has the added benefit of raising the perceived value of what you're offering. Most negotiations are, in the end, a matter of coming to a price agreement among two businesses. There are many other factors, but a negotiator's questions should always aim at this bottom line.

IF YOU ARE THE BUYER, ASK THE OTHER SIDE:

- What exactly is being sold?
- When?
  - When will the service be performed?
  - When will we receive the product?
- Where?
  - Where will the product be delivered?
- How?
  - How will the service be provided?
  - How much will it cost?
- Can you match the best price I've gotten?

- If not, what price can you give me?

- How are the payments timed?

- If I offer something (more flexibility, fewer options), will it lower the price?

- What will you do if the product or service is not as promised?

- Would you mind explaining _____ to me . . . ?

- Could I ask you a few questions to see whether my facts/understanding is right?

It may help in negotiations to ask "What are you asking for this?" rather than "How much?" The negotiation determines how much something is worth. The price should be found between what they want and what the service or product is worth to you.

If you need to make a critical decision, see section 13/4, Questions That Work When Making a Big Decision. If you are buying a business, see section 16/1, Questions That Work When Checking out a Business Opportunity.

8/11 Reaching Difficult Issues

Assessment

There is more room between yes and no than many think. In seeking the bottom line, you may find several related issues surrounding the main item. Questions discover what bargaining chips you have to work with. What may be almost worthless to you may be vital to the other side, something you won't know until you ask. Even ultimatums often have flexibility when the reasons behind them are probed. Care is required in questioning, for a casual query can be returned, forcing you to reveal information you would rather have hidden. If you request to know how much someone makes, expect to be asked the same.

ASK THE OTHER SIDE:

- What exactly is the obstacle you see?

  - What exactly is your complaint?

    - What exactly do you want us to do about it?

IF THE OTHER SIDE MAKES DEMANDS:

■ Why are you saying that?

  ■ Can you tell me the reasons behind this demand?

■ It seems you've reached certain conclusions; how do you support them?

■ What would it take to change your position just a little?

■ Can I get back to you?

IF YOU GET SIDETRACKED:

■ Can we finish with the original topic?

IF THE PERSON SAYS SHE DOESN'T HAVE THE AUTHORITY TO MAKE THE FINAL DECISION:

■ Who does have the authority to approve this agreement?

■ Can we meet with the person who can approve this?

■ When does the board of directors meet?

IF HE INVOKES A RULE:

■ Would you make an exception to the rule?

■ Have you ever made an exception to this rule?

■ Why does this rule exist?

WHEN YOU PROPOSE A SOLUTION:

■ What happens if we both agree to . . . ?

■ Does that sound fair to you?

If you need to hear the other side's concerns completely, see section 13/1, Questions That Work When Investigating a Problem. If negotiations can't start due to a dispute, see section 15/1, Questions That Work When Facing a Conflict.

8/12 Concluding the Negotiations

Assessment

If you can reach a commitment to some point or resolution of some issue in each meeting or phase of negotiation, you avoid being stuck in an endless cycle of discussions. Before you say yes to any point, use questions to check the other side's supporting facts. You wouldn't expect the other side to accept your statements on faith, yet often you may find yourself accepting facts and figures without close examination. You may need to check with your experts before making a final decision on accepting a proposal. If you do so, welcome the experts' questions as a final check. Before you arrive at a final offer, make any offer contingent upon getting answers to any remaining key questions.

ASK THE OTHER SIDE:

■ Can you put these commitments in writing?

....

Questions That Motivate

Are you growing?

Seth Godin[20]

....

Chapter 8 Conclusion

Ideas into Action

Sales and negotiation revolve around wants, needs, hopes, and dreams. Questions can not only remind customers of their needs but also help them sell themselves on the benefits of your product or service. The buying/negotiating atmosphere functions best when each side sees the other incorporating its ideas into a proposed solution. If you use written sales pitches and project proposals, the document is a proxy for you and should ask meaningful questions on your behalf. Curiosity is a more powerful force than fear. Scare tactics are not the best tool, since they do not inspire the customer or negotiating partner to continue or return to the discussions with enthusiasm. Create curiosity and the other party will eagerly listen.

Let's recognize sales questions as among the most important questions a businessperson asks. Ask for the order. It's either get the sales up or the costs down. In the end, any sales effort and business has to answer one question: Why would a customer buy from you instead of another business? The answer may give you a surprising focus, for no organization can be all things to all people. A business has finite resources and must limit its operations by deciding what and how much it should produce, service, or sell. This analysis also identifies your competitors, their prices, and their geographic reach, information that shapes every business playing field.

You will often hear that you get not what you deserve but what you negotiate, a thought that may be better expressed as you get not what you deserve but what you question. As you recognize the negotiations around you each day, you will start to appreciate the role inquiry plays in discovering the reasons behind people's positions. If you use positive questions, you will be known not as a tough negotiator but as an effective one. Questioning involves face-to-face conversations, the most effective way to conduct negotiations; in the age of the Internet, negotiators should remember the wisdom of Francis Bacon in his essay "Of Negotiating," where he observed, "It is generally better to deal by speech than by letter."

We leave this chapter on selling and negotiating with what Professor Charles Goeldner of the University of Colorado has said is the most important question you can ask a customer—"Will you be back?" Repeat business is critical.[21]

In chapter 9, we present the questions that can trigger creativity in the workplace.

QUESTIONS THAT WORK WHEN:
Creativity and New Thinking Are Needed

We should not only master questions, but also act upon them, and act definitely.

WOODROW WILSON

Is there a difference between creating a symphony and starting a business? Both take energy, discipline, and a burning desire to imagine something where nothing has been—in short, creativity. Creativity is closely linked to imagination, interpretation, and the individual. It is the art of the unforced question, the inquiry from inside, an intelligent gamble with irreverence. These mysterious qualities make many organizations think it is impossible to require employees to use creativity. Yet with positive questions, all employees can contribute new ideas.

Some people I surveyed for *Questions That Work* said that the best use of questions regarding creativity in the workplace is simply to discover who is creative and to encourage that skill. I disagree and argue that questions bring out latent abilities buried under years of discouragement. Debra Giampoli, director of consumer promotions for the New Meals Division at Kraft Foods, says she has a strong belief that human beings are "hard wired" for creativity and that to "deny it is tantamount to denying a primary drive." She believes many of us have had creativity "conditioned" out of us by the time we reach adulthood. "Once released," says Giampoli, "we are happier, more fulfilled, and better at what we do."[1]

Creativity can, in a practical sense, be defined as the ability to solve a given problem with the resources at hand. A firsthand demonstration of this was given during an interview with Maurice Kanbar, the inventor of Skyy vodka. Kanbar said there was a simple reason that he developed his superpure premium vodka: It his way of solving a very real problem of hangovers. He once asked a doctor sitting next to him at a dinner why his head hurt after an evening of drinking, even if he was enjoying only vodka. The doctor explained that the pain came from the body's processing of impurities in the drink. Kanbar soon was investigating how to further purify his vodka, saying, "I knew that if somebody could make a dependably pure vodka, that would be the only one I would drink, and one thing led to another."[2] His experimentation involved asking new questions. In the end, a triple filtration system produced a drink with fewer regrets the following morning, and a new product with international distribution was born. It wasn't a cure for cancer, but by following a pattern of creative inquiry, Kanbar found a creative solution to a universal problem. His technique shows why a business should encourage people to creatively question the relationship between different pieces of information. I was struck by a passage from Jacques Barzun:

> The genius, according to [Henry] James, has an enormous capacity for perceiving similarities among disparate things; his mind jumps across the grooves cut by common experience. His is also a sensitive mind, every stimulus starts multiple trains of thought, wildly free associations. "In such minds," says James, "subjects bud and sprout and grow."[3]

I propose a formula for questioning:

(Questions Who + What + When + Where) = Identified Issue ÷ Questions Why − Questions Why Not × Questions How = Solution.

Each step of this process is one of questions—adding up information, dividing the issue into parts this equation does add up again, multiplying inquiry until a practical solution is arrived at. Of course, creativity is more than any one formula. As Robert Buckman, chairman of the board of Bulab Holdings, Inc., suggested, the value of questions is that it causes us to look at the other side of any equation.[4] Creativity asks "Why?" and "Why not?" at the same time.

There is a creating power in any organization that supports curiosity and encourages questions, just as long as inquiry does not become a barrier. Professor John Bourne believes questions can kill half-baked ideas; indeed, he believes the typical "questioning" cultures he is familiar with are those that decrease workers creativity.[5] Imagine you've got a great idea for a new way to do something, and you share it with coworkers. At this moment, like a newborn child, a creative idea needs close care and comfort, not to be tossed to the wolves, who can rip and tear with their sharp interrogation. Questions requiring statements of hard facts also harm rather than help creativity, since creativity is often a feeling that is just beginning to reach out for new facts, creating new realities. This type of negative inquiry hurts creativity because it supports the status quo.

Graham Rawlinson, an innovation consultant and educational psychologist, says sometimes it is best to ban questions altogether when trying to innovate. "Many ideas are hidden by the question—have you tried to . . . answer no . . . move on."[6] His point: "The less you know, the more likely you will get an original idea." Anyone creating a questioning culture quickly realizes there are some who may not be open to new ways to think. Survey respondent Dale Parish says you should ask, "Whom in this department do you feel is the least receptive to change that could be moved to a position where they could be happy in doing noncreative work?"[7]

9/1 Creating the Right Environment

Assessment

Managers have to give up some of their control to nurture creativity, for, as one of those I surveyed points out, the price of creativity is a little chaos.[8] When I asked Dr. Richard J. Sojka about creativity in the workplace, he regretfully responded that he knew of no managers in large corporations who ask questions that foster creativity. In his mind, "managers really, really need to have an attitude adjustment just to operate in a creative culture."[9] We all know the type of manager he is referring to. They are those who prize predictability, order, and control above all. Lest you feel superior, everyone has built their own mental prisons. Questions help people break out of them.

If you can make it safe to learn, reduce tension, and reduce hostility, you may find that people's natural curiosity will reappear. Paul Plsek, a former Bell Labs engineer and corporate quality planning director, says that creativity needs a supportive environment and that managers are a big part of that environment.[10] Leaders need to open the door to creativity and ask their staff, "If you could ask me to do something that would most help you and your department to be more creative or innovative, what would that be?" Plsek says that managers should be asked, "Which area of your department's work needs some creative thinking?" He argues, "If there is no awareness of the need for creativity, creative thinking will not likely be encouraged."[11] Another survey respondent says that encouraging creativity is simply acting to "take out the off button."[12] This may require loosening old patterns of behavior and reexamining your relationships with others. There is often a social and internal dislocation that occurs when some people are creative, an almost uncomfortable shifting of mental gears. Questions encourage people to appreciate and to embrace differences.

ASK EMPLOYEES INVOLVED IN A PROCESS:

- Are we questioning assumptions, the routine way of doing things?

- What takes too long?

- What causes complaints?

- What is wasted?

- What is misunderstood?

- Do we really understand the situation?

  - Are we asking the right questions?

- Are our goals on target?

- How would you come up with workable ideas?

- Do we have adequate resources of time, knowledge, and information to be creative?[13]

  - Have we learned the skills that enable creativity?[14]

- Where can you go that helps you relax best?

- What setting would be most inspirational for you if you were asked for a really creative idea?[15]

- How would you describe the feelings of "aha" that you have experienced?[16]

- What gift would you seek from seven specific geniuses to enhance your own creative powers?[17]

Questions That Work

Madeleine Homan, president of a coaching business, says she doesn't believe people need motivation to be creative; she thinks they need to remove the obstacles to creativity. Her four questions to open up options are:

1. If you could wave a magic wand and have this project turn out exactly as planned, how would it look?

2. If you could have three wishes from a genie, but they all had to be work related, what would they be?

3. If money were no object, how would you proceed?

4. If you had more help than you needed, how would you go about doing this?[18]

If you need to encourage people to make fundamental changes in how they work, see section 18/1, Questions That Work When Encouraging Change. If you need to set up a creative team, see section 10/9, Questions That Work When Forming a Team.

9/2 Inspiring Creativity

Assessment

Inspiration is a tricky word to use in the business environment, even more vague than creativity but so necessary to a breakthrough idea. As Richard Scharchburg, Thompson Professor of Industrial History at Kettering University, summed it up, "Inspired minds make all the difference."[19] When examining inquiry that could inspire all employees, I was taken by a question from Paul Plsek, a former engineer now turned health care consultant. "If someone out there came along with a product or service that replaced your department's work, what would that product or service be?" Plsek says everything we take for granted will someday be replaced by something. He argues that if an organization cannot answer this replacement question, it is time to develop better skills in imagination. Once you realize that yes, there is something to replace your product or service, the follow-up question is simple: "What are we doing about it?" "If you don't innovate yourselves out of the market, your competitors will," says Plsek.[20]

The beginning of creativity can often be a challenging question. A Ford executive is said to have challenged his staff during the development of the Taurus by asking, "Why should I or anyone buy this car?" Alex D'Anci, a marketing manager for ABB Corporate Research, Finland, says creative questions and answers can come from an effort to "target a given customer and tell the people to live with them for a while to discover their latent needs."[21] A manager can likewise challenge employees to define what problems they are struggling with, what latent needs they have. The difference between creativity in the workplace and creativity in the artist's studio is that a creative business solution has to, in the final application, be useful.

Being creative doesn't require reinventing the wheel. Kristine Piazza Belser, a survey respondent, says creativity often means, "We just need to improve and tweak."[22] Exhortations do not help this process. You can't bully or demand that creativity suddenly appear. It has to be encouraged one-on-one. Barbara Waugh, the worldwide change manager for Hewlett-Packard Laboratories, says, "to everything anyone offers in that tentative small voice as they express passion for the first time, say, 'Great idea!'" Waugh says that "it keeps them going and builds and it dims the judgements roaring in your own brain and allows you to entertain how in fact it may very well *be* a great idea."[23]

ASK THOSE INVOLVED:

- Let's begin by talking about what got us to this point; can you describe the past?

  - Can you describe the present?

- How do we feel about our present situation?

  - Why do we look at things this way?

- If we were to storyboard our situation like a movie, what would happen next?

  - Wouldn't it be great if . . . ?[24]

- Have we stated any problems?

  - How is this problem solved elsewhere?

    - How is it solved in a completely different business?

■ What if solving this problem were a matter of life and death?[25]

■ Do we have to do it this way?

■ What would happen if . . . ?

■ If we did a one-page analysis, what three things would make it better?

■ What three things would make it worse?

■ What's the stupidest way we could do this?[26]

■ If we were starting as a competitor to ourselves, how would we do it?[27]

■ How would a small and entrepreneurial business do this? A big and bureaucratic business?

■ What mistakes have we made this week?

■ What have you created or designed this week?

■ What did you improve this week?

■ Why not?

■ What's the opposite?

■ How can we challenge assumptions?

■ What is this similar to?[28]

■ What's the metaphor? What happens when we try other metaphors?[29]

■ How can we have the most fun exploring the possibilities?[30]

■ If I were going to turn this into a competition for who could make the best _____, how would you start to create it?[31]

Questions That Work

As a former member of Price Waterhouse's Management Consulting Practice, Alain Rostain has studied change management and creative problem solving. As a former software developer and product manager in Silicon Valley, he's had up-close experience with creative people in high-tech cultures. Rostain is working on a model using four basic approaches to creative thinking, "all of which ask very different types of questions." He sees the question categories as Visioning, Exploring, Experimenting, and Modifying, with each of these four critical to innovation.

1. Visioning: What do we want? What would be the ideal?

2. Exploring: What assumptions can we challenge, what would be different?

3. Experimenting: How can we combine existing elements in new ways?

4. Modifying: How can we improve on what has been done before?[32]

If people are afraid to take the necessary risks, see section 18/2, Questions That Work When Taking Risks.

9/3 Increasing Your Creative Productivity

Assessment

Creativity requires continuous questioning of what is and what could be; it is sparking an innovation that explodes into new opportunities. You create a focus with questions but then branch off to discover new alternatives, definitions, and concepts. It is a process of disconnection and reconnection of ideas. Your future may depend on this ability to use questions to link problems with possible solutions. In your workplace, write down your questions before they disappear. You might not have a creative idea right then and there, but by writing down your questions you preserve the possibility. I keep a notepad for jotting down ideas, but I could better describe it as a question pad with lots of "what if" questions. To increase the number of creative ideas generated by your staff, you can challenge people to come up with their own questioning lists. If you don't go prospecting every day for creative ideas, you'll forget how. It is said that Thomas Edison had a quota of one minor invention every ten days and one major one every six months. Ask your staff, "What is your creative/questioning quota?" It is the simple idea of "use it or lose it."

ASK THOSE INVOLVED IN THE CREATIVE PROCESS:

■ What do we want to create?

■ How have we done this in the past?

　■ How effective was it?

　　■ Are there other ways to . . . ?

　■ Why do we do something this way? Could we . . . ?

■ How can we do this . . . ?

■ What would happen if . . . ?

　■ Would it be better if . . . ?

　■ What would be the benefits if . . . ?

　■ Can we do it cheaper if . . . ?

　■ Can we do it faster if . . . ?

■ What innovations do customers initiate?

　■ What is of value to customers?

■ How is this like (a piece of art, or bowl of fruit, or anything rich in visual images)?

■ How would this look ten years from now?[33]

■ How do you think Leonardo, Einstein, Whoopi Goldberg, Mother Theresa, and Picasso would perceive this issue?[34]

■ Why not?

If you are problem solving, see section, 13/1 Questions That Work When Investigating a Problem. If you are hiring creative employees, see section 11/1, Questions That Work When Examining How You Recruit and Pick People.

Questions That Work

Ellen Domb, an editor of a journal that focuses on innovation skills, says she has her own personal list to help inspire new ideas. Domb says that by answering the following questions, your employees can articulate what is preventing the success.[35]

1. Who is the customer?

2. What is the Ideal Final Result from the customer's point of view?

3. How do you know that?

4. How confident are you about what you think you know?

5. What is preventing us from achieving the Ideal Final Result?

9/4 Brainstorming about a Product

Assessment

Most businesspeople have had at least one bright idea for a new product, but the idea usually stopped when it came time to actually take it to the next step. Asking questions will help you not only design your product but also bring it to market. One of the most successful brainstorming companies in the world is IDEO, the design/think tank whose president, David Kelley, can claim to be one of the fathers of the first computer mouse designs, among many other innovations. Kelley's business is generating raw ideas and turning them into finished products you just can't wait to buy. He gave a powerful description of this creative process when he said, "The feeling of picking up the right product is really exciting . . . you get product lust, you lust after it from that moment forward."[36] Walking around his workplace, one gets the idea that it is bursting with questions in search of new answers. Kelley's work also demonstrates that brainstorming of new ideas can no longer depend on a single discipline or narrow set of skills. Questioning is the key to help you unlock an empathy for other perspectives, an empathy essential to innovation.

ASK YOUR STAFF:

■ How are people using our product or service?

  ■ Is our product or service an everyday activity?

    ■ Why not?

- What are the difficulties our customers face?
- What is our product not doing or providing?
  - Can we make it smaller?
  - What if we make it lighter?
  - How can we make it safer?
  - How can we make it easier to use?
  - What would make it last longer?
  - How can we make it more reliable?
  - Can we make it cheaper?
- What if?
  - What next?
- What ideas can we borrow?

If you need to check if your product meets customer needs, see section 8/1, Questions That Work When Understanding the Customer.

9/5 You Have What You Think Is a Good Idea

Assessment

If you have captured some good ideas, you've just begun the process of turning them into reality. Creativity in the workplace is increasingly a group effort. A manager's role in the creative process is to help people not only come up with creative ideas but successfully share them with others. If everyone feels she had a hand in the creative process, she is less likely to resist the outcome. To be sure creative ideas are worth the group's effort, survey respondent Arthur VanGundy believes you should be asking questions that check assumptions, exploring "What is the added value?"[37] You always have to remember that users and consumers of a new idea need to know what's in it for them, the added value they will receive. Questions make sure you haven't created an idea too far removed from the reality of the market.

ASK YOUR COCREATORS:

- How can we test this idea?
  - If we can test this idea, can we . . . ?
    - Who will have to be involved?
    - When can we try this out?
      - What will be the short-term and long-term consequences?
  - Is there an experiment we can perform?
    - What evidence do you need that the idea works?
- Is the idea unique?
  - Does it allow us to solve a problem that could not have been solved before?[38]
  - Does it enable us to do something we could never do before, by any means?[39]
- Do we have a customer who wants it?
- Who is going to have to implement the idea?
  - Whose cooperation is necessary?
- What resources do we need?
  - When do we need them?
- How much will it cost?
  - How much time do we need?
- Is this the right time to try this?
  - Why not?
- What will happen immediately?
  - What will happen in the short, medium, and long term?
- How can we reuse our idea for other applications?
  - How can we reuse equipment and supplies for other applications?
- Can I develop this idea?

- Can I run the department or office that tries it?

- Can I license the idea out?

Questions That Work

Bruce Ganem, a professor of chemistry and chemical biology and the J. Thomas Clark Professor of Entrepreneurship at Cornell, uses this set of questions to test the real-world uses of ideas:

1. Does it work?

2. Will it make our company more competitive?

3. If you can use it, can you make it better?

4. If you can make it better, can you raise the barrier to others using it?

5. Will the new technology lead to new opportunities?[40]

If you have to pitch your idea, see section 8/3, Questions That Work When Finding the Customers or the Right Person to Pitch To.

Questions That Motivate

Are you going to be a leader or are you going to be a follower?

Fred Damert[41]

Chapter 9 Conclusion

Ideas into Action

Creativity is born of the unconscious belief that we are capable of being better than we have been. The actual process of creativity is mysterious, but any understanding is sufficient because, in the end, none is. You will never fully understand the process, for, as Jacques Barzun said, "If creation was a process, by this time its operation would have been reduced to formulas, recipes, which intelligence and method could apply to produce great art and great science."[42] You need to invite unpredictable contradictions into the workplace, and you may find they stir the spirits of employees you never imagined were creative.

I share the thought of authors Alan Robinson and Sam Stern: "A company is creative when its employees do something new and potentially useful without being directly shown or taught."[43] I hope this chapter has supported my belief that questions are a fundamental factor in shaking up our thinking, in our becoming creative. Leaders recognize that questions are a positive destructive force. Taking something apart, starting over, can be a powerful source of innovation. If nothing else, inquiry discovers other people's ideas and pushes an idea forward.

When pursuing creative and innovative ideas, the question "What is the worst possible thing that could happen if we . . . ?" is important. Several survey respondents suggested the question, but the business trainer William Hodges gave the best explanation for why you should ask it. He says, "It is amazing how when we confront the worst possible scenario we find that there is little to fear and much to gain. Especially when the worst case is that people might laugh at us."[44] Sue Scott, the founder of Primal Lights, is a creative businessperson who has dealt with this question. Scott started a successful international company with the unique idea of changing Christmas lights into an all-year decoration by enclosing bulbs in transparent plastic fruits, animals, and other odd objects. She learned she had to take risks. The product lines she designed with "the market" in mind didn't do as well as those she dreamed up. Her observation about creativity? "Everybody says how do you come up with the ideas. The ideas are the easy part. It's when you have to begin a business to support it that the work starts."[45] In chapter 10, we discuss ways to turn ideas into action by questioning at meetings and in planning.

QUESTIONS THAT WORK WHEN:
Meeting and Planning

Do I contradict myself? Very well then, I contradict myself.

WALT WHITMAN

To transform ideas into reality, you need to capture information inside and outside the organization, create relationships, and master the evaluation and decision-making process. The playing field for many of these activities is the conference room, where questions need to be asked as the company officials meet, plan, and manage projects. Positive questions help keep people involved and focused as they decide the fundamental issues of quantity, quality, time, logistics, collaborations, and design.[1] In short, those who use inquiry can have greater confidence that they can deliver on time and on budget. It is a questioning discipline that should begin the moment anyone decides that something needs to be done.

When planning and meeting, your aim should be to tap into the experience of others (one of the most effective learning tools you can use). A successful meeting builds a chain of connections. The leaders of the meeting, while keeping to an agenda, should be open to new issues and developments, for inquiry is in part the science of surprise, and dissent and disagreement are part of any healthy process of project management. Successful businesspeople realize there is a close connection between the dollar sign and the question mark.

10/1 Having a Meeting

Assessment

How many productive hours of employees are slowly strangled in meetings? How many employees want meetings to be over before they begin? Those attending meetings often resist asking or inviting time-consuming questions, wanting only the orders for what to do, rather than a discussion of what is possible. As a result, meetings often are only sequential monologues, not dialogues. Let me argue an idea.

No meeting should be held without an agenda made up of questions.

No facilitator should run a meeting without prepared questions.

No meeting should end without the creation of a list of questions yet to be answered.

Questions focus you on the issues meeting participants are to discuss. Should we do this or stop doing that? Can we try this or sell that? These are issues the group can interact on and make a recommendation about. Think of your last productive meeting. Chances are a question sparked the most useful part of the time together, questions that discovered problems and the promise.

When I attended meetings at one company over a period of years, I noticed that the agenda topics tended to be the same time after time. This showed a clear focus but also that not much progress had been made. When it came time for me to help run the meeting, I tried an agenda based on a series of questions. The discussion then changed from what people had done to what they could do. When it came time to write up the meeting summary, rather than simply repeat what was said (which everyone could have picked up in the meeting), we were able to write up a series of questions yet to be answered. Those attending the meeting knew their actions would be the answers to these questions.

Here are some additional thoughts on questions and meetings.

■ *The meeting is a mix.* A good meeting requires the right people. It is pointless to meet without those who can suggest options or make options happen. This mix should include a sprinkling of original thinkers (at least one confident questioner), a meeting secretary to capture information and questions, and a maestro or meeting leader to keep the meeting going at the right pace and who knows how questions can direct the flow of information.

■ *Sometimes it's better not to have the meeting.* The meeting is not more important than the problem. A meeting or a question that gets in the way of acting on a pressing problem can represent a destructive delay. Everyone has to know when to stop seeking more information and begin to act. Ask, "Is this meeting really necessary?" A meeting to pass along information could be replaced by an e-mail or memo. Some information, of course, should never be put in an e-mail or memo, particularly bad news. Personal information is best shared one-on-one, never in a meeting.

■ *Put a limit on questions.* Any meeting can have too many questions. Limit q-and-a so that people don't wander off into areas over which they have no control or influence. While it may be good to raise broader questions, groups have to police themselves and keep questions focused on the topic at hand. Meeting leaders have to skillfully acknowledge questions but gracefully set aside off-track queries for future consideration.

■ *The boss should not chair the meeting.* A meeting's atmosphere should encourage everyone to speak; otherwise, the discussion's point might as well be the subject of another memo. When a boss is the meeting facilitator, few can risk expressing a completely honest reaction for fear of being cut off or cut down. The facilitator should be a neutral party charged only with the job of having the best meeting possible.

10/2 You Are Asked to Set up a Meeting

Assessment

Think of a meeting as a house. Built right, it is a sheltered place to learn, live, and work together. The raw material is the inquiry and ideas of others. If you want colleagues to be active participants in constructing your meeting, what better way to invite participation than to encourage curiosity and passions to surface in the form of questions? Meetings, like a house, can collapse if they are not carefully planned. A simple set of questions can help meeting organizers avoid many of the grinding annoyances and burdens so often found in conference rooms.

ASK YOUR TEAM MEMBERS OR THE PERSON WHO HAS
ASKED YOU TO HOLD THE MEETING:

■ Why do you want to hold this meeting?

   ■ What kind of a meeting is this going to be—information, discussion, or both?

   ■ Will we have workshops or panels as part of the meeting?

- What is the agenda?
  - What is the theme or feeling you would like to create?
  - Should I put out a memo telling everyone why we are holding the meeting?
  - Should I ask others for their ideas on what should be on the agenda?
  - What are we hoping to achieve in the meeting?
- Who else will be there or should be there?
  - Who are the original thinkers we need to include?
- Who will be the facilitator or meeting leader?
  - Whom do you want to take the minutes of the meeting?
- What is the exact time the meeting should start?
  - Is there a time or date I should avoid?
- Where is the best place to hold the meeting?
- Do we need any audiovisual equipment for the meeting?
  - Should I prepare any audiovisual elements or printed material?

The agenda should include the key questions that the meeting is designed to answer.

If your meeting is going to be a regular one, and you are becoming a team, see section 10/9, Questions That Work When Forming a Team. If the meeting involves negotiations see sections 8/7–12, Questions That Work When Negotiating.

10/3 You Are Asked to Attend a Meeting

Assessment

Questions asked before a meeting sharpen your line of inquiry during it. Despite the assurance of teachers and some coworkers, there *is* such a thing as a truly stupid question. It is one that has already been answered in the meeting or one that should wait. You need to ask yourself, "What questions must I have answered before the meeting is over?"

ASK THE PERSON WHO IS INVITING YOU:

- Is there an agenda?

- What are we trying to accomplish?

  - Will I need to present anything?

  - Will we be making any decisions?

- Who else is invited?

  - Which one of these people is a good planner?

- What do I need to bring to the meeting?

If you have to give a presentation during the meeting, see section 15/5, Questions That Work When Giving a Speech or Presentation.

10/4 You Are the Facilitator

Assessment

Why do so many meetings end with many members being ignored if everyone knows that someone who feels part of a team is more loyal and productive? Good facilitators foster a questioning atmosphere. The focused facilitator avoids ignoring important points of view by taking five steps:

1. Asking questions to corral the concepts to be discussed

2. Involving everyone by asking for opinions

3. Using questions to encourage quiet participants

4. Probing beyond yes or no answers

5. Listening to what is said and, in particular, what isn't

One survey respondent suggests that meeting organizers and anyone trying to advance an agenda ask, "Whose opinion matters most about how things are done here?"[2] The idea is to ask a question that pushes beyond organizational charts to understand the real sources of authority.

As already noted, it is generally not wise to have the boss lead meetings. One high-tech boss is described as firing inquiries from a corner chair as if it were a gun turret. Rapid-fire questions from a boss can shoot down the spirit of open collaboration.

ASK THE GROUP:

- What do we want to achieve?
  - What do we want to avoid?
- What's the best way to address this?
  - How do we want to make any decisions?
- What do we need to know?
  - What are we afraid to find out?
  - Does anyone have any questions about something she doesn't understand?
- What problems are we facing?
  - Can anyone help?
  - Would you like to share your thoughts?
- Are we finished with this part of the discussion?
- Do we know enough to make a decision?

If you have to find a new solution, see section 9/2, Questions That Work When Inspiring Creativity.

10/5 Conducting and Concluding a Meeting

Assessment

Meetings aim to create common understanding and coordinated response. Your meeting should give people a chance to participate, to interact with one another. Like a teacher writing a lesson plan, meeting organizers should preplan questions to be sure that they hit all key points before the end of the session. Their challenge is to think of questions that draw out both facts and opinions.

If you plan to finish a meeting with a question-and-answer session, it's a good idea to outline topics needing the group's focus. By putting a "fence" around a questioning period, you avoid being distracted from the matter at hand. Finishing with positive questions helps confirm what was learned while helping participants decide how to act on future challenges.

ASK THE GROUP:

- What is our decision?

- What is the schedule of what will happen next?

- Do we need to meet again?

  - When should the next meeting be?

- What questions do we need to follow up on?

  - What key issues need to be addressed that you now have in your notes?

- What has been set aside for us to follow up at another time?

- Can each of you write a follow-up memo outlining your plan of action?

If you have an idea you want to pursue, see section 9/5, Questions That Work When You Have What You Think Is a Good Idea.

10/6 Reviewing the Meeting

Assessment

After-meeting questions are powerful tools for improving the next session. You can't read people's minds, but careful questions can reveal flaws in the meeting. Consider attaching an evaluation to the minutes to invite feedback. Sharing these questions and answers helps the group see how the meeting process is being improved.

ASK PARTICIPANTS:

- How did this meeting go?

  - Was it worth the time we've invested?

- Did we do what needed to be done?

  - Did you get the information you needed?

    - Was the information effectively presented?

- What can we do to make the next meeting work better?

  - What should the meeting leader have done to make this a better meeting?

  - Did you participate in the meeting?

    - What could be done to encourage everyone to participate?

- Was there an alternative to holding this meeting?

If you want to be personally reviewed for your performance, see section 12/1, Questions That Work When Asking Your Boss to Give You Feedback.

10/7 Looking Ahead

Assessment

Headlights are turned on to help you see down a dark road ahead. If only looking into the future were as easy as flicking a switch. It takes time to concentrate and question, to reflect and discuss, time many businesses don't give employees. Pressing demands today crowd out the chance of questioning the possibilities of tomorrow. Leaders should ask themselves, "How can employees act in the company's long-term best interest if the employees never think about the next generation of the company?" Looking ahead is about positioning yourself, your colleagues, and your organization to be in the right place at the right time. When the going is dark, inquiry illuminates obstacles in the way.

ASK YOUR BOSS:

- Can I have time to brainstorm about the future?

  - Can I ask you about your point of view?

- What concerns do you have about the future of our company?

  - What concerns do our employees have about the future of our organization?

ASK YOUR COWORKERS:

- What concerns do you have about the future of the company?

- What trends will affect the future?

- What is the focus of the future for our organization?

  - What do we need to do to be ready for this future?

- What do we think the marketplace and competition will be?

  - What are the products and the markets we will target?

- What advantage will we offer customers?

  - How much is the customer willing to pay for that advantage?

- Is our technology cutting edge?

  - What alternative technology could replace us?

- How will we measure performance to make sure we are on track?

- How would Disney/Intel/Microsoft approach our challenge?[3]

If you need to encourage a vision for the group or effort, see section 18/6, Questions That Work When Creating a Vision.

10/8 Studying an Idea or Opportunity

Assessment

Why waste time duplicating existing work? When searching for an answer to a question (as you often are during a project), a first item of business is to make sure acceptable answers have not already been found elsewhere. If nothing else, your investigation of other people's ideas will help you find the right questions to explore during your project. Often, ideas being examined have been forwarded by upper management or demonstrated by a competitor. Think of idea checking as a criminal investigation. Talking to police detectives over the years, I came to appreciate how they approach any situation with a stream of structured questions. The questions are not just to prove a case to their own satisfaction. Detectives know their investigations have to discover evidence that will stand up in a court. This is not too different from proving a position to some executives, where judge and jury are one person. Such questioning should hold all explanations up to scrutiny and avoid a rush to judgment. You have to be open to unexpected ideas and even argue the other side of what might be your first answer. A "right" answer isn't the place to stop. A positive questioning culture tries to find out whether there is a better answer. You can inspire and circulate ideas with a simple question: "Is there a better way?"

ASK THOSE MOST FAMILIAR WITH THE IDEA:

■ How many times has this concept or idea been used?

   ■ How well did it work out?

■ What are the similarities between past successes and this situation?

   ■ What are the differences?

■ How can we establish a defensible competitive position?[4]

■ How can we attract the human and financial resources needed to pursue this opportunity?[5]

■ In order to make money, what assumptions do we have to make for the business model to make sense?[6]

   ■ How can we test those assumptions?[7]

■ Can you give me at least five different ways that this advice, item, or idea can be broken?[8]

■ Can you create a five- or ten-minute lesson plan on how you would teach this concept to a grade school class or high school class and present it?[9]

IF YOU NEED TO ANALYZE A STUDY REGARDING YOUR ISSUE:

■ Has anyone done a study about the issue we are facing?

   ■ What kind of study was it?

■ What was the point of the study?

■ Where did the study appear?

■ How many cases were in the study?

  ■ What is the margin of error?

If you find people do not have the information they need to think about an opportunity, see section 18/4, Questions That Work When Creating Knowledge.

10/9 Forming a Team

Assessment

Why do we have teams? For many of the same reasons you should ask questions. A team effort discovers new ways to tackle projects by sharing knowledge and opinions. A well-run team benefits from rapid communication and quick decision-making abilities, with the aim of high productivity and low conflict. Teams can be as intimate as a few coworkers sharing a task or as remote as boxes on an organizational chart. Teams are of two general types: temporary teams put together to problem solve and established teams for ongoing work. No matter what the size and purpose, all teams need a certain chemistry. Putting together a team is a psychological jigsaw puzzle where success can be denied by one missing piece.

A TV profile I worked on regarding the financial leader Jim Benham illustrated an important point of teamwork. It focused not on Benham's corporate work but on his trumpet playing in a jazz band. He spoke of liking the freedom of jazz, noting that such music doesn't have to be perfect. Benham said the jazz band taught teamwork: "We start our notes the same time. We swell and grow the note and we cut it off exactly the right time. Together . . . that's when it all clicks and comes out right."[10] Teams are jazz bands. Everyone shares the same concept, but you can play solo and creatively change the melody with questions. The point is to come together, to take advantage of one another's strengths and individuality to end on a positive note.

ASK POTENTIAL TEAM MEMBERS:

■ What is the history of a particularly successful team project you've worked on?

  ■ If you had a chance to redo your last team project, what would you do differently?

- What is your track record on projects you've been in charge of?

- What are your strengths as a team member?

  - What makes you think so?

- What areas are you willing to improve on?

- What is a team?

- Do you meet your deadlines?

- How are you going to keep management in the loop?

- What quality control will you put in place?

- What training is needed to work on this team?

If you need to hire people for your team, see section 11/2, Questions That Work When Doing Interviews.

10/10 Your Team Begins to Work Together

Assessment

Teams must find ways to disagree but in the end commit to one course of action. Team leaders should constantly ask their team how things are going. Such status review questions keep unrealistic expectations from being formed, encourage communication, and discover causes of future conflict.

Team leaders use questions to discover every group's opinion leaders. Inquiry also involves reaching out to quieter employees. This fosters loyalty and productivity by demonstrating the value of participating fully in a shared effort. Mark Sanborn, a leadership consultant, says that questions define teamwork. He sees their primary role as clarifying expectations: "What is expected of me as a team member, and what can I expect of the team?"[11] A team can be the best place to use questions to refine an idea. Ron MacNeil, principal research associate at MIT Architecture, says that, when presenting an idea to a group, you have to decide "How can I give this idea away so that the team will own it and develop it further until the *really really great idea* surfaces?"[12] Team leaders have to use questions to create what some call "aha" moments where everyone can make a discovery. This powerful concept requires using questions to introduce the idea, gauge reaction, and encourage further brainstorming.

One critical caveat: ask management whether it is serious about pursuing ideas you and your team might create. Nothing hurts future worker participation more than not being taken seriously.

ASK YOUR TEAM:

- What should this team accomplish?
  - What is a success for us?
- What kind of teamwork will be necessary to do this job right?
  - How are we going to support each other?
    - If something goes wrong, how are we going to get things back on track?
- What would this team do differently if we were a business on our own?
  - Who would do what?
  - How would we make decisions?
- What are the different ways we could do this project?
  - Which of these ideas excites you?
  - Which of these are you ready to do now?
- How much time do you think we'll need?
  - If this were the last minute, would we do this assignment differently?[13]
- What are the milestones we need to reach?
  - When do we need to reach them?
- Do you think all members of the team have enough information to participate?
- What do we already know?
  - What do we need to know?
    - Whom should we talk to?

- If we benchmark this, which companies or products should we compare?

  - What did you learn today that someone else could use tomorrow?

- Are we doing anything that is no longer important?

- What can go wrong with this team or this project?

  - How can we prevent it from going wrong?

  - What will you do to help prevent problems from coming up?

- How can we make this work more fun *and* faster?[14]

If you need to give feedback to a team member who is disrupting the group, see section 11/9, Questions That Work When Giving Feedback to Someone off Target.

10/11 Launching a New Product or Service

Assessment

Do successful products begin with a clear business goal in mind or occur through serendipity? Clear goal or not, any new product or service involves questions of risk. Dedicated questioners know the various kinds of risk to review, risks in resources consumed, reputation, and rewards to be gained or lost. One frequently neglected form of risk is failure to take advantage of new opportunities. A positive questioning culture is one of the most powerful forces for launching a new product, but businesses have to protect against focusing almost exclusively on deadlines of production and delivery. They may miss asking questions that could lead to future evolutionary and revolutionary ideas. Analysis of a possible new product or service often comes down to one question: "Can it make a profit?"

ASK YOUR STAFF:

- What is the big picture?

  - What are the industry trends?

  - What are the economic trends?

- What ideas do you have about new products or services?

- What is the market segment?
  - How big is it?
  - How will we market to that segment?
- What are the customer's needs?
- How important is price?
- What is the competition?
  - Who are they?
    - What position do they have?
      - What is the market they operate in?
      - What is the staff they have?
  - How do their products compare with ours?
  - What are their strengths?
    - What is their track record?
    - How loyal are their customers?
    - What is their financial backing?
      - What prices are our competitors charging?
- What difference can our product or service create?
  - What does it offer to the marketplace?
    - What makes it unique?
    - What makes it better than other products on the market?
- What resources do we need?
  - Which people in our company do we need?
  - What money do we need?
- What are the costs of materials?
  - Should product parts be manufactured or bought?
- What are the labor, marketing, and overhead costs?

■ What is the time frame for production?

  ■ What will we do if sales are faster or slower than expected?

■ What is a realistic timetable for introducing a product?

  ■ Is the timing right?

■ How will the product reach its market?

■ What is the sales strategy?

  ■ Who should represent the product?

    ■ Should we use brokers, distributors, reps, or telemarketers?

■ What could we do that would create "buzz value" among our customers and competitors?[15]

■ What is the planned price?

  ■ What is our planned profit percentage?

    ■ What levels of sales and what level of profit are necessary?

■ What governmental bodies have jurisdiction over this product?

  ■ What changes might occur in the regulations?

■ What competitive responses are anticipated?

  ■ How will we counter them?

If you have to market the product or service, see section 8/1, Questions That Work When Understanding the Customer.

10/12 Getting Something Done

Assessment

Sometimes nothing less than a direct and explicit order will do to get some employees started on a project, but, in general, questions are among the best way to motivate workers and clarify objectives. Begin by asking employees to repeat back to you their understanding of what they think should be done. When employees explain their concerns, you can repeat back what they said and ask whether you clearly understood. The gap between an idea and its implementation is bridged by inquiry.

For highly motivated and intelligent workers, one key to getting them moving is inspiring an emotional and intellectual commitment to the job at hand. Inquiry keeps employees involved throughout the process. Managers should pick two or three critical points to inspect, asking employees to check in as those points are completed, and can change the two or three points over time as earlier points are satisfactorily addressed. Managers can test to see whether someone is prepared to do tasks or interested in finishing projects by asking theoretical questions about how the employee would personally wish to accomplish something. Use positive questions to review the proposed solutions and the possible results, but welcome their initiative, for no manager has all the answers.

ASK OTHER MANAGERS OR THOSE RESPONSIBLE FOR THE TASK AT HAND:

- When would you like to discuss your plan/ideas?

- Why does it have to be done?

- What do we want to get done?

- Who is going to do it?

- When is it going to be done?

- Where is the best place to do it?

- How will it be done?

  - How can we make it as challenging in a good sense as possible?

- Do we have the basics under control, before we get too far ahead of ourselves?[16]

- What's the worst that can happen?

ASK THE EMPLOYEE:

- How would you do this task?

  - What would be the best way to accomplish it?

■ What's it going to take to . . . ?

   ■ Do you have a better way to . . . ?

■ Who should we ask to be part of this?

■ What will happen if you do nothing?

■ What are your objectives?

   ■ How will you measure your success?

■ Do you have any questions about this?

   ■ How does that sound to you?

■ What will happen if you do nothing?

IF YOU WANT TO REMIND EMPLOYEES OF THE AUTHORITY THEY HAVE, ASK THEM:

■ What have I said that you can't do?

If you are having trouble communicating what needs to be done, see section 15/2, Questions That Work When Communication Is the Problem. If you have to negotiate with the employee, see section 8/11, Questions That Work When Reaching Difficult Issues.

10/13 Doing Strategic Planning

Assessment

Those asked to engage in strategic planning are often chosen because of their knowledge of the culture and of the concepts behind a company or industry. However, strategic planners must be careful not to abandon questioning and work instead from assumptions. The strategic plan should begin and end with inquiry. Raising questions raises awareness of long-term issues. It is a fundamental way to anticipate and acknowledge problems. Margie Sweeny, a survey respondent, says that questions are essential to conducting what she refers to as "Future Search." In her definition of strategic planning, she sees everyone in the organization looking at the organization's past, present, and future to get everyone "on the same page." Each person may have his or her limited view, but it is a piece of the overall puzzle.[17]

While some think strategic planning happens only when the future is in doubt or is a process to go through only every few years, Grant Todd, the president of a firm that specializes in organizational knowledge development, says thinking about the future should happen even when times are good and no threats loom. He says that when no pressing problems exist, the company can apply "generative thinking." This type of thinking provides the horsepower that moves companies from good to better to best and helps them "survive their success."[18] Positive questioning makes strategic planning part of the routine. A natural flow of questions and answers creates daily goals that are the foundation for long-term change.

A few cautions before asking planning questions. Some businesspeople confuse thinking ahead with planning ahead. We all know of planners who can't act. Planning involves setting priorities and a course of action, not just wondering about options. Before you begin a plan, consider the question that Gary Lockwood, a strategic business coach, asks prospective clients. He tells them to imagine they have been working together for one year and then asks them, "What evidence do you see that proves the success of our efforts together?"[19] You could ask coworkers, "What result do you or will you see that proves the success of our planning?"

ASK YOUR BOSS:

- What will change the operating philosophy of our organization?

- How do we strategically plan?

  - How far ahead are we planning?

- How do we approach learning in this company?

- What do you think of my plan?

- What changes should I make?

- How are you going to commit our resources?

  - Is this how you want to go ahead?

ONCE A YEAR ASK YOUR STAFF:

- What are our major strengths we should be building on?

  - What are the best opportunities for growth and profits?

- What weaknesses do we have that we need to address?

  - What are our three biggest problems?

- What are our priorities?

- What regular risks do we face?

  - How do we deal with them?

- What complaints and compliments are we getting?

- What do you think the image of the company is to those outside it?

- What do you like best about our company?

- What are our competitors doing?

- What would you do if you were working for the competition and were trying to beat our company?

- If someone came along with a product or services that replaced our department's work, what would that product or service be?[20]

If you are looking into the very nature of your company, see sections 18/1–8, Questions That Work When Leading the Way.

10/14 Reviewing a Project or Event

Assessment

When profiling David Cohen, the man behind the successful *Day in the Life* series of books, I heard the best summary of what it is like to work on a big project. He described the first such book "as trying to build a glider on the back of a truck hurdling toward a cliff down a hill." He says he did it, "but just barely."[21] A repeated list of review questions gives everyone an organized process for gathering knowledge so that the next project is less of a cliffhanger. No project is done until essential review questions are asked. This can be painful, particularly if the project did not work as expected. Overcome exhaustion with the topic and make questioning a personal goal until you've learned something to use on your next project. The ultimate project feedback is determining that your earlier inquiry and decisions achieved their objectives.

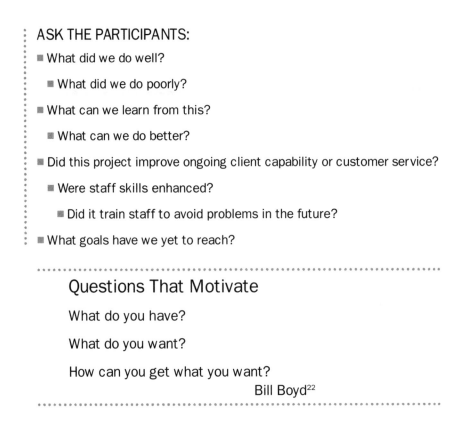

ASK THE PARTICIPANTS:

- What did we do well?

  - What did we do poorly?

- What can we learn from this?

  - What can we do better?

- Did this project improve ongoing client capability or customer service?

  - Were staff skills enhanced?

    - Did it train staff to avoid problems in the future?

- What goals have we yet to reach?

Questions That Motivate

What do you have?

What do you want?

How can you get what you want?

Bill Boyd[22]

Chapter 10 Conclusion

Ideas into Action

It is easy to feel helpless when looking to the future, to avoid questions and instead let events lead the way. Meetings and planning sessions often address issues that have not been fully confronted. Any group activity such as meetings and teams may involve personality clashes, but, as long as rules are not changed in the middle of the game, what better social incentive is there for action than the excitement of working together toward an agreed-upon goal? Questions stretch you and your staff.

Meetings often have a dynamic of win or lose, where the choice is to make points or lose face. They can be a high-stakes poker game, but skilled questioners know they have to treat the questioning process as a poker player treats the hands he is dealt. You need to look at the odds and the likely results if you continue questioning. Any questions you've already asked are like money in the pot; they are not yours anymore. Questioners have to know when to drop a line of inquiry if the cost of continuing is too high in lost relationships, damaged reputation, or wasted effort.

Strategy is about defining objectives and never losing sight of a goal. You have to use questions to focus your time, your energy, and your money. Any organization has a crunch in one or more of these areas. Meetings and planning should discover these constraints before they become life threatening or costly. Now is always a beginning point. Big projects begin in small meetings that give people something to identify with and work toward. A leader realizes his followers will be asking the question "What's in it for me?" Positive meetings and planning answer that question. In the end, any process designed to effect change and shape the future is concerned with asking workers three questions: "What's possible?" "What's not possible?" and "Why?" Think of questions as dynamite with which to blow up obstacles.

In chapter 11, we look at how questions shape your organization's future by looking at the questions to ask when hiring and managing staff.

QUESTIONS THAT WORK WHEN:
Hiring and Managing

Questions are never indiscreet; answers sometimes are.

OSCAR WILDE

Do you know the questions needed to hire someone with the right abilities and attitude? Once I had a choice of hiring one of two people, one thoughtful and quiet, the other outspoken and strident. I picked the fighter and spent days fighting with the employee. I hadn't asked the right questions and didn't know what to look for. I also violated the rule against giving the answers while asking for questions. I'm sure I said, "We're looking for someone who really can go after a story; do you think you can?" What else did I expect when the glibber of the two was better able to enthusiastically and elaborately reply, "Yes!" A subtle, slow probing is needed to discover hidden values of the prospective employee. As an interviewer, you can use questions to search for reactions that reveal subconscious patterns of thought. In the end, you hope to hire a colleague with enough mental horsepower and, more important, the spirit needed for the job.

Why is the interview process often neglected or short-circuited? Look at the math:

Interviewing Process = # of job qualities × # of questions ×
# of answers × # of applicants × # of interviewers

These factors add up to an extended question set, but hiring is a total effort that some of the most successful companies make. What organizations seek is meaningful and productive connections between employee and employer. Herb Kelleher, CEO of Southwest Airlines, says his company has prospered because of the care taken in hiring. "We're religious about it," said Kelleher. "We do it with a great deal of zeal. We will interview endlessly for a particular person."[1]

The hiring is not complete even when the position has been filled. Even the sweetest new employee sours when supervisor and supervisee fail to connect. What do you want in a job—freedom, money, respect? In the end, most people want a sense of personal growth, a sense that they are *doing something and going somewhere.* To go somewhere, you have to have a relationship with your superiors. Questions address concerns about making a connection.

Today's speed and complexity of business require a decreasing degree of direct control. The shortened reaction timeline for decisions does not allow workers to always consult senior managers. Supervisors find themselves doing a balancing act, giving employees responsibilities and rights to respond to situations while trying to make sure the employees' decisions and direction of action coordinate with the group's goals.

This chapter defines how questions set an agenda for hiring, helping you decide who to hire, how to give feedback, and do performance appraisals, and, when necessary, helping you fire employees; in other words, the questions that define the life cycle of an employee in your organization.

Positive questioning helps prevent any humiliation and hazing of employees. In some organizations, interviewing and initiation of new members involves grilling people to reveal their ignorance. College professors, drill sergeants, and other teachers use this technique to humble new students, seeing questions as part of a harsh rite of passage to build a sense of loyalty to and elitism within the group (such as practitioners of the law, journalism, or medicine). Questions can break down the individual's sense of self or build it up. Kind questions are unexpected and can often lead to the best answers. Too often, managers quiz others to show off how smart they are without thinking about the true purpose of the inquiry.

New employees bring an invaluable gift to your new workplace. Not only are they excited and motivated; they question how your organization works. With this fresh inquiry, they force you to see your all-too-familiar world through new eyes. Their questions help you figure out what makes your organization tick and what makes your workplace sick.

11/1 Examining How You Recruit and Pick People

A number of years ago I interviewed Milton Moskowitz, coauthor of *The 100 Best Companies to Work For in America.* This groundbreaking book examined companies from coast to coast from the employees' point of view. While the best companies shared some common attributes, there were also many differences among them. One common factor among the companies chosen appeared to be a sense of genuineness. They meant what they said, to the public and to their employees. An honest and open approach to questioning is one critical component to a quality of genuineness. This sense can be preserved only if new hires share the core beliefs of those already in the company. By asking questions internally in advance of hiring, you determine not only the qualifications but also the *character* of the person you are looking for and the company you are trying to create. As Charles Schwab described his hiring practices, "I try to hire people who had service in mind dealing with the customer as opposed to people who had the best sales capabilities."[2]

Certainly, hiring demands the same level of questioning as any significant financial investment. An employee hired at $50,000 over five years costs a quarter of a million dollars. Simple math; yet any machinery costing such an amount often is chosen by committee after weeks of meetings and research. The time and attention an organization spends on the interview process immediately sends a message to the prospective employee: You are worth our time. It also sends a message to employees: They are among the select few who made the grade, the first step in building the identity of an elite organization. Clearly, one of the criteria managers should be judged by is good hiring practices, yet I rarely hear of that being the subject to feedback or performance appraisals. *Questions That Work* includes the topic of hiring in a question set for a performance appraisal. How important is new talent? Roy Vagelos, CEO of Merck, has been said to begin meetings by asking, "Whom did you recruit lately?"[3]

ASK YOUR HUMAN RESOURCES DEPARTMENT:

■ Do you have any employment guidelines I should review?

  ■ Are we going to do a background check?

    ■ How quickly can that be done?

  ■ Should I review the state employment guidelines?

■ Can I advertise for this position?

  ■ Where should we be advertising?

    ■ How long will we be posting the position?

  ■ Does our job advertising speak to who we are?

■ Is there a recruitment firm that can help us with this position?

- Does the best candidate know about the position?[4]
- What is the pay scale I will be able to offer?

ASK YOUR MANAGER:

- Do you know of any executive I could ask to see whether she knows of a candidate?
- What is the relationship between qualifications and compensation?
  - How high are we willing to go to get the best qualified?
- Can I offer employees a cash incentive to help us find the right person?
- What employees should I bring in to help with the selection process?
- How quickly do I need to move?
- Which employees are already doing similar work successfully?
  - What are the traits they have that we should be looking for in this new hire?
- What are the critical skills and qualities needed for the job?
- Who will be doing the orientation about the company?

ASK OTHER EMPLOYEES:

- I want to find someone who will be a valued long-term member of our team; what qualities would you look for in a person who would fill this job?
  - What are the minimum qualifications you think someone should have?
- What kind of personality should the person have?
  - What are the essential qualities?
    - What is more important, nerves or brains?
      - What level of risk taking should this person be comfortable with?
- What skills does the new hire need?

■ What are the five major functions of this position?

■ What training should the person have?

■ What questions would you ask?

■ Whom would you recommend for the job?

■ How many employees do we need right away, and how many will we need in the future? Six months? A year?

11/2 Doing Interviews

Assessment

The Latin word for "interview" is *entre-voir*, "to have a glimpse of." What you are looking for is complex; it can be skills, knowledge, energy, honesty, or even companionship. In the end, no matter what the position, the best advice is to seek maturity. Psychological maturity is revealed in self-confidence and willingness to accept responsibility. Sadly, this is sometimes set aside for "job maturity," the technical skills and know-how. It is a disaster to hire someone who knows how to do a job but doesn't know how to interact with other people or is unwilling to be held accountable. You may never be able to see into other people's hearts, but questions give a glimpse of who the candidate is and, more important, *what his potential is.*

There are as many different styles and theories of interviews as there are interviewers. Some believe general questions are a waste of time, arguing for a focus on the task at hand. Others want to go all the way back to an interviewee's childhood. One style suggests focusing on discovering the intangibles, the qualities of heart and hustle; still others want to see how the person interacts with others. The right style depends in part on the position to be filled, but, in truth, your style of interviewing will depend largely on your personality. Those not interested in being amateur psychologists should not try to be; their apathy will tell in their lack of interest in asking such questions and listening to answers.

Job-interviewing goals should include discovering the traits the candidate can't buy—drive, determination, and discipline. Once I interviewed a candidate whose resume included several impressive schools, even more impressive companies, and work in several foreign countries, all signs of a fertile and ambitious mind. The interview, however, indicated that the credentials were largely the product of well-connected and well-to-do parents. Wealth creates opportunity, not commitment.

Here are some general rules to guide any interviewer:

- Don't spend all the time talking about the job, yourself, or the company.

- Do interviews with senior and junior people who will work with the person.

- Don't ask questions focusing on the resume: You hire people not that piece of paper.

- Do ask questions to reveal a person's ethics and energy level.

- Don't forget to take notes.

- Do ask everyone the same questions.

- Don't forget to follow up someone's train of thought.

- Do ask "describe how" questions to provoke in-depth answers.

- Don't finish the interview without asking whether the candidate has questions.

Your organization may have suggested sets of interview questions. These questions will likely cover the areas of education and experience, then turn to focus on how well the candidate meets the specific requirements for the job. A structured interview will ask specific questions designed to cover all parts of the job description without giving away too much information; otherwise the candidate will simply say what he thinks you want to hear. First, question candidates to make sure they are able to do basic job duties. Second, ask questions to discover how candidates will work, and whether they will fit into your workplace. Skilled interviewers ask questions about the person that reveal what can't be bought or taught, the person's core values. They also try to discover the passions of the person and how those passions might make the person an exceptional employee.

Many interviewers believe that confrontational interviewing is passé, since it can generate guarded answers. A conversational style of interviewing should, in theory, allow for candid answers in a more relaxed atmosphere. Whatever the style of questioning you pursue, list important questions before the interview; otherwise, the job candidate may end up interviewing you. Interviews should always be done in private and without distraction. Legal experts say that using the same set of questions for all interviews is one way to protect yourself in case a rejected applicant later sues for discrimination.

Candidates are primed to answer many standard interview questions. To avoid canned answers, ask specific questions about past behaviors on the job. People change basic attitudes little over the years and will likely conduct themselves the same way if hired. Asking the same question a different way will help you see whether answers are consistent. If you pause . . . for a long time . . . after each answer, the other person will often volunteer additional information to more clearly illuminate her past and state of mind. Not included in the list provided here are specific industry questions. You might ask at least one set of technical questions regarding an issue facing your business to see whether the person indeed has the background to succeed.

Overarching all the specifics of an interview is a larger question of why people work. Jim Naughton, the president of the Poynter Institute, says that, when hiring, he would ask candidates what their dream was, a conversation he says unfolds somewhat like this:

> This may sound strange, and feel free to just say so, and we'll go on with the interview, but I'd like to ask what your dream is. It doesn't have to be something directly related to a job, but it can be for some people. There was a time mine would have been to grow up one day and discover that I was Russell Baker, a wonderful humor writer for a paper like the *New York Times*. It can be as basic as wanting to be rich. Or owning a seventy-four-foot yacht and sailing it around the world. Or being a foreign correspondent. I'm thinking of the sort of thing that you'd discuss on a trip across the country in a car with a good friend, or maybe with a stranger over the third glass of scotch. I can't give you the scotch, but dream a little bit.

Naughton says the answers often illuminate the character of the applicant or explicit goals he could sometimes assist them in realizing. "The reply was almost never boring or disinterested," says Naughton, "and a number of people I hired later said the question had demonstrated to them that it was a place where it was permissible to dream. Damn straight."[5]

TO START THE INTERVIEW:

■ How did you hear about the opening?

 ■ What do you already know about the job?

- Why are you interested in our company?

    - Why are you interested in our job opening?

- Why would you like to work here?

    - How can you benefit the company?

- What's your definition of a job?

    - What are the responsibilities of a . . . ?

- Where else are you interviewing?

TO QUALIFY THAT THE PERSON CAN TAKE THE RESPONSIBILITIES AND TIME COMMITMENTS ASSOCIATED WITH THE JOB:

- Is there anything that would prevent you from performing the essential duties of the job?[6]

- If hired, when could you start?

    - Do you have any obligations or trips that would mean you must be absent for during the next twelve months?

- Do you have any problems working nights, early mornings, or weekends if needed?

- Are you willing to travel?

    - Do you have any problems accepting assignments that would take you out of town for two or more days, and on short notice?

- Are you usually able to work overtime on short notice?

- How much do you think this position should pay?

    - What kind of salary do you expect?

- Are there any limits on where you would be willing to relocate?

TO UNDERSTAND THE PERSON'S PAST:

- Can you tell me about yourself?

    - Can you describe your personality?

■ What was your academic rank in high school?

 ■ What particular academic achievement did you have at college?

■ Why have you chosen this field?

■ How is your career going?

 ■ What is your background, starting with your first important job?

■ Have you ever been fired?

 ■ Why?

■ Why did you move here?

See if your questions can elicit a description of how the candidate built his career.

TO UNDERSTAND THE PERSON'S CURRENT JOB AND EXPERIENCE:

■ What are or were your responsibilities on your current or last job?

 ■ What did you do yesterday?

■ What is the most crucial part of your work?

 ■ What was your most important achievement on your last job?

■ What was your favorite part of your current or last job?

 ■ What was your least favorite part?

■ How do you work under pressure?

 ■ Can you give me some examples?

 After a specific accomplishment is described, ask, "How did you do it?"

TO UNDERSTAND THE PERSON'S LEARNING ABILITY:

■ What are the most crucial things you learned on your first few jobs?

 ■ What experiences on your present job added most to your development?

- Everybody has his or her own problem-solving style; can you describe yours?
  - Can you give me some examples of some problems you've solved?
- What was your biggest failure in your current job?
  - What did you do after you failed?
- What was the last book you read?
  - Can you describe the main idea in the book?

TO UNDERSTAND THE PERSON'S JUDGMENT AND DECISION-MAKING ABILITY:

- If you're familiar with our organization, can you describe our main product or service?
  - What would you say are our strong points and weak points?
    - What do you think we can do to improve?
- What has been the biggest crisis you've ever faced?
  - What has been your greatest personal or professional challenge thus far?
- What kind of a decision maker are you?
  - What kind of risks do you take on the job?
- What parts of this job are the most crucial?
- Here's a situation in our workplace. How would you handle it?
- What was your last ethical conflict in the workplace?
  - Can you talk me through how you resolved it?

TO UNDERSTAND HOW THE PERSON LIKES TO BE SUPERVISED:

- Who was your favorite past boss?
  - Why was he or she a favorite?
    - Who was your least favorite boss?

- Can you describe your present boss?

- If I were to call your boss today for a job review, what would she say about you?

TO UNDERSTAND WHAT MOTIVATES THE PERSON:

- What sort of supervision most effectively motivates you?

- Where and when have you been the most successful?

- When can you remember being truly satisfied at work?

- Can you give some examples of projects on which you were highly motivated?

- We all have work-related strengths; what do you consider to be your three major strengths?

- What other companies are you talking to?

  - Why did you pick them?

TO UNDERSTAND HOW THE PERSON WORKS WITH OTHERS:

- What would your past coworkers say they admire about you?

- Can you describe the last time you were in a small, intense group working on a project?

- Can you give me some examples of how you used a sense of humor at work?

- What makes you upset?

- We all have areas dealing with others we need to improve in. What are some of yours?

TO UNDERSTAND THE PERSON'S LEVEL OF COMMITMENT:

- How long do you want to stay in this position?

- How important is it for a company to have a loyal workforce?

  - How do you show your loyalty?

■ What do you think an organization should do to encourage loyalty?

■ How do you feel about being honest and loyal?

■ Can you offer some on-the-job examples?

TO UNDERSTAND THE EMPLOYEE'S PHILOSOPHICAL NEEDS:

■ What is your ideal work environment?

■ What do you want from a job?

■ How do you like to be rewarded? (Money isn't the only way; what else matters?)

TO UNDERSTAND THE PERSON'S GOALS:

■ How would you describe your goal-setting style?

■ What are your goals?

■ Where do you want to be five years from now?

■ If you could choose to be a success in any job, what would it be?

■ What is your definition of success?

■ If we don't hire you, where would you like to work?

TO GAUGE CREATIVITY:

■ What are the most creative things you've done?

■ If you were to write a book, what would it be about?

■ Who are your favorite painters?

■ What poets do you like?

■ What was your dream when you were a kid?[7]

TO WRAP IT ALL UP:

■ Now, given what you know about us, why do you want this job?

■ Why do you think you can do this job?

■ Why are you the right person for me to hire?

 ■ Why should we hire you over the other people?

At the end of the interview, ask whether the person has any questions for you. See whether the inquiries indicate the priorities, the mental horsepower, and the passion of someone you would like to work with.

Questions That Work

Bill Hart, president of the Employers Resource Association, quoted Lewis Carroll's *Alice in Wonderland* when asked what questions could best serve a manager when hiring.

"Would you tell me, please, which way I ought to go from here?"

"That depends a good deal on where you want to get to," said the Cat.

"I don't much care where—" said Alice.

"Then it doesn't matter which way you go," said the Cat.

If you are worried about technical skills, focus your inquiry on those issues. If interested in the person's work ethic, turn your line of questioning there. Here are Hart's suggested questions for five equally qualified applicants:

1. What do you bring to us that we do not now have?

2. What past experiences do you have that directly relate to our position?

3. What is the ideal job for _____? (Insert applicant name.)

4. Who is _____?

5. Why should I hire you?[8]

IMPORTANT EXCEPTIONS

The law and common sense suggest that there are some questions you should not ask. The distinctions between what you can and cannot ask is confusing. You can ask how long someone has lived in a city or state but you can't ask his or her birthplace. You can ask whether someone is a citizen of the United States but not what other country she maintains citizenship in. You can ask whether someone has ever been convicted of a crime, but you can't ask about arrests that did not result in conviction. You can ask about organizations the applicant belongs to except those whose name or character indicates the race, color, religion, or national origin of its members. Ask your personnel office or state employment office what you can and cannot question candidates about.

If you have questions about the type of people you are hiring, see section 18/7, Questions That Work When Sharing a Culture.

11/3 Thinking of Promoting Someone

Assessment

When you think of promoting someone, you are measuring not just current performance but also potential. Promoting someone to be a manager, for example, requires finding someone who understands that the job is to create a whole larger than the sum of its parts. Promotions create role models for the rest of the organization by symbolizing what you want in employees. Whom you promote becomes the most visible demonstration of your values and priorities. They represent the shape and direction of the organization tomorrow. Albert Yu, an Intel executive, says you should promote people on the basis of how fast they learn, rather than how much experience they have.[9] Walking the halls of a number of high-tech companies, I saw that age was not a qualification for filling a corner office with a window; those were for fast learners and doers. Organizations should look for those capable of continuous rapid learning (often demonstrated by questioning abilities), and, when hiring a manager, they also must look for someone who can teach.

ASK OTHERS WHO WORK WITH THE PERSON:

- How smart is this person?

- Do you trust him?

  - Does this person keep their promises?

- How much responsibility can he handle?

- Does this person assume responsibility for his own mistakes?

- Does this person work well across many other departments?

- Would you seek this person as a key resource on an important task force?[10]

ASK THE PROSPECTIVE MANAGER:

- Why are you interested in this position?

  - What would you do with this job if you got it?

- How will you help us grow?

  - How will you set priorities?

- How do you measure whether you are getting the job done right?

  - What did you set out to accomplish at your last job but still haven't done?

    - Why not?

- What defines an outstanding supervisor?

  - Who was the best supervisor you've worked for?

    - What made him so good?

  - How would you pass information on to your employees?

- If you were teaching a course in supervision and you could cover only two major points, what would you cover?

- What kind of a leader are you?

  - Can you describe your leadership style?

- Whom have you personally hired?

  - How did they work out?

- What will happen when someone on your team isn't working out?

  - How would you manage me (if I joined your team)?

- How do you specifically handle criticism?

■ Let's run over a couple of scenarios:

■ What would you do if . . . ?

■ What if one of your assumptions is wrong?

■ What do you do if you have this problem _____?

■ What salary increase do you expect?

■ Is there anything else we should discuss?

By asking questions, you should understand that you are granting a reciprocal opportunity for the other person to interview you. The topic and tone of those inquiries often offer as much insight as the person's answers.

If you have a lack of leaders to promote, see section 18/5, Questions That Work When Teaching Leadership.

11/4 Checking References

Assessment

Reference calls are frustrating for both those placing and those taking the call. Most managers know the legal implications of criticizing former employees. Still, direct references offer some of the most powerful glimpses into a prospective employee's character and past performance. There are many questions even the most reluctant previous employer can answer.

ASK THE REFERENCE:

■ When did the person start to work for you?

■ What is/was this person's job with the company?

■ What is/was her salary?

■ What was her starting salary?

■ When did she leave your employment?

■ What was her pay when she left?

- Why did you let the person leave?

- How well did the person do in the job?

  - How did this person handle crisis assignments?

- Will this person be a problem?

  - How did she get along with other employees?

- How has the person progressed in her career?

- Let me describe the resume; is it accurate and up to date?

  - How many jobs has this person held?

- Is there someone else (preferably someone not on this reference list) I can call about the candidate?

11/5 Doing a Salary Review

Assessment

One of the most emotionally difficult questions managers are asked is "Can I have a pay raise?" Managers often sincerely wish they could say yes, but reality dictates a pie can be cut only so many ways. When approached about a possible raise, ask for time to consider the request, time to consider the following questions.

ASK THE MANAGER REQUESTING A RAISE FOR A STAFF MEMBER:

- What is the competitive compensation for similar talent in the marketplace?

  - What would it cost the company to replace this person?

- What are the contributions to the organization's success of this individual relative to those of others in the organization?

- How did the individual perform relative to the job expectations over the performance period?

- What is the potential value of this individual to the organization's future success?[11]

ASK THE PERSONNEL OFFICE:

- What are our competitors paying?

- What is the standard increase the company is granting?

- What can we afford to pay?

- What does it cost to hire someone with the specialized skills this person has?

If you are the one needing the raise, see section 12/1, Questions That Work When Asking Your Boss to Give You Feedback or section 12/3, Questions That Work When Asking for a Raise.

11/6 Hiring an Intern

Assessment

Having been an intern and having worked with interns who have gone on to become producers, reporters, and television anchors, I appreciate the opportunity internships offer. The key is finding interns who are not just passing time but instead are eager to learn.

ASK THE PROSPECTIVE INTERN:

- Why did you decide to go to college?

  - Why did you pick your major?

- How well have you done in school?

  - Do your grades reflect your abilities?

    - Why not?

- What course was your favorite, and why?

  - What was not your favorite, and why?

- How many days of school or work have you missed?

- What sort of work experience have you had?

If the person asks about a mentor, see section 17/1, Questions That Work When Looking for a Mentor.

11/7   Helping Someone Starting out on a Job

Assessment

If you've spent weeks searching for the right employee, imagine the importance of spending a few hours so that he has a good first workday. The importance of a first assignment in setting an employee on the right track cannot be overestimated. Negative experiences on the first day can color an employee's opinion for years. New employees are frightened because they may not know how to behave and don't know exactly what is expected of them. Since new employees are particularly eager not to appear stupid, you have to encourage and reassure them that it is okay to ask questions. Some businesses give new employees an orientation book made up of questions. The only way to answer the questions is to go around the building and ask them. This is a quick and easy way to encourage inquiry and build relationships.

ASK THE OTHER EMPLOYEES:

- Who can help answer this new employee's questions during the first few days?

- Who can give this new employee a tour?

- Who will take this new employee out to lunch the first day?

If you need to review what questions new employees often have, see sections 7/1–3, Questions That Work When Taking on a New Job or Career Change.

11/8   Someone Asks to Work Part-Time or on Flextime or at Home

Assessment

In place of pay raises or other perks, some organizations are giving employees the flexibility to change their schedules from the traditional nine to five. Workers can be proposing job sharing, telecommuting, or flextime, each of which offers different challenges to managers.

ASK THE EMPLOYEE:

■ Will your proposed schedule or change allow you to do your job?

　■ What problems could you have interacting with customers, coworkers, and management?

■ How does your proposal save money?

　■ Will it cost us more money?

■ How can we measure your performance or productivity?

If the proposal raises vague worries, see section 13/1, Questions That Work When Investigating a Problem.

11/9 Giving Feedback to Someone off Target

Assessment

Frustrations caused by not having enough returned information about "what," "why," and "how" in the workplace lead directly to productivity and personnel problems. We all want feedback, but how many of us really appreciate constructive criticism? We want a gentle process of self-discovery to be helped by a coach, not a cop. Managers who give feedback can use questions to critique not the employee but the work done, to describe a behavior without passing judgment.

Compliments can be shared in a few moments, but meaningful feedback often has to be shared when there is time to discuss deeper issues. Feedback can and should be positive when possible. A colleague once told me it took four positive forms of feedback to balance one negative, an observation with the ring of common sense to it. How corrective feedback is given depends entirely on the person and on time pressures. As one survey respondent put it, managers have to use feedback to lower the stress levels of some employees and to increase stress among others. The trick is to discover how much information the employee wants, how much he can absorb in his own way, and when it is needed. Managers must, in turn, be open to feedback from employees.

What follows are questions to inspire useful exchanges while giving feedback addressing disappointing performance.

ASK COWORKERS BEFORE GIVING FEEDBACK:

- What do you think is going on?

  - Are there any personal problems or pressures I should know about?

  - Is there a lack of confidence?

- Is there a misunderstanding of directions?

  - Was there simple human error?

  - Is this a new mistake or a repeat mistake?

ASK THE EMPLOYEE:

- Are you aware of your job duties?

  - Do you know what to do?

- Are the ways we measure performance accuracy?

  - How are you going to measure your own performances?

- Are you aware of your performance?

  - Are you aware of performance standards?

  - What is causing the gap between what you've done and your goals?

- If others were placed in the exact same circumstances, what's the likelihood some/many/most would have done the same thing?[12]

- What's the most important issue in your life right now?[13]

  - Is there anything causing problems away from work?

- Are you comfortable with my expectations of you? Please explain.[14]

  - What, if any, problems are you having with me as your supervisor?[15]

    - Are we focused on critical issues?

  - How can you tell whether you are making improvements?

- Is the job too simple?

  - Is the job too complex?

  - Are there distractions?

- Do you feel you lack the skills needed?

  - Do you lack the opportunity to practice skills?

- Do you have a lack of time?

- What resources are lacking?

  - Are there any tools you need?

- Do you see the importance of the job?

  - Do you see the need to act?

  - Do you feel apathetic?

- Is poor work being rewarded?

  - Is good work being discouraged?

- Do you not trust the company?

  - How would a highly motivated person do your job?

Questions That Work

Dick Barnett, co-owner of the Barnett & Kutz management and consulting firm, suggests that a set of three simple feedback-generating questions be used in a brief sit-down session between supervisor and supervisee once a week, or as often as necessary. As someone who works with companies that have plateaued, he says it is necessary to use questions to help senior leaders describe the current state of their business. Then, they can use more questions to help the company rediscover the core reason it exists. He says the company can "spend their energy being that mission, rather than struggling or suffering." A company is not that different from a person. Both can find that their best ideas no longer work for them. Barnett's three questions are these:

1. *How are you doing?* Barnett says, "You already have your own opinion, and a long list of concerns. Just get their concerns, *because that's the ones they're going to be willing to work on at the moment.*" (emphasis added)

2. *What are you going to do differently next week?* "Again, you probably have a lot of things you want the person to change," says

Barnett. "Just let them identify the one or two on the top of their list."

3. *How can I help?* Barnett says this "keeps them responsible, but tells you if there's legitimate support/interference you need to provide."[16]

If you cannot change the person's behavior and need to move to the next level, see section 15/3, Questions That Work When Disciplining an Employee.

11/10   Doing Performance Appraisals and Setting Goals

Assessment

Performance appraisals are loaded with perceived danger. Name another regular meeting you have with your employer that involves income, security, social standing, and future opportunity. Managers should acknowledge that appraisals are not once-a-year opportunities to play God. Mike Montefusco, a business adviser, urges a continuous two-way question-and-answer process to ensure that there "is good communication in both directions about organizational and individual needs and expectations."[17]

Before a manager asks an employee any appraisal questions, she should ask herself a set of questions to accurately document the employee's overall performance. The manager should first ask whether everyone has agreed on what is being evaluated. Imagine coming to a performance appraisal and being surprised by the criteria for success. The manager should ask what an employee has to do to make the manager and the organization happy. The manager and the organization should then agree what they would dismiss an employee for doing or not doing. These are the two extremes of any appraisal.

Managers can use positive questions to involve employees in the frequent appraisal process of setting goals, for the next five minutes or the next five years. Edward Miller, of the Poynter Institute, says that feedback "must provide *information on progress toward accomplishing a goal based on some specific standards.* Goals need to be specific; something vague like 'wanting to communicate better' is not a goal; it's a prayer."[18]

When Paul Hampel, of the St. Louis *Post-Dispatch,* was asked about his favorite questions, he said a newspaper editor should ask,

"Why did you become a journalist?" This simple question ("Why did you become a _____?") can inspire profound and useful answers in all professions. Hampel says, "If your staff became journalists because they wanted to help the world—great. Now ask them how they intend to do it." Hampel says the question is a "take on the old trick the German psychiatrist Victor Frankel used. When his patients told him they were considering suicide, Frankel would respond: 'Why haven't you done it already?' From there he would sift through their vague answers to challenge his patients to formulate the essence of their lives, which never failed to have life-sustaining value."[19]

ASK OTHER MANAGERS BEFORE DOING THE EVALUATIONS OR WHEN REVIEWING EVALUATIONS:

- What makes the difference between winners and losers?

  - Where does this person fall in that spectrum?

- Whom would you least want to lose to the competition?

  - Why?

- Is this someone who is pigeonholed?

  - Is this someone who should be promoted?

ASK THE EMPLOYEE'S COWORKERS:

- Is she reliable?

  - How has her attendance been?

- How is her speed and consistency of work?

- Does she communicate effectively?

- Does she promote teamwork?

  - Does she cooperate with others?

- How does she help others succeed?

- How well suited is her personality to the position?

  - Does she have the talent needed to do her job?

■ What should this person be doing in the future?

  ■ What additional duties could this person take on?

  ■ What training does she need?

■ Has she shown initiative?

  ■ Is there a lack of confidence?

■ How is she handling difficult people?

■ How did she contribute to a problem?

IF EVALUATING A MANAGER, ASK THE EMPLOYEES OF THAT MANAGER:

■ Do you have a clear sense of direction?

■ Is your manager leading change?

  ■ How?

■ Is your manager delegating?

■ Is he doing the necessary planning?

■ Who has he hired lately?

  ■ How do you feel that person is doing?

THE PHILOSOPHICAL QUESTIONS:

■ Does our organization need this person?

  ■ Does this person need our organization?

ASK THE EMPLOYEE:

■ Can you share with me some of your goals?

  ■ Can I ask you some questions to help me understand those goals?

  ■ How will you achieve those goals?

  ■ Here are some of the goals I think are important; can we talk about the differences?

■ How can we best measure the goals we've agreed on?

■ Do your current duties add value to the company, or are they just routine work?

■ What have been your accomplishments of the last period?

   ■ What impact did these accomplishments have on the company?[20]

■ What have you done to help the company make more money?

   ■ What have you done to help the company save money?

■ How have you looked ahead, been proactive?

■ What have been some of the problems you've faced over the past six months?

   ■ How did you contribute to that problem?

   ■ How have you been a problem solver?

■ How are you willing to help coworkers?

■ What do your coworkers admire about you?

■ This is a philosophical question, but if your life ended today, what is the one thing everyone who knows you would say about you?

   ■ What would you want them to say?

   ■ Why wouldn't or couldn't they say what you would like them to say?[21]

■ What is the satisfaction you get from doing your job?

   ■ What are your strengths?

   ■ What are your weaknesses?

   ■ What do you do best?

     ■ What brings out your best?

   ■ What are you bad at?

■ What does success mean to you?

■ What do you enjoy doing?

   ■ What do you dislike doing?

- What can you do that no one else can do?

- People sometimes get stuck on a certain path; is that a concern of yours?

  - Why does it feel hard to change?

- What setbacks or failures have you experienced in the past _____ months, and what did you learn from them?[22]

- What's the most challenging part of your job right now?[23]

  - Is there any specialized training that you need?

- Describe the last dispute you had in the workplace.

  - How did you resolve the conflict?

  - What would you do differently the next time?

WHEN THE PERSON HAS SUCCEEDED AT SOMETHING:

- What are you doing that is working so well?

  - What should be next?

  - What can I do to help?

WHEN COMMUNICATION MISHAPS MIGHT BE CAUSING PROBLEMS:

- Have you made any suggestions that you think were ignored?

- Is there a misunderstanding of instructions?

WHEN REVIEWING PAST GOALS:

- What have you accomplished during this rating or review period that is consistent with the goals we set?[24]

- How does what you are doing contribute to reaching our mutually agreed goals?[25]

  - How can we work together to improve in that area?

- Whom have you hired in this period?

■ How are they doing?

■ If you look at their performance, what are you doing to help them succeed?

WHEN LOOKING AT HOW THE WORKPLACE CAN IMPROVE:

■ Do you think the company is slowing down or failing?

■ Can you suggest a plan of improvement for an area where there is still a need for more attention?

■ How can you make this company a better place to work and live?

■ How do you think you can help the company, unit, and office objectives?

■ What dumb, nonvalue-adding things are you asked to do each day?[26]

■ What are you doing that doesn't need to be done by anyone?

WHEN SETTING GOALS:

■ What can you do to help the company succeed in the future?

■ What additional duties could you take on?

■ What would make your job more exciting?

■ In six months, what do you want to become?

■ Where would you like to be next quarter?

■ In six months, what do you want your department to become?

■ What are your larger plans for the future?

■ What do you want to be doing next at our company?

■ Of all the jobs we have, what jobs would you like to be doing?[27]

■ What planning are you doing toward that goal?

■ What do you need to do your job better?

■ Do these long-range goals make sense?

■ Do you feel they are realistic?

■ Are they specific?

■ How can your goals contribute to the unit's overall performance?

■ What do you need to learn?[28]

  ■ How can I help you learn that?

WHEN ASKING HOW THE EMPLOYEE FEELS ABOUT THE WORKPLACE ENVIRONMENT:

■ What do you like about your job?[29]

  ■ Are you having fun in your work?[30]

■ How do you view your coworkers?

  ■ Whom do you need to help to succeed?[31]

■ What's one thing I can do better for you?

  ■ What would you do if you were in my job?

    ■ If you had my job, what would you do differently?[32]

■ What are you doing that could be done as well or better by someone else?

■ What person, alive or dead, would you like to have as your work partner?[33]

■ If I gave you one million dollars to renovate your working environment, how would you spend the money?[34]

Questions That Work

Mary Cusack, a former department manager of manufacturing at Procter & Gamble, describes an informal review process called "Stop, Start, & Continue" that she said was performed about every six months with many of her employees. As someone who challenged a traditional union manufacturing plant to become a high-performance work system, Cusack says she successfully revamped the pay system from being based on titles to being based on skills performance and moved daily decision making from the office to the factory floor. Cusack says the review process was based on three questions managers would ask themselves and each other:

1. What do you want this person to stop doing?

2. What do you want this person to start doing?

3. What do you want this person to continue doing that is already effective?

These questions made up a form filled out by the manager and employee and discussed in a face-to-face meeting after which the employee kept all the forms. Cusack says that "over time people found it to be more worthwhile than the formal review process each year." She concluded that the questions are "simple and straightforward," but that it is the process that gives them value.[35]

If you need to encourage someone to move toward his goals, use the "Questions That Motivate," which are found at the end of each chapter, or see section 18/3, Questions That Work When Taking Action.

11/11 ## A Valued Employee Is Leaving

Assessment

When employees leave, companies often take one last shot at getting an honest read of how they saw the workplace. Even employees who are leaving want to feel that their opinions count. The final interview has one specific value—to discover issues that might provoke others to leave.

ASK THE PERSON'S DIRECT SUPERVISOR AND OTHER MANAGERS:

■ Are we concerned about any trade secret issues or organizational material being taken?

■ Is this employee underpaid?

  ■ Can we offer more money?

    ■ Should we?

ASK THE EMPLOYEE:

■ What are your long-term career plans?

  ■ Can our company offer a better long-term situation?

- Will your new employer still be around in a few years?

- What did you feel was the best thing about working here?

  - What did you like least about working here?

- What did you accomplish?

- What helped you reach your goals?

  - What stood in your way of reaching your goals?

- How would you improve the company?

  - How do you feel about the direction the company is headed in?

    - Did you think the vision of the company was clearly communicated?

      - What would you do to improve communication?

If you need to hire to replace someone, you can ask the employee who is leaving some questions about the position she is vacating. For suggestions, see section 11/1, Questions That Work When Examining How You Recruit and Pick People.

11/12 Dismissing an Employee

Assessment

While physical violence may be unlikely after you dismiss an employee, a courtroom fight is another matter. You can be sued for a discriminatory firing; for undertaking a retaliatory discharge after the employee exercised her rights under the law; or for slander, libel, or defamation of character. There are few easy dismissals, even if you believe the firing will help the person move on to a position she is better suited for. It sounds harsh to "fire" anyone, but, as has often been observed, a business is not a church. Inquiry can introduce the specter of dismissal, while preserving the employee's ability to save face and change her attitude.

ASK THE PERSON'S DIRECT SUPERVISOR AND A HUMAN RESOURCES PERSON:

- Does the employee in question have fair notice?

- Are our procedures being properly followed?

- Has the discipline used been fair and consistent with past applications?

- Does the personnel file have all the documentation of our concerns?

- Are we getting the results we hoped for?

ASK THE EMPLOYEE:

- What do you think will be the consequences if you cannot change the situation?

  - What do you think will happen if you cannot come up to our standards?

- Would you like to take a day off and think about the job and whether you are up to the requirements, or would you like to look for work elsewhere?

- What is a fair resolution for this problem for both sides?

If you need to attack other problems created by the employee, see section 13/3, Questions That Work When There Is a Problem You Need to Act On.

. . . .

Questions That Motivate

What is the one thing, which if practiced consistently,
would make the most impact in your life?
Mike Turner[36]

. . . .

Chapter 11 Conclusion

Ideas into Action

Personnel issues are often the first and most important task of managers each day. You will be known for whom you hire, remembered for those you taught and encouraged. Identifying, hiring, and retaining talent are the key issues in any organization. Even high-flying high-tech companies where capital is not a top constraint cannot grow beyond the talents of their employees. While many people can master a job's technical skills, it takes a far finer mind to recognize emerging talent in another and to cultivate and creatively challenge it. Organizations that track how interviews are done and who hires which employees will have a powerful tool to judge each manager's contributions to the institution. Retention is still another measure of a manager; a department with rapid turnover may need closer attention.

Managers should use questions to invest in and build the true capital of any enterprise—human capital. Inquiry can discover the untapped value in people. Satisfied employees and a happy workplace are important points of differentiation in a world of keen competition between employers. If you find you've become a rich ground for others to recruit from, you can take some satisfaction from this inconvenient compliment. If you create a positive questioning culture, other organizations will turn to you for their future planners, thinkers, and leaders.

Hiring and retaining are complicated because you hire and promote for where you will be, not where you are. Hiring and promotion decisions are future forecasts. By identifying strong, questioning candidates, you take the first step toward hiring those who are future oriented. While you are evaluating potential employees, they are doing the same, asking themselves who they are and what are their talents, gifts, and skills. They are asking where they can make a contribution and get the best salary and what tradeoffs they must make among workload, institutional grief, and on-the-job satisfaction. For some employees, the job is evaluated almost exclusively as a matter of salary, the money-as-scorecard philosophy. For most other employees, the psychic paycheck, the emotional rewards, are an equally important factor.

The emotional connection grows when feedback and performance appraisals become regular parts of the exchange between employee and employer. These are a form of pay to be given as regularly as a paycheck. Just as the payroll department is given time and resources to do its job, managers have to have time and resources to give employees meaningful emotional compensation. Constant inquiry shows you are reaching out and you understand the goals of your managers and coworkers. Not asking any questions about an assignment shows you are not fully considering the implications of the work ahead. Positive questioning when managing creates conversations, connections, and competitive advantages. In chapter 12, we look at how to use questions to manage your career.

QUESTIONS THAT WORK WHEN:
Managing Your Career

Try not to become a man of success but rather to become a man of value.
ALBERT EINSTEIN

Planned progress depends on promptly possessing information about the actions and decisions of others, information most efficiently and directly gathered with questions. Continuous positive questioning creates deep knowledge. New challenges and the rewards that come with them are thus the result of questions asked of your boss and coworkers. During negotiations over pay and status that define so much of the work world, you do get what you ask for. In short, management of your career results from management of your inquiry.

If you agree that work should be more than a title on the door and a six-figure paycheck, questions will lead you to work you truly love doing. Lucetta Marty, a survey respondent, and director of the Creativity Tank, asks a question everyone should consider: "What do you try without being forced?"[1] The answer tells you a great deal. Variations on the question include, "When did you do something that no one taught you?" and "Where have you been that no one took or sent you?" The answer shows you where your heart has taken you, the skill, task, and place you could happily make a living. It is a matter of, as Peller Marion, a career counselor, once said, of redefining success to fit your desires. She said that you need to "develop a plan just the way you have a strategy to put money away for retirement or a plan to save money for your kids' education. [You have] to develop a strategy and a plan to look at your career and redefine it." She warned against becoming one of the many people who "get into a routine that's very comfortable and [that] solves 70 percent of their problems and so they settle."[2] Questions keep you from settling for less than what you want. Inquiry accelerates ambitions and accomplishments.

12/1 Asking Your Boss to Give You Feedback

Assessment

Independent of performance reviews, you should constantly seek feedback on what you could do better. This can be bruising but is better than finding out about problems in front of the rest of the staff or when you are being shown the door. You can ask for feedback by alluding to a success while asking for advice: "We beat them this time, but what do you think I need to do to make sure I win the next time?" This technique helps if strained communication between you and your boss makes you think twice about asking for a critique. If you think that asking for feedback suggests that you're not capable or up to speed, you should think as great athletes do. They seek continual training and coaching, a constant cycle of performance and feedback.

ASK YOUR COWORKERS OR BOSS:

■ If my performance appraisal were done right now, how would I do?

■ Are you happy with my work?

  ■ What part of my work do you think is best?

■ What should I do to make our department run better?

  ■ Have we had any shortcomings lately?

■ Are there any challenges ahead that I should prepare my department for?

  ■ Are there any changing priorities we should focus on now?

■ Has there been any personality issues I might be missing?

  ■ Are you aware of any unsatisfied employees in my department?

■ What would you like to see me do more of?

  ■ How would you improve my work?

■ Would you like for me to elaborate with lots of detail or a little?[3]

  ■ What can I do to enhance the way you and I communicate?

■ What do I need to know in order to deliver?

Ask your boss out to lunch, where you might get uninterrupted time to ask your questions.

Questions That Work

Bert Decker, chairman of Decker Communications Inc., uses his Three-by-Three Rule to create constructive feedback. He says feedback requests should ask for three strengths and three distractions. Why three of each? Too much positive feedback doesn't give you the information you need to improve, and too much negative criticism "throttles your confidence." Decker says each of us has strengths to be acknowledged and distractions we need to pay attention to. Asking for just three pros and three cons has an additional benefit. Decker says any more feedback is too much to ask someone to give and too much for you to remember.[4]

12/2 Having Someone Review Your Performance

Assessment

Many employees don't openly question the performance review process or the result. It is an important employment practice you need to participate in fully. Performance appraisals can be based on numbers—sales increased or widgets produced—but chances are much of the performance appraisal will be based on perceptions of how effective you are. Looking at last year's review before heading into your latest one will generate a list of questions for you to focus on. Such inquiry increases your chances of receiving honest feedback.

BEFORE THE APPRAISAL, ASK YOUR SUPERVISOR OR HUMAN RESOURCES DEPARTMENT:

- Can I see a copy of the evaluation form?

- Which parts of this form are particularly important for me to focus on?

- When will we have time to sit down and review the results?

- Which assignments or tasks are the priorities we will focus on?

AT THE REVIEW, ASK YOUR SUPERVISOR:

■ May I read your appraisal?

   ■ When was I watched or evaluated?

   ■ How did you arrive at these conclusions?

■ What are the directions or duties I should pursue to succeed with our company?

   ■ How can I become a more valued employee?

■ Given my achievements, which jobs might I be considered for?

■ Is there a way you can compare my performance to those of other people doing the same job at our company?

■ Can I suggest a plan of improvement?

12/3 Asking for a Raise

Assessment

Asking for a larger than standard raise requires more than arguing that your performance went beyond agreed-upon goals. Such a raise requires you to keep a list of your accomplishments, in particular what money you saved or made for the company. If you can't easily look at your salary as a proportion of money made for the company, you need to ask questions to find the market value of your specific skills. Ask others how to quantify your value to the company or your results of the past year. Your questions will remind you, your coworkers, and managers of what is new in your job and how you have been a catalyst for change. With such insights, you should be able to outline why your compensation no longer equals your contribution.

If you are offered a promotion, negotiations become more complicated, because the pay raise should be based on what is commensurate for the new job, not on your existing salary. Ask around to see how much the company would pay someone from the outside to take the job. Before beginning a big new project with the expectation that there will be a raise, ask to be sure you and your supervisor agree on how much it will be. Don't be trapped by the starving-artist theory of compensation—if you love it, you can't make a living at it. In the end, you want an answer to your own internal question: "Do I expect a decent payoff for putting in the time and effort needed to do the job right?"

Questions can help you look into your organization's pay philosophy, giving insights as to who is rewarded and promoted. Enter a salary negotiation prepared to ask for a specific figure. Why? A figure gives the discussion a focus, helping you avoid a debate about whether you deserve a raise at all. Common sense suggests asking for more than you think will be offered, since any negotiated figure is likely to be lower than what you ask for. The worst a boss can say is no, but it is a humbling no that speaks directly to your value as an employee. Anticipate questions you may be asked about your last raise or your accomplishments since that increase. It is better to ask for a raise when the organization is doing well, but you also want to make sure to ask when the approving authority is personally in a good frame of mind. It helps to have an effective continuing dialogue with the manager so that you know that person's moods. If you ask for a raise in the questioning form we suggest, you won't put a manager on the spot because you will be allowing time to respond. By suggesting that you don't expect an answer right away, you allow the supervisor to come back with an offer. You want your boss to feel he won't regret a decision in your favor.

ASK OTHERS, INCLUDING ANY PROFESSIONAL OR TRADE ASSOCIATIONS:

■ How much do you think someone taking on such a position should be paid?

■ How much are my peers paid?

■ Are there any loose industry guidelines for what the pay should be?

■ How closely are they followed in our area?

ASK YOUR COWORKERS, HUMAN RESOURCES DEPARTMENT, AND EVEN YOUR SUPERVISOR:

■ What are pay raises looking like in general?

■ What is the maximum raise?

■ Are there any guidelines for the company?

■ What are the pay ranges for specific job titles?

■ Who are the exceptions?

■ When are raises given?

■ Should I send a memo to my boss before I meet with her to ask for a raise?

■ What can I do to make myself more valuable?

■ How can I advance to the next level?

ASK YOUR SUPERVISOR:

■ Could I have some time with you today to discuss an important matter?

■ What is a good time to have a meeting to discuss my performance?

■ How am I doing?

■ Here is an outline of some of my accomplishments; would you look it over?

■ Given how many goals I've met, how much money I've saved, what do you think a fair salary should be?

■ Would you consider me for a raise?

■ Would you consider me for a promotion that would include a raise?

■ I don't need an answer right now, but can I have an answer in the near future?

■ What information do you need to get approval for a raise or promotion?

IF THE RAISE IS NOT FORTHCOMING, ASK YOUR SUPERVISOR:

■ Can you give me a sense of priorities of what must be done so that my pay is fair for the amount of work I need to do?

■ What advice and support can you give me to help me make improvements?

■ I know you want to be fair to all employees, but fair doesn't mean equal, does it?

■ Is there someone up the chain of command who might have the power to help with my compensation?

■ Who has the final say on whether a pay raise is granted?

■ Can I have your permission to talk to her?

■ Does the company really demand perfect performance before giving raises?

IF THE SUPERVISOR SAYS TIMES ARE TIGHT:

■ Do I deserve a raise but can't have one at this moment?

■ Can we find a date to begin that raise?

■ Could we make it retroactive?

■ When will the salary freeze be lifted?

■ Can we agree my salary should be increased right after the freeze is ended and made retroactive?

■ Are there other benefits we might be able to discuss?

■ Could we look at noncash alternatives?

■ Is there a car I might be able to use?

■ Could I have additional vacation time?

■ Could we be more flexible about my hours?

■ What training or educational benefits are available?

IF THE MEETING IS POSITIVE BUT DOES NOT LEAD TO A RAISE:

■ What would you do if you were in my shoes?

■ What skills do I need to have to get a raise in the future?

■ Can we schedule another meeting after I've had time to consider our conversation?

Whatever agreement you get, try to get it in writing. At the very least, write a note back confirming any agreement, saying you'll move forward on the basis of what you've just outlined, and be sure to express your thanks.

12/4 Asking for a Promotion

Assessment

A positive relationship is essential with those who can promote you. Asking focused questions about your job is one way of improving your relationship with your supervisors. You can ask for:

- More responsibility

- A review of your current work

- Information on future opportunities

- Suggestions on company needs you can meet

You can ask the person who has or has had the job you are seeking for advice. This person can outline the challenges you are likely to face and the opportunities you might have.

ASK YOUR BOSS:

- How can I help you?
  - How can I make a larger contribution?
    - What additional training can I get that will help me do more?
- Do I have a chance at a promotion?
  - How good is that chance?
- Can you give me an example of what I would need to achieve to be considered for a promotion?
- Who is in charge of making the decision?

IF THE PROMOTION IS NOT FORTHCOMING:

- What goals do I need to achieve?
  - What are the chances I'll be considered for a promotion if I make those goals?
- What areas do I need to work on?

- Are my people skills up to par?

- How can I improve those skills and my expertise?

Questions That Motivate

What is your real passion?

Barbara Waugh[5]

Chapter 12 Conclusion

Ideas into Action

There are few questions that compel attention as much as those that can change our careers. The workplace has changed from organized advancement on the basis of age and title to promotion on the basis of personal experience and potential. Managing your career requires effective problem-solving responses, not emotional reactions; this can be difficult when you are dealing with issues of pay, perks, power, and prestige. The hard truth is there is a direct relationship between pay and perceived value to the company.

Questions discover and define the value you bring to the workplace. Consider asking yourself a key question, the question your supervisor is asking: "Does this person directly contribute to the success of our company?" *Questions That Work* also helps you understand the big picture in your industry and the larger issues of change in your career. Positive questions also help you discover and form the growing relationships every employee needs. Throughout your career, you need to know whom to ask the important question "Will you help me?" It is a question with a quality common to all great inquiry: directness and deceptive simplicity. Asking the right people to help you can transform your career.

The day of checking your brain at the factory gate is over. Can you think like an owner? That is the question that will in the end determine your success. If you can ask the same questions an owner would, you will find new opportunities and be the CEO of your own career. In chapter 13 we explore how questions can help you help others. It's a look at the powerful role inquiry plays in investigating, solving, and preventing problems.

Part IV

Crisis Questions

QUESTIONS THAT WORK WHEN:
Dealing with a Problem

Good questions outrank easy answers.

PAUL SAMUELSON

John F. Kennedy said, "When written in Chinese, the word 'crisis' is composed of two characters. One represents danger, and the other represents opportunity." The link between the two makes managers who are facing a crisis or key decision anxious. The fear of mistakes, of missing an opportunity, or of committing other errors of omission paralyze at one extreme and lead to a frenzy of unfocused activity at the other. Uncertainty naturally grows in gray areas, where there are no regulations or clear rules, the places where there is a large degree of subjectivity. It is an environment where people feel worried, threatened, impatient, or suspicious, the place where problems grow.

One reason for anxiety is that we often don't understand our own problem-solving or decision-making processes. We must gather information, create a logical explanation for what has happened, and design a realistic response. Question asking is a way to turn problems into opportunities. I appreciate that that phrase may have a hollow ring. The commentator Christopher Fildes tells the story about a chairman who used to tell his troops, "We don't have problems. We have opportunities, opportunities. Is that clear?" to which someone finally said, "Well, yes, chairman. We do seem to face a large number of insurmountable opportunities."[1] Audrey Rice Oliver knows that problems can be turned around. She is a woman who went from being a teenage single mother living in poverty to running her own software company. Oliver, who was once invited to speak at a White House economic summit, had her own philosophy of handling problems. She said, "Many people are told no in many walks of life and I think you have to evaluate what 'no' means to you. . . . 'No' means never to some and to me it means for the moment."[2] To overcome obstacles, you need to keep asking a series of positive, progressive questions.

219

I've worked in newsrooms that appear to be filled with nothing but problems and difficult decisions to be handled every hour, on deadlines that sometimes are a matter of seconds. Those who prosper in such an environment are those who quickly define problems, figure out what needs to be achieved, consider options, and act on the plan at hand, all while making contingency plans. These decision makers are not experts in any one area, but, know what questions to ask when they are facing a difficult situation. They know the value of what Rudy and Kipling once said,

> I keep six honest serving-men.
> (They taught me all I knew);
> Their names are What and Why and When
> and How and Where and Who.

13/1 Investigating a Problem

Assessment

Today's complex world demands that you have a variety of techniques to investigate problems. What is a problem? One long-standing definition says it is the difference between what you have and what you would like to have. Problems are as varied as workplaces and people but can be broadly classified as irregular or regular, critical or annoying, equipment driven or people driven. Inquiry helps you determine the most important indications of the problem, which is crucial, since the right remedy is different in each case. It is important to recognize that a complaint is not always a problem. Complaints are often a venting of temporary emotions or a cloaked request for guidance.

Writing a problem statement in the form of a question is one of the quickest ways to creatively begin to move toward a solution. Solving problems often involves finding a question relevant to the people involved. The key is coming up with the right words that everyone understands and agrees upon. Once a problem is defined and identified, energy has to be applied to confront it. When no one is questioning, things go back to the way they were. Attacking a problem is a process of clarify and narrow, clarify and narrow. Of Kipling's servicemen "who what why when and where,"—the variations of "why" may be the most valuable. Many problem solvers have learned to ask the simple question "Why?" five times in a row:

The assembly line broke down.
Why?
Because this belt broke.
Why?
Because we didn't replace it.
Why?
Because we were not keeping track of the wear.
Why?
Because we didn't assign someone to do this as part of their job.
Why?
Because we didn't think it would be a problem. Now I think we need
   to assign someone to check the belts each week before we start
   up the line.

One advantage of such short "why" questions is that they focus on the outcome, not the process. It is simple to remember to ask "Why?" five times when encountering a problem. Questioning is such an organic process, constantly changing according to time, place, and personalities, that it always helps overcome the first obstacle to problem solving, the assumptions that often create a crisis. As Gail Taylor, a survey respondent, says, "You don't solve a problem, you dissolve it."[3]

Attacking Assumptions

We fashion ways to cope with almost any problem. Rather than question where they are stuck or questioning whether there is a new way around an obstacle, many people live inside comforting walls of assumptions and cherished beliefs. Questions should force you out of denial and help others to acknowledge the scope of the matter. Problems almost always present a conflict with what you think you know for if all your assumptions are correct, you would anticipate and solve problems before they become an issue. Ian Haynes, a senior pharmaceutical engineer at AstraZeneca Pharmaceuticals, has studied how assumptions lie at the heart of many problems. His review of the process of problem solving points to the need to get to the "innovation zone" before beginning to innovate effectively. In his mind, asking questions is the first essential step to getting to that zone. He says that managers have to ask, "What is the real problem here?" and "What assumptions are we making (data we are inventing and data we are ignoring) in addressing this problem?"[4]

Not knowing, what some call an "impoverished awareness," lies at the heart of many problems.

A manager who says he doesn't have all the answers challenges one of the first assumptions (the boss is all knowing) that needs to be attacked to begin sincere problem solving. Many employees are used to asking the boss what to do. It is interesting to see what happens when the boss asks his staff what the problem really is and what they think the solution is.

Another assumption is that employees can read the manager's mind when a problem occurs. Chances are you've dealt with a manager who, when pressured by a problem, quickly becomes frustrated with your lack of understanding of the issue. Since emotion and ego are part of all problem solving, you should not assume you know what the other person is thinking or feeling. Positive questions push people to see what's going on and what is possible.

ASK OTHERS:

- Are we trying to defend a belief because we want it to be true?

- What are the frequent problems we are experiencing we thought we had fixed?

- Since you are closest to the job, can you come up with specific measures of success?

Using a Positive Approach

Researching a problem can be a positive experience if you look at what works, not just at what has failed. If you focus exclusively on what is wrong, what Paul Chaffee describes as "deficit" data, the process of problem examination can be "life killing." Identifying and asking about what you would like more of, what works, can be exciting.[5] Not every attempt to solve a problem will have a satisfactory answer, but, by using a positive questioning process, you accept the necessity of small failures that are part of learning. It is a process of support, communicating clearly with people and bringing them into the problem-solving process. Try to put personalities out of the question so you can understand first, judge later. Dr. Serge Bouwens, senior research consultant at ID Research in the Netherlands, says that, to avoid personalizing the problem and involving egos, you can phrase questions tactfully: "This is a really difficult problem, and I am sure many other organizations have to deal with it. Can you address this problem?" This allows you to rise above the case itself and to suggest looking for references and ways to improve upon the standard solutions.[6]

Much alienation and tension in the problem-solving process grow out of fear. Cross-examinations will not help you open up people. A frank exchange can take place only with open and positive questioning. It may help to ask whether a crisis does present an opportunity. Barbara Waugh, of Hewlett-Packard, suggests asking every time one encounters an obstacle, "What if this is a gift?"[7] Cynics may consider the question Pollyannaish, but it can elicit feelings of optimism among others. Positive questioners recognize that where facts end, you must confront a sense of confusion before you find a new direction. This uncertainty can be a gift, a vague yet not uncomfortable sense of possibility.

It's Discovering a Story . . .

While engaged in fact finding, you can invite people to tell their side of the story. If they find you are attacking the problem, not them, people will give the information needed more freely. Doctors ask questions in private rooms, and managers who wish for spontaneity should remember to carry on conversations behind closed doors. Like a doctor, you should welcome those with complaints in a place that provides comfort and privacy if you wish to discover the history and symptoms of what is the matter. Inquiry helps you avoid confusing the symptoms of the pain someone might be feeling, and the real cause of the illness, the hidden problem that causes the pain.

Listen first, and use positive questions to empathize. As you listen to the story, gradually explore the problems the person is facing. Slow storytelling relaxes both parties, allowing people to let down their guard and to offer opinions. Grant Todd, an organizational knowledge teacher, says it is important to ask, "How do you feel about this issue" (as opposed to "How do you think about it?").[8] In listening to the story, you will test and weigh the generic and strategic elements of the situation. You are likely familiar with the common issues; the unique ones will need to be addressed specifically before you move forward. Your questions need to bring up the pertinent past that has led up to the current situation and list the issues that need to be addressed.

Those you question can be in trouble. Inquiry has to allow tactical retreats rather than suggesting total surrender. Pressing a question may give you a feeling of victory but destroy the openness you need to have with your partner to reach a shared solution. It is important not to immediately discount another's information, unless your aim is to generate anger. View shared information as the glue that holds together a relationship, for, if information is weak, it compromises any future communication. Questions discover what was and what needs to be, what you need to do and what needs to be undone.

ASK THOSE DIRECTLY INVOLVED IN THE PROBLEM:

- Can you tell me what happened?
  - Is this an accident?
    - Is this a situation that has occurred before; if so, how often?
  - Is this a surprise, or did we think it could happen?
- What is our current reality? Describe it; don't judge it.[9]
- Can you bring me up to date?
  - What has changed since we last talked?
- What reliable information do we have about the problem?
  - What made you think that . . . ?
    - What evidence do you have?
  - Who was involved?
    - What was our department's role in this problem?
  - Where did it happen?
  - When did it happen?
- When is it not happening?
- Why do you feel it happened?
  - What is the history of this type of problem?
    - Can you give me a chronology of this most recent problem?
    - When did the problem start?
    - How did it start?
  - What do we currently do?
    - How do we do it?

- Why did it happen this way?

  - What was the logic?

- How widespread is the problem?

  - How large could it become?

  - Have others had similar problems?

- Would you explain this to me?

  - What didn't we foresee?

  - What didn't we understand?

  - How are these issues related to each other?

  - How can we make the issue simpler?

- Is our analysis clear so far?

  - What could be other causes for this problem?

- How can we break this problem apart?

  - How significant is the problem?

  - Who is affected?

  - How are they affected?

    - Who might complain about this?

- What are the customer complaints?

  - How quickly do we respond to complaints?

There are always "customers" in every problem. It may be you. Try to figure out who all the "customers" are for each problem statement.

IF SOMEONE IS NONRESPONSIVE OR UNCERTAIN ABOUT THE PROBLEM:

- Is there anything else you would like to say?

- What is your opinion?

- Do you need more information?

■ Whom else can you check with?

■ Can you try something or think about something a new way?

■ What's draining to you about this situation?

■ Does this work for you?

Questions That Work

Dr. Jim Botkin, member of the global think tank The Group of Rome and president of the International Corporate Learning Association, says often *what is not happening* is important when making decisions. He relates a passage from Arthur Conan Doyle's "Hound of the Baskervilles."

> "Is there any other point to which you wish to draw my attention?"
> "Yes, to the curious incident of the dog in the nighttime."
> "The dog did nothing in the nighttime."
> "That was the curious incident," remarked Sherlock Holmes.

He says military commanders are trained to use that concept in the context of these three variations:

1. What is happening?

2. What is not happening?

3. What can I do to influence the action?[10]

If you are asked to hold a meeting or form a team to problem solve, see section 10/1, Questions That Work When Having a Meeting.

13/2 Investigating a Problem with Your Supervisor

Assessment

A time will come when you have to investigate a problem directly with upper management. You can't make bad news good, so you shouldn't try. While you may find yourself taking direct orders and not being permitted to question, the opportunity to pose a few short questions can help you divine the less obvious attitudes of supervisors. Plan to put forward your most urgent questions first so that the opportunity is not lost. Ask your question, and pause, giving your supervisor plenty of time to respond. When people feel pressed, they cannot be creative problem solvers.

ASK YOUR BOSS:

- Can I have your advice on a problem I've been looking into?

  - Can I have your feedback on this problem?

- What problem do you think has created the situation?

- Here is what I've been told. Is that an accurate account of what happened?

  - I think I've narrowed down what is the problem. Do you agree with this summary?

- What is the objective?

  - What are the changes I should make from what I had been doing?

- What is our strategy, the general course of action we want to take?

  - What have been the steps we have been taking to deal with this?

  - What have been the results?

- What are your priorities?

  - How can I correct this problem?

If you are being questioned about your part in the problem, see chapter 15, Questions That Work When You Are Put on the Spot. If you are being asked to be creative about how you will solve the problem, see section 9/2, Questions That Work When Inspiring Creativity.

13/3 There Is a Problem You Need to Act On

Assessment

After your initial reality check, you will hear the larger dimensions of the problem. Now comes the time to soak yourself and others in the problem. Fred Martin, of MIT's Media Lab, likes to ask, "What are you thinking?" when a student is immersed in a problem.[11] That's one way to explore solutions that are subtly surfacing. Good managers know that when they get into a troubled situation they bring their people together. In many cases, you can ask, "What do you think?" and stay out of their way so that your staff can do its own thing. This latitude is what many of us prize about our jobs. Mike Montefusco, a business adviser, says that inviting others into the problem-solving process creates a "buy-in" to the solution and creates a form of vesting.[12] Of course, supervisors can't just let their people fail without sharing the responsibility. Managers who delegate authority may pick the wrong person to solve the problem. They need to regularly review their staff to see whether the right person with the right skills is on the most pressing problem.

Problem solving requires a flexible process, but one in which you take certain steps in a certain order. Once you've established what happened (and the when, where, who, and why involved), you have to repeat the process to discover what needs to be done to move beyond or prevent the problem from occurring. Some problems don't need to be addressed right away. They may be a distraction from more serious problems or greater opportunities. You need to move quickly toward discovering what the options are (perhaps someone has already solved a similar problem), why a proposed answer will work, and how others can buy into the solution.

Watch for the red lights in conversations, the places where communication stops. Barbara McRae, a consultant and business coach, warns that "why" questions "tend to trigger defensive responses and 'who' questions imply the intent to blame." She coaches managers to ask "what" and "how" questions in order to stay focused on the solution.[13]

WHEN SETTING UP A TIME FRAME, ASK THOSE WHO ARE GOING TO HELP YOU SOLVE THE PROBLEM:

- Since time is often the first factor, when do we have to have this problem solved by?

  - What is the latest we can have this problem solved by?

  - What is most urgent?

■ How likely is the problem to occur again?

■ What are the two or three things you want to accomplish first?

WHEN SEEING WHETHER SOMEONE HAS ALREADY FOUND A SOLUTION OR CAN GIVE YOU A SOLUTION:

■ Can you help me out of this mess?

■ How have people responded to this problem?

■ Has someone already solved this problem?

   ■ How?

■ What have you tried so far?

   ■ How did that work?

■ What is the precedent for solutions to this problem?

   ■ Will we be setting a precedent?

■ What does the rest of the company do?

   ■ What is different about our situation?

■ Who else can help us with our problem?[14]

■ Can you show me how to do it?

   ■ How would you handle it?

   ■ Do you have any tips?

■ What is your solution?

   ■ How did you figure out that solution?

WHEN SOLICITING IDEAS:

■ What do we want to achieve?

   ■ Where do we need to direct our focus?

■ How should we go about developing a plan to deal with this problem?

- What solution do you have for our needs?
- If such and such causes the problem, what would happen if . . . ?
  - Would it be helpful if . . . ?
- What are the issues?
  - What opportunities are hidden in those issues?
- What if . . . ?
  - What if we need more resources?
- What are the options or alternatives?
  - Are the options realistic?
- What are we going to do about this?
  - What plans have we made to deal with this problem?
  - Why didn't they work?
    - When there is a failure, why is it not stopped right away?
  - Do we need a new plan to solve this problem?
- Have you had any other suggestions?
  - What are the alternatives you identified?
    - What are the additional alternatives?[15]
- If we knew we couldn't fail, how could we approach this challenge?[16]
- What are all the different solutions?
  - Can you give me the specifics of that solution?
  - What alternatives have we yet to consider?
- What are our competitors doing when they face this problem?
- What outcome might create an audible "wow" in the organization?[17]
- Can you write down your suggestions on how to solve the problem?
- How would you rank these ideas in private?

IF INFORMATION IS NOT FORTHCOMING:
- Can I have you write up your opinions anonymously?

WHEN YOU HAVE TO EVALUATE A POSSIBLE SOLUTION:
- Why did you choose your solution?
  - How will you manage the solution chosen?
- What limitations are we operating under?
  - What short-term limitations are we facing?
  - What about the long term?
- Where might information be wrong?
  - What are the consequences of wrong information?
- Do you think this would work better?
  - Why not?
    - Do you see any flaws in this proposed solution?
      - What could go wrong with this solution?
        - Does this solution fit overall?
        - Does this solution hit all the key problem areas?
    - What kind of a response is this solution likely to get from others?
- What about our solution bothers you?
  - What is the worst that can happen if this solution doesn't work?
    - What is the best that can happen if it does work?
  - What's the most likely outcome of this solution?
    - Will solving this problem create other problems we can foresee?
- What other concerns do you have about . . . ?
- What do you see as the best resolution to this problem?
  - What is your preference?

Try to use questions to come up with two solutions. You can come up with a more creative alternative and use it as an option if the first solution fails.

WHEN YOU NEED TO IMPLEMENT A SOLUTION:

■ How can the system be improved?

■ What major jobs are needed to solve this problem?

  ■ What major functions of those jobs are needed?

  ■ What results are required?

  ■ What are the relevant skills?

    ■ Who needs more training?

      ■ How can we get them more training?

  ■ How can we design this process to make your job easier?

    ■ How can we improve your workplace to make your job easier to do?

    ■ What equipment can we get you to improve your work?

■ After we make the fix, how will we check to see that it is working?

  ■ Will we give this solution a tryout?

    ■ How, who, when, and where?

      ■ How will information be gathered?

■ What are the consequences if we don't solve this problem with this solution?

  ■ What is our contingency plan?

If you need to assemble or work with a team to solve a problem, see chapter 10, Questions That Work When Meeting and Planning. If you are asked to solve a problem creatively, see chapter 9, Questions That Work When Creativity and New Thinking Are Needed.

Questions That Work

When Darrell Mann, a survey respondent, replied to my request for inquiries to use in problem solving, he provided a list of questions and topics he explores when doing a study. These include:

- *Why not?* Mann says he looks for "trigger words like *can't, won't, never, always,* etc." He challenges them because "experience says they're rarely as definitive as the writer or speaker believes."

- *Where are the contradictions?* Mann says they are always present.

- *What's the problem definition?* Mann says it helps to try to "translate the problem into a vivid emotive phrase" such as "instant camera."

- *Who's already done it?* Mann says 99.9 percent of the time "someone, somewhere has already solved your problem."[18]

13/4 Making a Big Decision

Assessment

Businesspeople may not like uncertainty, but Christopher Fildes, a commentator, has a perspective. "If there were no uncertainty there would be no markets, just as if every race were a walkover there would be no betting, and if business were easier [a maxim of his father's] more people would be in it."[19] In other words, those who have to make difficult decisions in business typically receive rewards that reflect that difficulty. It is the moment when options are unclear, when they must give up the familiar for the unknown, that good decision makers show the right stuff. The old saw about success being the result of opportunity meeting preparation is particularly true when a big decision is to be made.

When facing an important decision, pull together a team, the advisers you can quiz to provide the information you need. You can "hear" decisions being made through the process of q-and-a. The art of making good decisions is often the art of asking good questions. The rapidity of business interaction today, the compression of time created by technology, makes it all the more important to have focused questions at your fingertips. The faster you evaluate a situation and get a grasp of the problem and alternative solutions, the better off you will be. As the software creator Linus Torvalds put it, "The fact that you question means that suddenly you start looking at alternatives."[20]

You cannot endlessly question but must instead move forward not knowing everything. If you can back up your decision and show that your recommendation is tied to the best projectable end result, you have done your best. Do you have a clear and explainable method of making a decision, other then just "thinking" about it? A growing number of newsrooms are adopting series of questions that force journalists to argue through a variety of options. The point is not only to make the right decision but also to be able to explain the decision process to others, including the public. Here are questions to help you think through your decision.

ASK THE OTHER DECISION MAKERS:

- How are we doing?
  - What did you see as the decision?
- Why is a decision necessary?
  - What is the history that brought us to this point?
  - What past decisions created this situation?
  - Are the prior decisions still valid?
    - Is this a periodic decision or a unique decision?
- What in the environment has changed—our competition, supply situation, personalities?
- What will be accomplished for the business, rather than who will be pleased?[21]
- What is the aim of this decision?
  - What is the mission?
    - What are the objectives?
      - What will help us meet those objectives; what strategy will we use?
      - What are the specific tactics?
- What's the big picture?

- How does upper management feel about this issue?
- If we do this, what are some of the possible unintended consequences?[22]
- If we don't do this, what are some certain, likely, and possible impacts?[23]
- What are the long-term and short-term repercussions of this decision?
  - How much impact will this have on the entire company?
- Is this the right course for the short term?
  - Is it the right course for the long term?
    - How far into the future does this decision commit us?
- What is the impact on the rest of the operation?
- Who will do what?
  - How can we make this a reality?
- What equipment will we need to buy?
- What will it cost?
- What are the alternatives?
  - What is the best alternative?
  - How do we do the best alternative?
- How would someone else approach this issue—our boss, our competitor?[24]
- What if we don't do anything?
- How does this decision make you feel?
  - Does this sound about right?
- What do we get out of this?
- How does this help our customers?

If you are facing a decision with significant ethical factors, see section 18/8, Questions That Work When Creating an Ethical Workplace.

Questions That Work

Rita Rizzo, the CEO of Rizzo & Associates, who has consulted with General Electric and JC Penney, says she has five favorite questions to help develop managers' judgment skills:

1. What is the result you would like in this situation?

2. What options exist for achieving the desired result?

3. What risks are attached to each of those options?

4. Which risk set is most manageable and how will you manage them?

5. What is your plan?[25]

If you have to reveal your decision in a speech, see section 15/5, Questions That Work When Giving a Speech or Presentation. If you need to develop a vision and framework for the types of decisions, see section 18/6, Questions That Work When Creating a Vision.

··

Questions That Motivate

What part of this decision/direction/next proposed action is in alignment with your values, gifts, and life purpose?

Peter Reding[26]

··

Chapter 13 Conclusion

Ideas into Action

It is the essence of the human experience to seek answers. Positive questions are a technique and a strategy for handling a wide range of problems and decisions. Brainstorming, listing the parts of the problem and listing the questions that must be answered to solve those problems, helps you discover the real issues and avoid the cookie-cutter solutions. If you list your business activities and decisions, you will see they are defined by a series of questions. If nothing else, positive questioning helps you realize that most crises and decisions offer a choice between not perfection and its opposite but two forms of imperfection. As one wise manager once told me, removing a cause of dissatisfaction does not create satisfaction. He knew that solving people's problems rarely made them happy. He knew that, instead, lasting satisfaction had to do with achievement and the recognition that comes with it. That was why he helped each employee who raised a problem to come up with a recommended solution. He used questions to help employees consider the problem and changed their whole outlook as he uncovered *their* ideas. Consistent positive questioning helps you start getting solutions from other people. It taps into the wide range of experiences in the workplace. Aggressive questioners, when faced with a problem, ask how many people they can reach with their inquiry.

A crisis triggers stress that disconnects people from one another. Negative stress is like an illness; those suffering are unable to listen and focus with complete attention. Rather than see crises as a curse, positive questioners find that crises can make a job worth doing and are what make each day challenging. We all know we are more responsible when put in charge of our own actions. Imagine a job that surrounds you with various crises but that does not allow you to question and respond. Employees put into such impossible positions tend to give their time but not their minds or hearts to the job. This is particularly true when managers use questions to be tough on the people and not the problem, where the manager's inquiry is better at generating reports than results. Managers tend to pursue obvious answers to any given situation, while leaders look for better solutions to the larger problem.

Inquiry in crises and decision making do more than just address what is wrong; they open up new opportunities. It has been said that if you spend your days solving problems, all you restore is normality. Organizations always seem to be learning and focusing on problems in the past; even countries typically fight the next war by relying on the lessons of the last. Positive questions explore opportunities that the situation can conceal. All organizations must prioritize; growing companies must realize that resources need to go to new opportunities, not just to old problems.

There is a saying that there is a lot more managerial "won't" than managerial "will." Questions create the needed conviction and energy to face problems and make tough decisions. T. J. Rogers, the CEO of Cypress Semiconductor, says, "If you endure and emerge stronger on the other side of a struggle, you will win. So don't worry about having everything go right. Worry about struggling with your problems and defeating your problems one at a time and over the long haul, and you will succeed."[27] There are some problems that are, for the time, insoluble, but deeper exploration of any dilemma will, if nothing else, suggest new questions that will be needed should a similar problem occur. Those who need to encourage positive questioning can suggest that questions are a form of insurance, to be taken out before a disaster occurs. In chapter 14, we discuss how to face difficult decisions when a relationship with an employer is not working out.

QUESTIONS THAT WORK WHEN:
You Are Fired or Laid Off

No question is so difficult to answer as that which the answer is obvious.
GEORGE BERNARD SHAW

What's it like to get the ax? When downsizing entered the national vocabulary, Maynard Brusman, a San Francisco–based corporate psychologist, had the walking wounded coming to his office. His first task was to let people know "the whole world of work has changed, there is no longer that psychological contract, no one owes you a job for life any more." While many realize this at one level, it doesn't change their feelings when they are dismissed, feelings so intense that Brusman had people coming in, "feeling that there is a death"[1] when a job went away. Dr. Brusman's second concern? Those left behind after a downsizing were being scarred by anxiety so severe that managers needed to rebuild employee morale and dedication. Positive questioning attitudes and cultures can help to do both.

Mergers, acquisitions, personality conflicts, or outgrowing a job can lead to your needing to move to another position. Middle managers are not immune, since they are among the most expensive employees a company has (don't think top management is about to cut itself). The best definition of job security is the ability to find another job right away, which means people today are always looking for work. If nothing else, having an outward vision of what they can do and their worth helps protect employees from a state of shock if their employment situation suddenly changes. Asking questions is the first skill you need; it will lead to many other skills needed to keep you employed.

14/1 You Are Worried about Your Company's Future

Assessment

During the depths of one recession, I interviewed many middle and senior managers who had never thought they would be fired. One had worked for what was once one of the largest corporations in America. In his recently bought upper-middle-class home, surrounded by polished wood and silver, he talked of having been out of work for more than six months without any promising interviews. I realized why the wood shone so bright. He had all the time in the world to polish it. The victim of a merger, he clearly had to recalculate his worth and the measure of his career success.

Since any company can be sold or broken up, you need to be constantly questioning what your company is doing. Francis Quittel, a management consultant, says most people are not fired for cause but are restructured or reorganized out of a job, and "most of the time there have been signals all along the way that people choose to ignore."[2] If there is word of cutbacks or your star is fading, the rumor mill will be running at full speed. Careful inquiry will keep you from wearing the blinders of denial and warn you if your career is headed for an unscheduled interruption.

ASK FRIENDS, COWORKERS, AND MANAGERS:

- Are we the targets of any sort of merger or takeover effort?
  - What companies would most likely want to acquire us?
  - What is the future focus of our company?
- Is our company profitable?
  - Is our division profitable?
  - Are we seen as a high-cost division?
  - Is our product seen as a less desirable technology to produce?
    - Are we dying, or are we seen as growing?
- Have any senior managers who were on the rise in our division recently quit?
- What would you do in this situation?
  - Where would you suggest I apply for work?
- If we merge or acquire, which company or division is the most important?
  - Which management team will take control of where I work?

If you are unsure what your status is in the company, see section 12/1, Questions That Work When Asking Your Boss to Give You Feedback.

14/2 There Is the Threat of Being Fired or Offered Early Retirement

Assessment

Do not vent if you think you are being shown the door; this is the time for cool, calm questioning. Be smart so that you walk away with all you deserve. Don't feel automatically obligated to help train the next person or finish off any projects; focus on your future. You could be out of work for many months, and you'll need all the resources you can muster to cover the gap.

If you are called into a meeting to discuss your uncertain future, you will want to be prepared to question all issues of your reputation and compensation. Unlike in other business situations, you may not be around the next day to ask for further explanation. If your position is being eliminated immediately and you are being rushed through the discharge process, ask politely and calmly to have the agreement in writing so that you can come back the next day to negotiate the entire severance package. You need to ask for time to think about all the issues that need to be addressed so that you can make the most of this unfortunate circumstance. While you may feel powerless and worthless, there will also be a sense of guilt among those firing you. You can leverage their short-lived concern to help smooth your way through unemployment. Make no threats and shed no tears; instead, use positive questions to be all business. There are many issues you can negotiate, although you may have to go beyond your boss for answers to some of your queries. The organization will want you out of the door as soon as possible, so you may have only a couple of days to work on the negotiations and play off the guilt they may feel. Move quickly but decisively.

While you can't get fired again for asking for any benefits or severance, don't ask for your job back. If they turn down requests for items such as additional time in your office or secretarial help, use the denial to ask for more money. This is one case where taking too many notes might hurt your situation. In such an emotionally charged situation, it might come off as your trying to document their words for legal purposes. Take some notes, but, above all, listen carefully; you are negotiating your future. One of my bosses used to advise employees that how they left the workforce was how they would reenter it, either bitter and angry or confident and assured. The choice was theirs. Take the situation when two self-assured and aggressive people had their employment coming to an end. One took the news with disbelief and shut down all positive communication with the company. The other surveyed the boss and coworkers for suggestions on what to do and what future employment opportunities existed elsewhere. The one who asked the questions lined up work that began on the moment his current position ended, and the other faded out of view and took several months to find new work, a powerful lesson to those who witnessed the difference.

The most important question for you is how much severance pay you can negotiate. The most fundamental figure is enough to get you to your next job. You may need to call another company or industry trade group for the standard severance package in your field. These can range from one week's pay to a month's pay for each year of service. Those who see a dismissal coming can question to find the high end their organization offers. You can always say, "I'm just asking for fair treatment by the company."

Think about asking coworkers and bosses for letters of recommendation.

ASK YOUR PERSONNEL OFFICE OR COWORKERS:

- What kind of severance package would I likely get if fired or laid off?

- What unemployment benefits might I get?

  - How long would they last, and how much might they add up to?

- Does receiving a severance package make me ineligible for unemployment?

- Will the company give references?

- What kind of outplacement support is it offering?

- What kind of latitude does my boss have in constructing a severance package?

ASK YOUR ATTORNEY:

- What can I take from this job?

  - Are contract lists company property or my property?

ASK THE PERSON FIRING YOU:

■ What will be said about why I am leaving the company?

■ Can I work with you on a rough draft of a letter of recommendation?

  ■ How soon can I get that letter?

■ Can I have more severance pay?

■ How will I be paid for my unused vacation or sick days?

  ■ Will I get part of my year-end bonus for the time worked?

■ What will happen to my insurance benefits?

■ What will happen to my pension?

■ Can we add some time to my record so that I can qualify for an early pension? (only if you are near retirement)

■ When will I be eligible for unemployment benefits?

■ How close am I to being vested?

  ■ Can we continue my employment until I am vested?

■ What are my options with my 401K?

  ■ When will I receive the check for my 401K?

■ Can we shift the termination date to the next month? (This can extend your health benefits another month and save you money.)

RESOURCES FOR FINDING THE NEXT JOB:

■ Can I have an office to use for job hunting?

  ■ How about:

    ■ voice mail?

    ■ a computer with my e-mail address?

    ■ a laptop and a pager?

    ■ my company car?

    ■ stationery?

- business cards I can use?

- Are there any retraining or training programs I can take advantage of?

  - I'd like to work on my computer skills, etc. If I can't take a class through the company, is there any money for retraining?

  - What training programs does our company offer or has it offered that I can look at?

- What outplacement counseling will be provided?

  - If I have to travel for a job interview, will you pay for it?

- If you can't get more severance pay, can you trade for support in looking for a new job?

IF YOU ARE NOT HAVING ANY SUCCESS WITH YOUR REQUESTS, ASK THE PERSON YOU ARE NEGOTIATING WITH:

- I understand you may not be able to address all these issues. Who has the authority to grant my request?

IF YOU GET A MEETING WITH SOMEONE HIGHER UP, ASK THE PERSON YOU WERE NEGOTIATING WITH:

- Would you like to come to my meeting with _____ to discuss these issues?

IF LEAVING ON RELATIVELY GOOD TERMS, ASK YOUR BOSS:

- Can I finish the project I am working on?

  - Can I return as a freelancer?

- Can I finish the degree program I am currently working on?

ASK YOUR COWORKERS, THE RECRUITER WHO PLACED YOU IN THE JOB, YOUR MENTOR, OR IMPORTANT CLIENTS:

- Since we've had such a good working relationship, can you put in a good word for me as I negotiate my package?

- Is there anything you can do to help me?

If looking for a new job, see section 6/1, Questions That Work When Looking for a Job.

14/3 You Are Offered the Services of an Outplacement Agency or Job Search Company

Assessment

Outplacement help can be a useful part of the severance package, if only to keep you on track while pursuing the next job. Like pay, it can be negotiated.

ASK THE HUMAN RESOURCES DEPARTMENT:

■ Do I get to pick the outplacement agency?

　■ Can I interview the outplacement firms?

　　■ I would give first preference to the one you recommended, but is it okay to check out a few other firms that might be able to help?

■ How long will I be able to use the service?

　■ Is this a limited program or until I find a job?

■ Can I take the money you would spend on the outplacement firm and use it for something else?

ASK THE AGENCY:

■ How long has this company been in business?

■ What are this company's qualifications?

　■ Is it a member of any associations for outplacement firms?

　　■ Has it been certified by the National Board for Certified Counselors?

　　■ Is it a member of the National Career Development Association?

■ Is it licensed by the state (if needed)?

■ Are there classes I have to attend?

　■ How personal are the services it will offer?

- Do I have to request services in advance?

  - Do new clients have to wait behind older clients?

- Does it provide secretarial help?

  - Is there any limit on sending out letters?

  - If I like to send out customized letters, is that a problem?

  - Is there an overnight mail limit?

- Can I come in every day?

  - Is there any limit on telephone calls?

- What access will I have to reference materials and directories?

- How will calls be answered at the outplacement firm?

- Will it provide any practice interviews?

  - Will it record those for my review?

- Will it charge extra to write a resume?

- Do I have to pay even if I do not get a job that meets the minimum we agree upon?

  - What if the job does not work out?

- Can I have a copy of the contract?

  - Can we review the payment requirements and refund conditions?

  - If the job search is not working out and I don't want to continue, how much money will it refund?

- When can I talk to the counselor?

  - Can I ask for someone else if this person isn't a good fit?

ASK THE COUNSELOR:

- Tell me about some of your success stories.

  - Whom have you worked with who has a background or career similar to mine?

■ What types of searches have you done in my area of expertise?

■ What counseling techniques do you use?

■ How much of the job hunting will I have to do?

■ How long should the search process take?

■ How are interviews scheduled?

■ Who are some of the people you have helped place that I can talk to?

ASK THE COMPANY:

■ Can I have a copy of the contract?

   ■ What are the total costs?

   ■ What is your refund policy?

■ Are you a consultant, or are you selling employment information?

■ Are you licensed?

14/4 Using an Alternative Dispute Resolution Program

Assessment

Alternative dispute resolution programs may help the two parties avoid the full court process, but you can't avoid carefully questioning and preparing for the process. You may still want to consult an attorney to check your case, review options, and help present the best possible case.

ASK YOUR COMPANY:

■ Who will be hearing the case?

   ■ Are they neutral?

■ Who are some of the possible mediators?

   ■ What are their backgrounds?

■ Who will be paying for the mediator?

   ■ Is there a statistical summary of the arbitrators' past rulings?

. . . .

Questions That Motivate

What are you most proud of that I might not have
noticed?

Mary Key, Ph.D.[3]

. . . .

Chapter 14 Conclusion

Ideas into Action

Inquiry, as I have said, offers the infinite capacity for renewal. Any end,
through questioning, becomes a new beginning. Positive questions direct
energy into the productive zone between disorganized hyperactivity and
frustrated introspection. If you need to change your job, you first need to
overcome the emotional roadblocks of fear of the unknown, satisfaction
with the status quo, and comfort with your current job title before you
can be ready to move on. You need to constantly ask what you really want
to change about your work right now and then follow up by finding out
what you need to do to make those changes. You must then collect all
the facts, figures, and contacts you'll need to make the changes. Questions keep you from overpersonalizing failure and open the door to new
opportunities, especially when you remember that networking is the
cheapest and most effective form of personal marketing.

Ralph Waldo Emerson said, "Make yourself necessary to somebody."
The workplace's new rules say you cannot count on seniority or experience
for security. You need to have skills that employers will seek in the future.
Future security comes from what you constantly create with your questions: your networks, your reputation, and your workplace initiatives. If
your boss asks you, "What kind of future do you see for yourself here?"
start to wonder what kind of future he has in mind. Questioning skills
give each employee a contingency plan, a way to respond if the unexpected
and unhappy event of termination threatens. Asking about termination
policy in advance may help you keep a cool head if you are laid off. As you
change companies and even careers, positive questions help prevent you
from burning bridges you may need to cross again and also help you build
new ones to your next job. Just remember—in delicate human matters,
even with positive questions, just because you can ask a question doesn't
mean you should. In chapter 15, we look at ways to protect yourself from
career-ending disputes and other situations that put you on the spot.

QUESTIONS THAT WORK WHEN:
You Are Put on the Spot

Truth is often the best alternative.

HENRY KISSINGER

When you are on the spot, whether because of a conflict with an employee or a reporter on the line, you can use positive questions to shift power back into balance. If we had our way, we would want unilateral control over any situation in our life; we want to be in charge of what happens. The less control we have, the more anxiety, paranoia, and hostility we may feel. If we are using questions to control the conversation from our point of view, it still should not threaten the other person. Questions do not live up to their potential if they make the other party feel that she is defending herself. Instead, we need to use questions to decrease the potential for confrontation. Inquiry should not be used to criticize feelings. The more the other person constructively releases emotions and has them recognized, the more comfortable or calm she may be. The questions should help the sides to work together to create solutions. In any conversation, both sides will be tested, with questions shaping the discussion and each discovering the other side's expectations. In the end, you typically want the other side to either reconsider its position or consider the merits of your position. You will have a psychological shield and sword to do battle if you use questions to identify and challenge threats.

15/1 Facing a Conflict

Assessment

Conflict often creates meaning, as the fight among facts, beliefs, and competing motives defines differences. Positive questioners do not avoid conflict; they make it constructive. Much of conflict resolution theory comes down to one thought—no argument will be settled until both

249

sides understand each other. Conflict management, when done correctly, creates clear opportunities for communication and learning. Inquiry identifies the key points of difference and the shared issues that make up the main themes of any dispute.

How can positive questions help? They help the parties to the conflict to:

- Start and maintain important contacts.

- Be aware of each other's attitudes.

- Encourage the expression of reactions.

- Restate and clarify their positions.

- Discover what they have in common.

- Soften their attitudes when meeting the opposition.

- Deal with the inevitable rifts.

The positive questioner's game plan first deals directly with both the questioner's fear and the other party's fear. Ask the other party why it feels the way it does without criticizing its emotions. Once you know your opponent's feelings you can legitimize them and move the discussion forward from the individual to the issue. Your questions will discover whether the other person is stage acting and keep you from letting their exaggerated feelings cloud your judgment.

If you are on the spot, asking questions instead of spontaneously giving information can protect you. Not only does it limit what the other side can attack; the other party may be forced to reconsider its demands as they explain them. You can use questions to clarify the charges against you. It puts the ball back in the other person's court.

> *Attack:* You don't pay attention to my needs.
> *Question:* Why do you think I don't pay attention to your needs?

Exploration of any problem often reveals that at the heart of the matter is miscommunication. Adding new information helps both sides better understand the values behind the other's position. To encourage this exchange of values, restate hostile questions or rephrase them in a question.

Attack: Why didn't you take steps to prevent this from happening?
Question: What specifically do you think our separate responsibilities are?

In a conflict, some people constantly attack to interrupt the flow of the other's opinions. The art comes in following up on phrases that express disapproval, using inquiry to gently encourage the completion of an unfinished thought.

Attack: Let's not waste time on that idea.
Question: Why do you think it is a waste of time?

At this point you are not directly challenging the other side's reasoning. Instead, you are using inquiry to reflect feelings while not getting caught up in blaming. You even might consider asking for permission before expressing an opinion to make sure you don't introduce it before the other side is ready to listen. This process of checking into feelings and checking out ideas is aimed at gradually building rapport. If you are asked a complex question, ask the other person to repeat and refine the question (unless it is your boss and he will be insulted).

Attack: Why did you not complete the assignment on time, and when did you know you were not going to finish the assignment?
Question: I'm sorry, could you rephrase that question?

You can request a clarification and ask the exact nature of the concern or request further specific detail. This can take the wind out of the attacker's sails if you do everything you can to understand his point of view.

Attack: Your product is too expensive; why should I buy it?
Question: I want to understand your concern. From what specific facts does your question come?

If such questioning sounds expensive in terms of time, remember that conflict is never cost-free and that meaningful solutions always require time and energy. Avoid setting traps or using the trick questions that so many use to play with their opponents. A continual lack of sincere questions and straight answers results in a maddening circular discussion without end.

Complaints vs Conflict

While conflicts often begin with a complaint, complaints do not necessarily lead to or indicate conflict. Some people complain just to make a connection. Any defensiveness on your part can shut down an opportunity to understand the other side's facts and feelings. By recognizing the other person's emotions when listening to a complaint, you may find you can use the opportunity to learn from each other, rather than argue. With a complaint, you can offer the following:

> I know you want a fair solution; what do you think that would be?

Before dealing with a conflict, the psychologist Dr. Sylvia Mills recommends that you examine two issues. Do you have reactions or feelings you don't want the other person to detect? and, if you do, Is there anyone to whom you can freely express these feelings?[1] These questions identify "noise" that can be so deafening that you can't hear the other party.

Small points of order may help set up a better environment for positive questioning. Power relationship theory suggests you have the home field advantage if you meet on your territory. If this is not available, some advisers suggest that the other side will be more flexible if you meet outside that side's normal surroundings. Common courtesy suggests offering a coffee or soft drink, holding your calls, and politely looking the person in the eye. Having a sense of humor about yourself diffuses tension. Ask what the person wants you to do and see whether you can help get the person what she wants. Listening to an employee's long answers is sometimes the most important job a manager has.

ASK THE PERSON:

- Is this a good time for you to listen to me?[2]

- Would you like to talk now?

  - Where would you like to talk?

- What's on your mind?

  - I want to understand the concerns you have. Can you give me specifics?

- What may I have misunderstood?

- Is there something that has offended you?
- Can you clarify what you just said?
  - What did you mean by those remarks?
- How reliable is this information?
  - Who told you?
  - Can you confirm that?
- How can I help?
- What do you think?
  - Can you explain the connection?
- Do you have any other ideas?
  - Okay, what would you say if you were me?
- What would get you to change your mind?
  - What would be the best outcome regarding this in your opinion?[3]
- What will this choice produce?
  - Are we ready to accept the consequences?
- If you could say whatever you wanted without repercussions or being misunderstood by the other party to make this matter right, what would you say?[4]
- Where would you like this discussion to be at the end of ten minutes?
- Did that answer your question?
  - Have I got it right?
- What exactly were you trying to accomplish?
  - Can you sum up what needs to be done?
- What's the next item we need to deal with?
  - Anything else I need to know as we move forward?

Beware of asking, "Do you agree?" before hearing the other person's point of view.

Questions That Work

Dr. Richard Rathe, of the University of Florida, has examined the questioning techniques doctors use when consulting with patients. He agreed that there is some similarity between a doctor's questions and problem solving in the business world and specifically referenced a technique known as BATHE that he says he has used successfully with staff, family, and friends during conflicts. Its tenets include the following:

1. Ask questions about the *Background*. Your aim is to have the situation described in a few sentences. Dr. Rathe cautions about asking for more details at this point, saying they are not important and can waste time.[5]

2. You can then ask about how the situation *Affects* the person and how it makes her feel.

3. You can then move on to determine what is it that *Troubles* the person most about the situation. Dr. Rathe says you should be looking for the reason behind the emotion (it often is not what you expect).

4. The insightful interviewer can then see how the patient is *Handling* the conflict or crisis. This opens up questioning about similar circumstances in the past. The questions can help discover options, including at least one positive step that can be taken.

5. Finally, when you've gathered the information, it is time to express *Empathy*, both understanding and support for the person.

One of Dr. Rathe's favorite quotes is Tom Rusk's saying: "Feelings are facts to the person experiencing them."

15/2 Communication Is the Problem

Assessment

The human condition is one of misunderstanding. Employees often hear one thing when the speaker means something else. Yet managers must consistently create a communicated consensus to succeed. Leaders must not articulate only their ideas but must hear and act on the thoughts of others. With all the buck-passing and sloppy thinking, with workers being put on the hot seat and cringing around the conference table, the typical organization sometimes seems dedicated to discouraging honest communication.

When verbal fog is the problem, positive questions burn away the cold mist of misunderstanding. When emotional steam is the problem, questions safely vent the pressure of overheated opinions. Encouraging inquiry prevents a cycle of despair and passivity from settling in, a cycle created by ignored feelings and unheard concerns. When clear communication is not taking place, you need to quickly find out what is causing the interference. It could be cultural differences, language difficulties, or diverging goals. You want to elevate the discussion to where you are reasoning together, not engaged in verbal combat. Questions help discover whether the other party is listening "against you," for if trust is missing, the other side will misconstrue even the simplest statements. Rejection will lead to more caution, and there will be no straight answers, no direct route to agreement. As Irving Lee, in a *Harvard Business Review* article, once put it, there has to be respect for "questions for clarification." These questions "forestall the impulse to disagreement until there is an effort at understanding . . . that a proponent is entitled to every consideration in making his position clear, and that it will not be argued down before it is adequately stated."[6] Positive questions help discover what both parties agree on, the first steps to trust. This mutual respect has a hidden benefit; when the other side finds flaws in your thinking, you won't be automatically offended but can objectively analyze their objection. When you find yourself being questioned by someone you believe has the right motive and qualifications to instruct you, that person's concerns ring true. A questioning culture can't exist without a listening culture. Asking questions without an agreement to listen risks conversational death.

ASK THE PERSON YOU ARE TALKING WITH:

■ Can we talk about this?

  ■ Can we sort this out?

  ■ Can we work together to solve this problem?

■ What do you mean?

  ■ Why did you say that?

■ My confusion is interfering with my understanding what you want done; can you repeat your chief concerns?

■ Here is my view, and here is how I have arrived at it. How does it sound to you?[7]

- Do you want a just-the-facts kind of conversation or more detail?

- How can you help me look at things from your point of view?

  - Is your answer based on firsthand knowledge?

- I wish I'd heard it directly from you, but it sounds like we should talk, okay?

- What can we do to take the tension out of our conversations?

- Is there something that's offended you?

IF YOU ARE ADDRESSING A COMMUNICATION PROBLEM BETWEEN TWO OTHER PEOPLE, ASK THEM:

- What are the channels of communication?

  - Would a more open relationship help with getting what you want from another person?

- When is the best time to talk?

  - When would be another good time to try you?

- Do you listen carefully while the other person is talking?[8]

  - Are you really listening to me?[9]

- Would you like me to elaborate with lots of detail or a little?[10]

- What kind of communication from your manager do you feel is most effective?[11]

  - How do you know when someone is a good communicator?

If you need to give constructive feedback, see section 12/1, Questions That Work When Asking Your Boss to Give You Feedback.

15/3 Disciplining an Employee

Assessment

Questions are an essential tool when giving or receiving criticism. Creative inquiry allows you to move beyond what was possible to what is. If you are not dismissing the employee, you are focusing on her future.

This requires you to ask her how she is capable of performing better than she currently is. This focus on the future requires that you not attack and not reveal anger; your focus begins with a question, not an accusation. Positive questioning puts criticism on hold until you hear the employee's side of the story. Such open-ended questions show you empathize with her feelings or problems and detect subtle issues before they fuel greater disagreement.

When an employee needs to be disciplined, you need to examine how you would like to be treated in a similar situation. The discussion should be private, the manager should be clear about what he wants to happen, and there should be follow-through. If goals and a timetable are set, both sides should prepare follow-up conversations and questions to check the progress against the goals.

ASK OTHERS WHO WORK WITH THE EMPLOYEE:

■ Do you think this negative behavior or act was a willful violation?

■ How serious is this negative behavior or act?

   ■ How many employees are affected?

   ■ What are the long-term consequences?

■ What skill do you expect this person to have?

   ■ What are the important steps this person needs to take?

      ■ What are the key points this person should understand?

   ■ When does she have to have this skill?

ASK THE EMPLOYEE:

■ Why do you feel you need to do (a negative behavior)?

■ Why is there this problem?

   ■ Do you have a suitable solution?

■ What do you think will happen if you don't do this work or the deadline isn't made?

■ How do you plan to prevent such problems in the future?

- How does that strike you?

- What kind of training do you think is needed?

- Do you have the right equipment?

  - Do you have the right materials or supplies to do your job?

If you need to reset the goals for an employee, see section 11/10, Questions That Work When Doing Performance Appraisals and Setting Goals.

15/4 Disagreeing with Another

Assessment

Positive questions allow you to gracefully disagree with another party. Careful inquiry helps you take a pass on potential professional suicide missions or to decline situations that do not use your strengths. Focused inquiry determines just what the assignment is really designed to accomplish. A task may be a loyalty test, a test of how much you can take without breaking, or a test to see whether you are ready for a bigger opportunity. Questions illuminate whether an awful job is something that could actually lead to bigger and better opportunity. If you decide the assignment is clearly a dead end, you can ask questions that suggest more pleasant alternatives while carefully listening for any hidden agendas.

Coworkers and bosses who stifle disagreement hurt themselves in the long run, but if you bluntly point that out, you may end up fired in the short term. It may be difficult to raise any objection if a boss is surrounded by smiling toadies who agree to any assignment. Since such bosses feel they hold all the cards, bluffing by suggesting that you won't do a job is not an option; you need instead to use positive questions to articulate other options while defusing any anger. Try to anticipate superiors' real long-term needs and how you can help achieve them by doing something other than what has been proposed: "I understand you are concerned about this new project, but I wonder, do I need to finish my current effort first so we can hit our numbers at the end of the year?"

If your boss tells you to do something you think is wrong or dangerous to your career, one option is to ask gently pointed questions. Examples include:

- "Don't you think we might also try . . . ?"

- "What would you think if we tried . . . ?"

Questions can deflect bad ideas by opening the door to other small suggestions. Reference what someone else has done and ask whether you might do the same: "We seem to be stuck on this problem. Should we do what an article I just read suggested?"

With positive questions, you ask coworkers or your boss to explain their frustrations. The project or task they have proposed may not be the answer to their problem. Discovering those frustrations might be a key to discovering a solution the other party has not considered. Open-ended questions deflect or challenge questionable ideas without coming out directly in opposition.

ASK THE OTHER PERSON:

- Did you consider . . . ?

- How would your idea . . . ?

- This is an interesting idea. Where did it come from?

- What would be the starting point if we were to use your idea?

- Who else needs to be involved before we make a decision on this?

- What would be the biggest obstacle to this idea succeeding?

- Has this idea been tried before?

ASK YOUR BOSS:

- You are the boss, and I respect your position/decision, I just wonder if . . . ?

- If you tell me to, I will, but could . . . ?

- Can I use my best judgment on this?

- Can we look at how we communicate and make decisions?

- What can we work out that would make everyone happy?

- I need to understand this new direction. Can you help me define my priorities?

- What should I be working on first?

  - What needs to be done right now?

  - Would you like me to do my job well by using my best judgment?

- When presented with a conflict, which assignment do you want me to focus on first?

  - Do you want to put some duties on hold or give them to others?

  - Can you help me out of my current assignments before I tackle something new?

- If you would like me to work on this, what do I need to know about the future of my current project?

- What specifically do you want me to do?

- Can this assignment be temporary?

- Are there others who are better qualified?

  - Do you want me to tackle this on my own?

- Can I have a little time to think about this assignment?

If you are told to do a project you disagree with for ethical reasons, see section 18/8, Questions That Work When Creating an Ethical Workplace.

15/5 Giving a Speech or Presentation

Assessment

Every day we give talks, whether in the hallways with coworkers or in convention centers with stockholders. Before you speak, a questioning process insures that you have a benefit to present, a reason that people should listen. Your speech can be based on posing a single question to the audience, a query your speech answers with authority. This technique of presenting a problem and asking people to hear how you would solve it encourages people to listen to see where you will end up. Throughout your speech, you can pose questions and either invite the audience to answer or pause and answer them yourself. Questions keep the energy level up in both the speaker and the audience. Audiences now expect speeches, just like the Internet, to be interactive.

If you want people to act on your speech, you should construct it so that it ends with a clear question or command. That should not be "Well, what do you think?" It's better to risk rejection than never to get around to the reason you spoke in the first place. Inviting inquiries at the end of your speech gives the audience a chance to fill any information gap they might have. If no one has any issues, you might say, "A question I am often asked is. . . ." This allows you to reinforce a point already made or overcome a common objection to your agenda.

ASK THE ORGANIZER OR PERSON YOU ARE PRESENTING TO:

- What led to my being asked to speak?

- To whom will I be speaking?

  - What is the audience interested in?

- How will they use the information?

  - What are the decisions the audience has to make or will be making?

- How am I going to be introduced?

  - Can I write my own introduction or check your introduction for accuracy?

- How long will I be expected to speak?

- What will happen before I speak?

  - What will happen after I speak?

- Will you be serving food?

  - When will food service stop?

  - How close is the kitchen?

- Who will be a partner in my presentation?

- What will be the backup computers and audiovisual equipment?

  - Is there power for my laptop?

- What is the dress code?

- What questions do you think I will be asked?

ASK THE AUDIENCE:

■ What in my presentation excited you?

   ■ What was a turnoff?

■ Did I address the issues you wanted?

■ Was the information given in an understandable way?

■ Did you have enough of a chance to participate?

■ Can you use what you learned?

If you need to research a customer before speaking, see section 8/1, Questions That Work When Understanding the Customer, or section 10/8, Questions That Work When Studying an Idea or Opportunity.

Questions That Work

In the final part of any presentation, ask about what the audience has just heard to check how clearly you communicated your concerns. You can also ask for a review of your performance. Earlier in *Questions That Work* we reviewed a rule of three used by communications consultant Bert Decker. To use this rule of three when seeking audience response, Decker recommends against asking "Could you give me feedback on my speaking?" He says you'll receive only empty compliments. Instead, he recommends you ask, "What are three strengths I have as a communicator? And what are three distractions I have?"[12]

15/6 Mixing with a Roomful of Strangers

Assessment

I recently attended a business event for senior managers of a leading U.S. corporation. A speaker who was exploring executive fears asked, "How many would like to walk into a roomful of complete strangers?" Out of several dozen top managers, only three or four enthusiastically raised their hands, for almost no one likes feeling alone among many. After the speech, I asked what made these few people socially confident. As I discovered, they were the masters of the quick story and conversation-starting questions. They asked questions that expressed interest in anything other people brought up, anything from the weather forecast to forecasts of the economy. Not only did these conversationalists query persons they had just met; they invited others to join in, keeping the conversation circulating by surveying more than one topic or person. Simple questions were just fine.

When you are stuck in a conversation, two quick questions can get it moving. You can always say, "That's interesting, can you tell me more?" or "What happened then?" Conversation expert Dana May Casperson says that asking about family is generally safe (assuming you know that the person is involved in one). It is best to stay away from questions about specifics or personal relationships. She advises that you not quiz others all the time and instead comment about something you saw in a recent newspaper or newsmagazine the other person might read.[13] The same caution also comes from the TV journalist Barbara Walters, who warns against an endless stream of questions, for if a conversation is "poked along with tiny cattle-prod questions, it isn't a conversation any more. It is a strained, manipulative game, tiring and perhaps even lonely."[14]

ASK THE OTHER PERSON:

- Can I have your name?

- Where are you from?

- What work do you do?

  - How did you get into this line of business?

- Do you have any hobbies?

- I'm curious:

  - Can you tell me about . . . ?

  - Can you explain . . . ?

  - What's your secret for _____?

  - What do you think about (current general news topic?)

- Have you traveled to any interesting places recently?[15]

- Have you read or been inspired by any great books lately?

If you are aware of the company you are going to be mixing with, see section 6/1, Questions That Work When Looking for a Job and section 6/3, Questions That Work When Needing an Informational Interview.

15/7 Responding to a Sexual Harassment Complaint

Assessment

Any harassment concern can quickly become a complicated matter requiring careful investigation. Your organization should have a clear policy including a follow-up to any complaints made. Question the alleged victim, the alleged perpetrator, and any witnesses with discretion and sensitivity. Be objective and take notes as you gather corroborative evidence. You may need to quickly turn the matter over to a more experienced investigator. This investigator cannot be someone involved in the situation in any way. In this way, the questioner can be counted on to remain objective and effectively interview each individual.

ASK THE PERSON MAKING THE COMPLAINT:

- What happened?
- Who was involved?
- When did it happen?
- What was your reaction?
- Were there any witnesses?
- Do you have any evidence?
  - Do you have any documents that confirm your account?
- What has happened since?

ASK WITNESSES:

- How is everyone getting along?
- Do you recall any specific interaction between _____ and _____?
- What is your recollection of the incident?

■ What do you know about the person making the complaint?

■ How long have you known this person?

■ How closely do you work together?

■ What do you know about how these two people relate to each other?

■ Anything else we should know?

ASK THE SUBJECT OF THE COMPLAINT:

■ How is everyone getting along?

■ Do you recall an incident such as _____ ever occurring?

Some advise not mentioning names and being general rather than specific during your initial investigation. Careless questioning can reveal too much information. Sometimes the subject of the complaint will seek to learn what the other side said happened as he attempts to justify or excuse his own behavior.

15/8 Being Interviewed by a Journalist

Assessment

Journalists are under a general obligation to immediately disclose who they are and why they are calling. Most reporters are open and honest and just want you to be the same. Should you be asked something you are uncomfortable answering, ask to get back to the reporter once you've nailed down accurate information. Watch for leading questions and hypothetical questions that put you on the spot. Saying "no comment" can be like waving a red flag in front of a bull. It is simple psychology that when someone won't answer your question, you are naturally intrigued.

ASK YOUR BOSS:

■ Is it okay for me to talk to this reporter?

    ■ Should someone come along with me from our communications department?

- Is there any point you want me to try to get across?
- Have we dealt with this reporter before?
  - What is her reputation?

ASK THE REPORTER:

- What kind of deadline are you on?
- What type of story are you writing?
  - Is it a feature story, a profile, or an overview of our industry?
- Can I help you with any future stories?
  - Would you like my pager/cell phone number in case you have follow-up questions?

IF YOU HAVE MORE TIME AND THE ARTICLE IS MORE IN-DEPTH:

- What kind of audience do you reach?
- Can I see some of your prior clippings?
- Can I get a copy of the article after it is published?

Questions That Motivate

How good can we be? How do we get there?

Joel Kurtzman[16]

15/9 **Needing to Complain**

Assessment

Complaining effectively takes time. You begin by identifying and articulating your problem. Questions define your concern by helping you compare your experience or product to what you expected. Your answers will give you some idea of what will be a fair solution. Once you've gathered your records, you are ready to officially complain. Begin with the person who sold you the service or good before you move on to the department or store manager. You can then go on to the company's headquarters, a consumer protection agency, or even a lawyer. Questions overcome "written-in-stone" policies and help you become a more sympathetic figure in the other person's eyes. If you can stress the positive of past performances, you will find a more receptive audience for the specific concern you need to resolve. As with all questioning, be pleasant but firm.

ASK THE CUSTOMER SERVICE PERSON:

- What would you do in my situation?

- What do you think is fair?

- What is the rule you are following?

  - What are the exceptions to that rule?

- Can I speak to your supervisor?

Questions That Motivate

What is the one thing, which if practiced consistently, would make the most impact in your life?

Mike Turner[17]

Chapter 15 Conclusion

Ideas into Action

Those who react calmly and clearly when put on the spot are those who have mastered questions that help them ascertain the situation, allaying their own and others' fears and creating control and direction. Others, especially those able to promote you, will be watching how you handle a crisis. Deft handling of a conflict with diplomatic yet precise questions will make you a better coworker and leader. Mastering the art of using questions to perform precise information appraisal is critical. We have entered an age of new personal responsibility, where inquiry is an everyday requirement. Inquiry can be a vaccine protecting you from rumormongers and office schemers who live to put people on the spot. If you want to know what it is like to face crisis situations day after day, start your own business. In chapter 16, we present the powerful positive questions many use to take an idea and turn it into a business.

Part V

Questions When on Your Own

QUESTIONS THAT WORK WHEN:
Starting Your Own Business

In all affairs it's a healthy thing now and then to hang a question mark on the things you have long taken for granted.

BERTRAND RUSSELL

How well do you know your business? Entrepreneurs have said it was good that they didn't know too much at the beginning, or their hopes would have been dashed before they started. George Zimmer of The Men's Wearhouse said, "You have to really be able to believe in your own idea and your own vision regardless of how many qualified people tell you you're walking a thin line between total failure and success."[1] Still, it is foolish to gamble on a venture without examining the risks and scrutinizing how competitive the market will be. Questions are the essential risk analysis tool. Risk analysis is paramount because failure when running your own business threatens not only your personal finances but your future professional prospects.

Your first questions should focus on whether the business idea offers enough uniqueness to get people to buy or to switch from an existing service. The head dreamer of new products at the design facility IDEO, David Kelley, was asked what someone with a new business idea needed to do. He warned that most people fall in love with their idea without knowing whether it will actually sell. It is a question of putting your money where your mouth is, he said. He suggested, "Build a few of them if it's low cost enough and then take them out and convince the local mom and pop grocery store to try and to sell them." Kelley said you need to ask for reactions to your idea but it's "no fair using your best friend . . . if someone you don't know buys it then you know you have a good idea."[2] The market is the ultimate q-and-a test. You have to invite hard, critical questions of your plan

271

before you go there. You should then ask others whether they think you have the personal characteristics to carry through on the business idea. These could include leadership, personal drive, and the ability to take risks and skills in planning ahead for the future—all characteristics linked to questioning.

16/1 Checking out a Business Opportunity

Assessment

There are thousands of business opportunities that promise a better life and more money. Before you invest, remember any business equation has a bottom line: What is being sold and for how much? If you are selling a product, examine how quickly you can turn over the inventory. If you are offering a service, examine how you can make your time and effort more valuable.

ASK THE PERSON YOU ARE SPEAKING TO:

- Are you an authorized agent of the company?
  - Can I get written information on the company's financial status and ownership?
- Where is the company based?
  - Where is it incorporated?
  - Do you have any offices in this state?
- Who are the top executives?
  - What is their experience?
  - Have they been in legal trouble?
- What will I be able to sell or offer as a service or product?
  - Where will I get my supplies?
    - What is the quality of these supplies?
- What claims do you make for the product or service?
  - How do you handle complaints?

■ What are the company policies and procedures for dealing with me?

  ■ Will you honor these guarantees?

■ What will this opportunity cost me?

■ Who are some customers I can talk to?

If you need to examine a business's reputation in general, see section 6/5, Questions That Work When Preparing for an Interview.

16/2 Buying a Business

Assessment

Buying a business rather than starting one from scratch has one significant advantage; you can see whether the business has been successful. Asking questions can take you only so far, so don't be shy about sitting in the store or going out on cold calls. You are looking for someone who is selling not because the business is failing but for a less threatening reason, such as relocation or retirement. Don't be too discouraged by some negative answers to your questions. Most successful businesses are very expensive to buy, and so you may need to look for a weak one that you can turn around. Any business is, in the final analysis, an issue of numbers. Enough bad numbers will in the end kill any enterprise. You need to understand all the numbers before you buy.

ASK OWNERS OF SIMILAR BUSINESSES TO THE TYPE YOU ARE INTERESTED INVESTING IN:

■ Do you know someone in your business who is selling now?

  ■ Do you know someone who might be interested in selling in the future?

■ Where can I collect information?

■ What trade shows can I visit?

■ Whom would you recommend as an intermediary, a broker, to work on my behalf?

  ■ Does the broker work on a retainer, what businesses has the broker helped to locate, and how can the broker help me negotiate?

- Considering the company I am thinking of buying, do you think it would be less expensive to start from ground zero and try and build my own business?

ASK THE COMPANY'S OWNER ABOUT THE BUSINESS:

- Why have you been thinking of selling your business?
  - Is a major customer changing in the future?
- What's the toughest part of this business?
  - What are your war stories?
- What are this business's strengths?
- What have been the biggest problems in building the company up to now?
  - What are the most important decisions you've made here?
- Before I buy, what experience do you recommend I have?
  - Is there a way I can work part-time in your business?
- Who are the competitors?
  - Are there any new competitors soon to appear?
- How seasonal is this business?
  - What ebb and flow do you see, and what does that mean to your hours?
  - Where can growth occur?
- How has your location worked out?
  - Where else would you see a location working out?
- How do you define the demographics of your customers?
  - What is their age, gender, and location?
- Who are the key suppliers?
  - What are your contracts with them, and when do they end?
- How could new capital best be used?

■ Where can I cut costs without cutting quality?

■ When you leave, what do you think will be the impact on the business?

   ■ How will customers react?

■ Would you be a consultant after the sale?

■ What other help can you give me or refer me to during this transition?

ASK THE COMPANY'S OWNER ABOUT THE SALE:

■ What are the assets that go with the business purchase?

■ Is the property owned free and clear?

   ■ Are there any issues with toxic contamination?

■ Can I see a valuation?

   ■ Have you had a professional business appraiser review the company's ability to make money?

■ Do you mind if I have an independent CPA review the books for the past five years?

■ Are you willing to finance the sale?

   ■ What collateral would I need to put up?

■ How will I have to pay for this purchase?

16/3 Buying a Franchise

Assessment

You are familiar with many of the biggest success stories in franchising. They are restaurants, stores, and businesses you use each day. There are, however, failures that do not make it and take investors' money with them. As a result, there have been many lawsuits involving the financial risks of franchises. Even if the business you invest in does break even, you don't want it to be simply because you have sacrificed your entire life to it. In that case, all you've done is given the parent company an expansion at your expense. Franchise agreements give you a connection with a much larger organization, but they can cost you a significant amount of freedom. This makes it even more essential that you ask the right questions.

You might consider having accountants or attorneys review the documents. You will be spending a good deal of time with the Uniform Franchise Offering Circular, but don't count on this disclosure prospectus for all your answers. The questions to be asked of a business owner extend beyond this list. Marketing, pricing, suppliers, production, and distribution all form part of the chain of inquiry. You'll have to ask owners, former owners, suppliers, and customers about the reality of the business. This process of questioning will serve you well once you start to run your business, for a successful business is one that masters information management.

ASK A CURRENT FRANCHISEE ABOUT THE OPPORTUNITY:

- What do you enjoy about this job?

  - What's the biggest downside?

- How successful have you been?

  - What is the market for this product or service?

- Would you invest in the franchise all over again?

  - What are the positives and the negatives about this franchise?

- Are you going to buy a second franchise?

  - Why not?

- What can this franchise do that its competitors cannot?

  - Do you wish you'd chosen to go with a competitor?

- What does the franchisor do for you?

  - If you have a problem, how do you find a solution with the franchisor?

- Did you feel that the franchisor gave you what you needed to succeed?

  - What else could it have done to help you get started?

- Can I work here for a couple of weeks to see how it goes?

- What background do you have in business?

■ Is there any special training or expertise you would recommend?

■ What background do other successful franchisees have?

ASK A CURRENT FRANCHISEE ABOUT THE COST:

■ What was the initial franchise fee?

  ■ Was it nonrefundable?

■ How much did it cost to get started?

  ■ Was the amount you were told you would need satisfactory?

  ■ Were there any hidden or unexpected costs?

  ■ Did you find the estimates of initial expenses to be accurate?

■ Was there a grand-opening fee?

  ■ How much did you spend on your grand opening?

■ What were the gross sales last year?

  ■ What were they the year before?

  ■ What volume of business do you do?

■ Does the royalty structure allow you to make a profit now and in the future?

■ Do you have to purchase supplies or services from the franchisor?

  ■ Could you do a better deal on your own?

    ■ How satisfied are you with the cost and quality of the supplies and services?

■ Was the information you received before you bought the franchise accurate?

  ■ What information did you have to give the company?

■ Are you able to find enough qualified people to work for your operation?

  ■ How much do you have to pay them?

■ Are there seasonal changes you have to make?

  ■ Do you have to pay for any regular renovations?

ASK A CURRENT FRANCHISEE ABOUT THE CUSTOMERS:

- How do you define the demographics of your customers?
  - What are their ages, gender, and location?
- How seasonal is this business?
  - What ebb and flow do you see, and what does that mean to your hours?
- What are the hours you need to be open for business?
  - What are the days per week you have to be open?
  - When do you personally have to be working?
  - Are there any rules about being out sick or taking vacations?
- Is this franchise a fad or something long-lasting?
- How do you identify your customers?
  - How do you promote what is unique in this business to those customers?

ASK A CURRENT FRANCHISEE ABOUT THE FUTURE:

- How long did it take for the franchise to reach its current strength?
- How is the company growing?
  - Is the company adapting to change fast enough?
- How thorough is the training your receive?
- What restrictions exist on the way you do business that you feel are unnecessary?

ASK A CURRENT FRANCHISEE ABOUT THE LOCATION:

- Do you get to choose your site?
  - Were the rules on where you had to put your site too restrictive?
- How has your location worked out?
  - Where else would you see a location working out?

■ Did another franchisee come into your territory or near it?

   ■ What happened then?

■ Was the geographic definition of miles between franchises as the crow flies or road miles?

■ Any problem with the franchisers building plans receiving local building permits?

■ How is your market like the one I might be entering?

■ Is there a similar business nearby?

   ■ Is there enough room in the area to support another similar business?

■ How much does it cost to buy or rent space for the business?

ASK A CURRENT FRANCHISEE ABOUT DEALING WITH THE FRANCHISOR:

■ Has the franchisor been fair?

   ■ How has it fulfilled its contractual obligations?

   ■ When you have a dispute, how is it usually resolved?

■ What do you think of the current management team?

   ■ How much turnover has there been in the franchisor's management?

■ Have you heard of any problems when contracts come up for renewal?

   ■ What are the additional costs when renewing?

■ How good of a support system is there with other owners?

   ■ To what groups do you belong?

■ What terms govern how you would get out of the franchise?

■ Are there quotas?

   ■ What happens if you don't meet them?

■ Was the risk you took joining this company worth it?

ASK FORMER FRANCHISEES:

■ Why are you out of the business?

■ Did you lose money when you sold out?

■ What's the one thing you would do differently?

■ What risks would you warn me about?

■ How was your market like the one I'm thinking of entering?

ASK YOUR ATTORNEY/CONSULTANT/ACCOUNTANT:

■ Can you carefully review the franchise contract and disclosure?

■ How can I confirm the earnings claims?

   ■ Are they based on at least three years of operation of a comparable franchise?

■ Can you review the lawsuits against the company?

   ■ What do you know about the company? Is this a company that likes to sue its franchisees?

■ What risks do you see?

ASK STATE AUTHORITIES:

■ Has your consumer affairs department had any complaints about this company?

   ■ Has it been involved in any legal problems?

   ■ Whom else should I check with?

ASK THE CITY WHERE THE FRANCHISE IS TO BE LOCATED:

■ Are there any rules on how signs have to be displayed?

   ■ Are there other image restrictions?

■ How accessible will the facility be to traffic?

   ■ Do you know of any planned construction near this location?

ASK THE FRANCHISOR ABOUT ITS BUSINESS:

■ Can I see some back copies of your company newsletter?

■ How stable is the top management at your business?

   ■ What is the track record, the experience of officers and directors of the company?

■ What litigation is this company involved in?

   ■ Has this company ever been the subject of legal action by law enforcement or regulatory agencies?

■ Are there any state or federal regulations I need to be aware of?

   ■ What local or state business licensing laws am I subject to?

■ What is the financial condition of the company?

ASK THE FRANCHISOR ABOUT THE CONTRACT:

■ Is there any noncompete clause?

   ■ How am I compensated for such?

■ How can the franchise be terminated?

   ■ How do I appeal?

■ If the franchise were to be terminated, what would I be paid?

   ■ Would an independent appraisal be done?

■ What happens if I die or am disabled?

■ Are the trademarks registered?

   ■ Will you provide legal protection if there is a dispute about trademarks?

■ How are conflicts resolved?

   ■ If litigation is involved, will it take place in my home state?

■ Who pays for mediation or arbitration?

■ Can I assign or sell my business?

■ Do I need your involvement or approval?

■ What insurance do I need?

■ How often will I be audited?

   ■ Who does it, and who pays?

ASK THE FRANCHISOR ABOUT THE OPERATION OF A FRANCHISE:

■ What is the background or experience you look for in new franchise owners?

   ■ What hours and personal commitment are necessary to run the business?

■ How long do I have to correct any problems?

   ■ How long does the franchisor have to correct any contract violations?

■ How do I acquire the initial inventory?

   ■ Can it be purchased on credit?

■ Have you done a market survey in my area?

   ■ Does it show the need for a franchise in my area?

■ Will I be testing the area for the company?

ASK THE FRANCHISOR ABOUT OTHER FRANCHISEES:

■ Are franchisees well coordinated (are there any bad eggs)?

   ■ How are other franchisees in the same system doing?

■ Who are some of the recent buyers in my state?

   ■ How many have left the system during the past few years?

   ■ How many have been closed or terminated?

■ How active is the franchise association?

■ How many franchise outlets are there today?

   ■ Where are they?

ASK THE FRANCHISOR ABOUT FEES:

- What are the charges?

  - How can they change?

- What do these charges include?

- How much will I have to pay for the continuing right to operate the business?

  - What is the term of the agreement?

- Are there continuing royalty payments?

  - How much are those payments?

- Can the royalty fees be raised?

  - Are there any products or services I must buy from the franchisor?

    - How and by whom are they supplied?

  - What if I want to find another supplier?

ASK THE FRANCHISOR ABOUT TRAINING:

- Where is training provided?

- When is training provided?

  - How long are the training sessions?

  - Is there a time limit?

  - Who teaches the training sessions?

    - What are their qualifications?

- Do you offer ongoing training?

- How much does it cost to send other people from my operation in for training?

- How many employees are eligible for training?

  - Can new employees I hire in the future receive training?

    - What would be the cost?

ASK THE FRANCHISOR ABOUT ADVERTISING:

- What is your marketing plan?
  - What does the next advertising campaign look like?
    - When does it start?
  - For the opening, what advertising support will you give?
    - What displays or banners do you provide?
- How much is spent on advertising?
  - Is it local, regional, or national?
  - Do the franchisees have a say in how the money is spent?
- How much will it cost me?
  - How much advertising will appear in my market?
  - Who is the celebrity used in your advertising?
- Can I advertise on my own?
  - Will you help me with my own advertising?
  - How do you rebate or discount my advertising fees if I spend my money on advertising?
- Do company-owned operations contribute the same amount as franchisees?

ASK THE FRANCHISOR ABOUT THE LOCATION:

- Do you locate the site?
  - What if I don't like the site?
- Will a feasibility study be done?
  - Where is the competition located?
- Do I have to sublease from the franchisor?
  - What happens if the lease is lost?

■ What are the restrictions on the location and placement of new franchises in my region?

■ How close will other stores allowed to be?

■ How can my territory be altered?

■ Can I purchase any new franchise in my area?

■ Do you keep any rights that limit my activity within my territory?

■ Can I move my operation if the first location isn't working out?

■ What will it cost me?

■ Will you help me negotiate a better lease if the traffic isn't what we expected?

■ When will I be required to do any remodeling in the future?

ASK THE FRANCHISOR ABOUT THE EQUIPMENT YOU'LL BE USING:

■ What are the total costs?

■ How complicated is the actual operation?

■ What is its reliability?

■ How expensive are repairs?

ASK THE FRANCHISOR ABOUT THE SUPPORT STAFF YOU'LL BE PROVIDING:

■ How many support people will be assigned to my area?

■ How many franchisees will support this service?

■ If I need individual assistance, will someone come to my location?

■ To whom do I speak if there is a problem?

If you ask about past litigation, be aware that franchisors may try to conceal an executive's litigation by removing the individual's name from their disclosure documents.

One final thought on franchises. The virtual space and openness of the Internet have led to an explosion of competition in every business category. The elimination of geographical barriers for commerce and communication has forever changed equations of supply and demand. While the Internet in theory evens the playing field for everyone, the overwhelming number of choices may lead many buyers to choose familiar brand names. The urgent nature of many decisions discourages some people from asking questions if they see a known quantity as a quick solution. This may be a virtue if you are allied with one of the big names, and the ongoing consolidation in so many fields suggests that in the end the big names may win out.

16/4 Looking for an Investor

Assessment

Investors will closely inspect your business plan, what could be described as the bones of your organization without the flesh put on. They will try to discover any discrepancies between your strategy and the prevailing reality. To prevent being confused to the point of paralysis, you must anticipate the questions investors will ask. You also need to look into who is interested in investing, for, as some entrepreneurs have learned, an investor can be an angel or the devil in disguise.

ASK YOUR TEAM:

■ Can you check out the investor's bankers, accountants, or attorneys?

■ What is the reputation of these people?

ASK PEOPLE WHO HAVE RECEIVED INVESTMENT CAPITAL FROM THE INVESTOR:

■ Did you trust the investor?

■ How did you get along?

■ Was the money there as promised and when promised?

■ How much of a role did the investor want in your business?

■ What useful advice did the investor give you?

■ Would you recommend the investor to me?

ASK THE INVESTOR:

- Can you give me the names of your bankers, accountants, and attorneys?

- Who are your references?

- Do you have a resume?

Questions That Motivate

How would you like to be involved?

Kathryn McKee[3]

Chapter 16 Conclusion

Ideas into Action

The best description I have ever heard of starting a business came from one small businessman who said life was so intense in his start-up that it was like building an airplane while flying it at the same time. Starting and owning your own business is not only financially rewarding, but there is also the self-fulfillment that comes from asking meaningful questions. If you ask a question as an employee, you may not really care what the answer is. When you own the business, every answer takes on a great deal more meaning. Questions may not cut down the long hours needed to start a new business, but they can reduce the risk of failure. If your business is successful, your questioning insights will serve you in the future as you consider having others franchise your business.

If you are interested in buying an existing business or franchise and feel pressure to buy, slow down, rather then speed up, and remember to get in writing the answers that promise you anything. If you document the answers to your questions, who promises what and when, you have a record of your relationship with the franchisor or the person selling the business. Remember, a wise seller will be checking you out just as you are checking him out. The transaction, if done fairly, can be exciting for both the buyer and the seller. Any promises by any business promoter that you will reap quick, big profits at little or no risk, or any evasive answers, are warning signs of problems ahead.

One final thought on running your own business. I once interviewed the well-known chef and cookbook author Bradley Ogden, who was expanding a group of restaurants. His recipe for starting a successful business on your own? "I think the most important thing is that you manage people as well as yourself and your time. Begin to train and develop individuals so that you can make sure the product is perfect when you're not there."[4] Questions play a role in each step of building a business. In chapter 17, we focus on questions you can ask when continuing your education.

QUESTIONS THAT WORK WHEN:
You Are Educating Yourself

Much learning does not teach sense.

HERACLITUS

College graduates have dedicated some sixteen years to pursuing an education. Yet, once they enter the workforce, they often suddenly stop seeking further formal education. Why does this happen? Traditional learning focuses on young people, but, in our rapidly changing world, we cannot have a divide between work and learning. In workplace after workplace, more money is spent on the upkeep of machines than on staff education. There are exceptions; some companies make training and executive education a priority, but often these are cut when money gets tight. Learning how to ask questions can guarantee that you continue your education no matter what the corporate bottom line.

Education can be seen as the pursuit of ambition in the face of annihilation. Can you learn enough to become successful enough to defy the odds of failure and falling behind? Certainly, our view of the world is only as good as the lenses we use to look at it. If that lens is cloudy or narrowly focused, an organization won't get a clear picture of the world around it. Individual or corporate education is one of the best ways to sharpen that vision. Questions tap into the world's experience.

MBA students often learn by the case study method, which stresses the role of questions. The students study a scenario that ends with pointed questions and an aggressive Socratic dialogue. This type of inquiry creates in-depth discussions, challenges assumptions, and reveals new ways of thinking. We should all keep alive the spirit of learning, always questioning our own actions, exploring new options, and being skeptical of easy solutions. The best education gives us the ability to recognize changing circumstances and inspires questions to ask when circumstances change or you want to change your situation.

17/1 Looking for a Mentor

Assessment

You'll probably never ask someone directly to be your mentor. It is a special relationship built out of ongoing questions and answers. A mentor is not just someone high up and well connected, the critical quality to seek in a mentor is the ability to look into the future, to see potential in others and opportunities in an industry. Dr. Mike Turner, a survey respondent, suggests that mentors can be anyone who asks questions that get you thinking about tomorrow. "What patterns, trends, or themes seem to be emerging your life? In what ways do they seem significant? Which would you like to encourage? How could you do that?"[1] The definition of a mentor thus can be a broad one, and most employees would be best served by having multiple mentors. To Jennifer Sedlock, another survey respondent, anyone can be a mentor, even if the relationship involves just one conversation. She recommends you ask potential mentors how the person started and do this with several people. This, she says, "will cut your learning time in at least half in whatever it is that you want to do." After these interviews you can find someone to spend ongoing time with.[2]

Respect how busy potential mentors are and appreciate the help they give. Dr. Rey Carr, who worked with the Canadian government on a national mentoring strategy to encourage young people to stay in school, says you need to know what you hope to gain from a mentor and the characteristics you are looking for. He suggests you know what you have to offer a mentor so that both parties will benefit from the relationship.[3] If you tell someone you are looking for insights, don't arrive at the first meeting with generic "How did you become so successful?" questions. A carefully prepared list of questions specific to the person's expertise will maximize the opportunity. Note taking lets your mentor know you are listening, and a thank-you later lets the mentor know you appreciate the value of her advice.

ASK THE POTENTIAL MENTOR:

■ Can I ask for your advice?

■ If the person says no, ask whether he knows someone else in the company who would be willing to help you.

■ Where do you see my career going?

■ Where do you see our industry going?

■ What publications do you see as absolutely necessary that you read each month?

■ What are the key groups and professional meetings you attend?

■ What are some leadership opportunities I should look for?

■ What would you do if you were me?

■ Whom else should I talk to?

If you need to ask about the mentor's career and what opportunities you should seek, see section 6/3, Questions That Work When Needing an Informational Interview.

17/2 Hiring a Coach

Assessment

A wide range of professionals are hiring personal coaches to give advice, enforce goals, and provide encouragement. A coach can be on your side looking at your personal and professional goals, giving you advice a company mentor might not think of or might resist giving you, since it might challenge her or the company. It might be important to have a dialogue with your coach. Survey respondent Bruce Elkin says he wouldn't work with a prospective coach if the coach simply wanted to tell him how to do something and didn't ask questions. You can apply many of the following questions to a potential coach or prospective teacher.

ASK THE COACH:

■ Are you a consultant or a coach?

  ■ How do you give advice?

■ What do you regularly do?

  ■ What background and experience do you have in coaching?

■ Do you have any certification or credentials? (Be aware there is no industry standard, although you could ask if the person is a member of the International Coaching Federation.)

- How do you handle confidentiality?[4]

  - Will you provide a commitment of confidentiality in writing?

- What specifically can you do for me?

  - What if I don't get the results I expect?[5]

- How much do you charge?

  - How will I be billed?

- How do we meet?[6]

- Do you have a specialty?

  - Do you work with anyone in my line of business?

- Which areas are most challenging to you?[7]

  - Where do you have the least experience?[8]

- Do you have examples of successes with clients in similar situations?[9]

  - Can I experience a thirty-minute sample session with you at no cost?[10]

- What is your worst crash-and-burn as a coach?[11]

- How might you personally benefit me that other coaches cannot?[12]

- Do you have a track record working with people in similar situations?[13]

  - Can you give me an overview of how would you handle my situation?

- Will you cut to the chase, be direct, not just talk?[14]

- What do you want most for your clients?[15]

- How can we measure progress or success?[16]

  - What would you suggest me to focus on within the first week, month, and half-year?[17]

- How do you keep yourself in peak performance shape?[18]

- What do you get out of coaching?[19]

- Do you have a coach of your own?[20]

  - Could you arrange for me to meet with that coach?[21]

17/3 Setting up a Training Program

Assessment

Training occurs at three levels: organizationwide, local, or individual. Strong training offers many benefits for those who want to improve their questioning skills. It creates opportunities for interaction with others and increases confidence and the desire for more information. Training has one clear value in that it raises new questions. Imagine eating the same meal each day; this is the reality for many employees who have no choice in the work they do each day. Training brings up new questions, new brain food to try. Margie Sweeny, of Training and Seminar Locators, says that the first question to ask is whether employees already know what they are about to be trained in. She says there is nothing deadlier than being trained in something you know.[22] You should be able to draw a straight line from training to improving performance of the job at hand.

ASK THOSE WHO WANT THE TRAINING:

- What is our goal?

- What are the objectives to reach our goal?

  - What are we trying to accomplish with this training?[23]

- Who is the target audience?

- What will people be able to do differently when they leave?

- Is the training interactive?

- What is the experience of those who created this training?

17/4 Attending a Seminar or Training Class

Assessment

Too often classes are based on monologues, not a dialogue. Writing down questions in advance will focus you on what you need to get out of a seminar. By asking questions, you engage in the seminar and get the most out of it. When looking for a job, you should check to see what training programs the organization offers or will pay for. If nothing else, if you ever have to look for a new job, your constant updating of skills will keep your resume up to date.

ASK THE SEMINAR LEADER OR TEACHER:

- Can I have an outline of the class?

- What's your area of expertise?

  - Do you have recent work experience?

- Can I let you know in advance the types of questions I would like to have answered?

- What reading is required?

  - Can I get a copy of the reading list now?

- How much time does the class take?

  - How much time will I have to spend doing homework outside the class?

- Will we have access to the top people and the latest types of equipment used in this industry?

  - How much access will I have to equipment?

17/5 Seeking an MBA

Assessment

The MBA degree has been described as the union card of the managerial elite. Getting this "card" is an expensive proposition. Going to school full time not only costs thousands of dollars but also costs the significant amount of income you could be earning if you weren't in school. Is it worth it? Graduating from a top business school can be seen as an investment in the ultimate networking and resume building experience. There are traditional programs, executive MBA courses for those with significant work experience, and part-time courses with classes on weekends and nights. All require careful shopping around and questioning.

ASK THE SCHOOLS:

- What accreditation does your school have?

  - What licensing does it have?

- Is it more advantageous to get a specialized MBA or a general one?

- If I already have an undergraduate business degree, does that reduce the number of credits I need for an MBA?

- Who are your teachers?

  - How involved are they with the students?

- What experience do they have?

  - What connections can they offer to work opportunities?

- What is the workload of the classes?

  - How much time will it take to do the work?

- How are the classes taught?

  - Are they taught with actual case studies or through lessons out of a textbook?

- How large are the classes?

- What classes do you offer in my area of interest?

  - How hard is it to get into those classes?

- What classes do you offer for entrepreneurs?

  - Are there opportunities for mentoring from the business community?

- What flexibility do we have in choosing classes?

  - What is the recommended course of study for someone with my interests?

- How much is tuition for the entire program?

  - What are the total costs of everything for the program?

    - What other extras might I have to pay for?

  - What is the school's refund policy?

    - What are the cancellation policies?

- What student aid is available?

- Are students eligible for federal student grants or loans?

- Are scholarships available?

- How can you help with student loan packages?

  - Can I make deferred payments?

- How long does the program take?

  - What is the longest someone can take to complete it?

- Who are the other students?

  - What is the ratio of those with work experience to recent college graduates?

- What job placement programs do you have?

  - What are the placement rates?

- What percentage of students who start the program finish it successfully?

- What success has the school had in placing students?

  - Have those interested in my career path had success?

- What businesses have hired recent graduates?

  - Can I have the names of some graduates who share my interests?

- What is the timetable for applying?

  - What tests, recommendations, applications, or essays are needed?

ASK RECENT GRADUATES:

- Was it worth the effort?

  - How much time did you spend studying?

- Did the school's reputation help you?

  - Given your experience, would you go there again?

- What would you recommend to someone in my situation?

- Which classes were the most useful?

  - Which professors did you think did the best job?

All of these questions can help you see whether recent graduates' answers are different from what the school is telling you.

ASK EMPLOYERS:

■ What is the reputation of the school in your eyes?

■ What experience do you have with graduates of this school?

  ■ How do they perform?

■ Is a specialized or general MBA more valuable?

■ What would you recommend to someone in my situation?

ASK YOUR CURRENT EMPLOYER:

■ Given the considerable benefits to the company of the courses I would take, will the company help with my tuition costs?

■ Can we be somewhat flexible about my work schedule to accommodate the course workload?

  ■ What opportunities might an MBA open up for me here at our company?

Questions That Motivate

What is a problem or obstacle that, if solved, would cause an immeasurable change in your life for the better?

Michael Ray[24]

Chapter 17 Conclusion

Ideas into Action

When we are young we don't know who we are or where we are going. The world seems to be all questions and few answers. Later in life, what answers we do find are fragile, and we realize how few "right" answers there are. In a vague and changing world, questioning skills offer a very attractive return on investment. Perhaps for this reason a growing number of organizations are offering ongoing professional training, including the establishment of corporate universities such as the Charles Schwab, Motorola, and Dell universities. Teachers and managers must remember that the most valuable lesson they can offer their students or employees is that no matter what the answer, there is a value in asking the question. This reassurance is important, for it encourages lifelong enthusiasm for learning. A positive questioning culture should inspire us to review our days carefully, to ask, "What did I learn?" and "What do I need to learn next?" In chapter 18, we review the leadership questions that can contribute to lasting satisfaction on the job and the inquiry that can change our world.

Part VI

Leaders and Questions

QUESTIONS THAT WORK WHEN:
Leading the Way

Life's most urgent question is: what are you doing for others?

MARTIN LUTHER KING

It is often said that you cannot manage what you cannot measure. How can you, then, measure the qualities of leadership? Is there a way to quantify taking risk, encouraging change, taking action, creating knowledge, teaching the next generation, defining a vision, sharing a culture, or being ethical? What a leader does—take on great responsibility and great adversity—is difficult to measure. Often the only measurement is the final result, the success or failure of an entire enterprise. What remains behind—the organization, the standards, the spirit—when the leader is gone tells the story. In the end, the greatest praise for a leader is the lasting, unspoken dignity of those who worked with the leader.

Jeff DeCagna, a commentator on business learning, was troubled by my repeated use of the word "manager" when I asked for his ideas. He refers to managers as those who "do things right," while leaders "do the right things." He asked whether I was talking about leaders instead of managers when applying the concept of question asking. In his mind, leaders are leaders because they take the wider view of the organization or are more focused on the mission.[1] We can agree that people want to be led, not managed. I'll share an experience of interpreting the words "leadership" and "management." On my first day at the Poynter Institute, participating in a six-month program to study leadership development, the class was asked (in the first of many questions) why we were there. I argued that the world needs fewer managers and more leaders, since leaders make things happen, while managers simply follow up. At the end of the entire program, I reconsidered my position when the same question was asked again. I acknowledged that "management" is the foundation upon which leadership can be built. There may be leaders who can motivate and inspire a workforce, despite a lack of any notable planning, hiring, and training skills, but I suspect they stand squarely on the backs of others who have those qualities. This thought creates one more definition of a leader rather than a manager: A manager thinks he needs to know all the answers; a leader knows where to get answers.

In positive questioning cultures, great leaders use authority (the right to make decisions), power (the ability to reward or punish), and influence (both good and bad persuasive force) to ask big questions that:

- Decide the priorities an organization should address.

- Forecast long-range issues.

- Identify risks and consequences of future action.

- Understand adversaries.

- See and build relationships.

- Deal with institutional problems.

- Gather viewpoints.

- Create enthusiasm.

- Forge agreement on what is to be done.

Leaders use questions to help define the right outcome. A leader tells the group where it is heading, how the future is changing. A leader focuses on the right outcome. What is it? The right outcome takes care of an organization's people while ethically bringing the product or service to the marketplace with greater speed, efficiency, and quality.

Leaders, by their openness to questioning, give followers the confidence to pursue their dreams. One of my bosses asked his employees what they really wanted to be. He encouraged employees to pursue their ideas even if it meant quitting and moving on to a new job. This leader knew that all any organization can hope for is the best efforts of employees as they pass through the company.

What follows are positive questions that look into the very nature of an organization. Mark Sanborn, a leadership consultant, says that he sees managers who have questions about what is going on around their organizations but "not so much what is going on with in them." They seldom challenge the existing thinking about how they operate.[2] Leaders must resist institutional inertia, change the way they and their followers see the world, and, as a result of that inquiry, encourage the innovation that will shape the future.

18/1 Encouraging Change

Assessment

Change has been a constant theme in *Questions That Work*. Inquiry is the most powerful mental tool we have for coping with the flux of the marketplace. As times change, inquiry helps us to be ready to change with them. Questions move organizations move beyond familiar and seemingly secure patterns. There is an oft-repeated saying that you can't treat change like an enemy; otherwise, you will always be under attack. Employees often see change as implying that there is a problem (why change if not to respond to a problem?); if there is a problem, there is a threat. In such a paranoid frame of mind, many employees worry that the cure (change) will be worse than the illness. If you don't have an open question-and-answer process with people about what the change will be, people will ask their own questions, and in the hallways and the lunchroom they'll find their own answers. Leaders recognize that change causes anxiety, fears that can be dispelled by encouraging hope and inviting questions. Without participation, there is no real, lasting change. Inquiry invokes curiosity, which in turn triggers creative problem solving. This is why positive questions are so important in goal setting. As Edward Miller, of the Poynter Institute, put it, "Goals describe a new and different state of affairs. They seek change, something to be accomplished in the future, not the equilibrium of the present."[3]

While change is all around us, organizations devote more time and energy to maintaining the institution than they apply to changing the work of the organization. The management theorist Peter Drucker once pointed out that U.S. businesses rarely prepare for change: "To my knowledge few if any American businesses have asked themselves: What does this change mean for us? What does it mean for employment and labor force? What does it mean in terms of new markets? . . . What does it mean for our customers? Our products? Our entire business posture?"[4] Great organizations manage the opportunities change brings. A leader would understand why Warren Bennis asks executives the questions "In your company, what's the mean time between surprises?" and "How do you get people to improvise?"[5] Change unleashes benefits beyond the bottom line. It revitalizes organizations and gives employees a sense of purpose by making the workplace a more meaningful and exciting place to be. Questions serve an underappreciated function when change is taking place, for all constructive change requires communication, and all clear communication encourages questions.

External pressure or internal leadership creates change. If change is to be a positive experience, leaders at all levels have to predict, understand, and direct change. Leaders know they need to stand for an enduring set of standards, while all else is flexible. There must be some continuity even during change, or all is chaos. The art of leadership often lies in encouraging employees to keep what energizes (positive values), while shedding everything else (negative habits, technology, or traditions). Questions decide which is which. TV newsrooms are an example of a place where use of technology has radically changed over the past thirty years, from using film that took days to ship from the other side of the world to accessing video transmitted live from anywhere on earth. The leadership in the TV station I work in encourages new ways to work while never losing the value of providing clear, complete, and compassionate news coverage.

Great leaders plant seeds of change around them with their questions, cultivate these seeds with constant inquiry, and harvest the results by asking whether the change is working. Leaders know organizations must continually make small improvements to maintain and grow their market positions. They do so by sending pulses of questions throughout the organization that can raise the alarm and warn the organization over and over to be prepared for sudden and permanent change. Like it or not we all face a perpetual process of retooling and shifting resources to face new challenges. Questions are a way to push people to think about the future. I've watched leaders up close who know that when they stop asking questions, they stop pushing for a better way. If nothing else, change should encourage one habit among managers and leaders—the habit of calling around to various people in their organization to ask, "What's new?" and "What's important?" Leaders also ask, "What does it take to make change occur?"

ASK YOUR ORGANIZATION:

■ What's new?

   ■ What phenomenon are we currently experiencing?

■ What's going on in the world?

- What is the state-of-the-art direction?[6]
- What are things you control that you can change?
- What would you do to change the status quo within our company?
  - How will the change we are making help the customers?
- What are we already doing well?[7]
  - What are we doing to maintain it? Increase it?
- Where are standards not being met?
  - Where are they being exceeded?[8]
- Where can we create the most leverage?[9]
- Where should we focus?
  - Who should we partner with?
- What markets should we be entering?
- How do you deal with discontent?
  - This is what you want?
- What are our three biggest problems?
  - How can they be measured?
  - How much do they cost?
- What are our handicaps?
  - How do we overcome them?
- What are the resources we need to succeed?
- If you look at our place as a buyer would, what would you buy?
  - What would you leave behind?
  - What is obsolete?
  - What should be replaced?
- How do we buy?
  - What changes do we need to make in our purchasing to remain competitive?

- Why should a customer buy from us?

  - Can we compete on quality?

  - Can we compete on cost?

- Whom do we choose as customers?

  - Have we kept our promises to customers?

- What three things have you and your department changed in the last month?[10]

- How can we improve?

- What is your honest feeling about my leadership relating to taking risks and losing within this company?

- If I were to give you 20 percent of all savings or increased profits we realized from your suggested changes, what would your first change be?[11]

- How should we challenge the most creative and talented people who work here?

  - How should this company credit or reward the originator of a new idea that does not fit into our business culture or product line?[12]

18/2 Taking Risks

Assessment

The work world is such an arduous daily climb toward stability that we all fear that taking any risk can lead us into a sudden free fall of failure. Every decision is an attempt to influence something that will always be a mystery—the future. Since most of us can't see too far into tomorrow, risk enters into every choice we make. Inquiries identify those risks by helping one be intellectually rigorous and honest.

The trouble is that not all institutions reward risk takers. Managers speak of encouraging others to take chances but often punish those who venture outside set boundaries. This defines one role of leaders as compared to managers: Leaders encourage workers to take risks and back up the employees. They encourage, as one of my coworkers once called it, "aggressive mistakes," so long as the risks have been taken into consideration. One boss I have worked for regularly forgives mistakes of commission, less frequently errors of omission. His theory: It is acceptable for you to fail as long as you anticipated the risks, but it is unacceptable to act without studying the risks. It is an echo of Greek tragedies, which warn of acting without thought of the consequences.

Much of risk taking is really courageous decision making in disguise. You question and review the options to decide the best outcomes, to support what is called the educated guess, a guess that often only one person can make. Henry Kissinger once spoke of the role of a leader in decision making: "Crises are distinguished by a stillness born of the awareness that choices are disappearing. The number of decision makers shrinks to those still in a position to affect events, their solitude magnified because, the more severe the crisis, the fewer the volunteers who are willing to assume responsibility."[13]

Leaders encourage risk taking while setting goals. They know a worthy goal is realistic but on the far side of realistic. All great goals thus involve the risk of failure. Any performance system such as annual appraisals simply preserves the status quo unless it challenges, unless it poses a risk of the unknown. Employees with goals are better able to handle risk. When there is a risk, a danger, people who have goals can take hold of and move toward those goals, rather than flounder about or stand still.

Entrepreneurs are defined by the risks they take. They live in the future, asking themselves and others what will happen next. Successful organizations cultivate internal entrepreneurs, creating a dynamic brain trust. Encouraging questions encourages prudent risk taking in another dimension. Workers who are self-motivated to ask questions discover a way to self-monitor risk levels. These employees can take on more responsibility and be trusted to try more experiments, because they know to ask questions that can keep them from going too far off course. Positive questions give employees a form of radar to help them constantly locate answers. The first question leaders need to ask themselves is, "How do I treat risk takers?"

ASK YOUR COWORKERS:

■ What changes are anticipated that will create threats or opportunities?[14]

■ Who is creeping up on us?[15]

- How would you attack us if you were our competitor?[16]

- Who are our competitors?

  - Who are our real competitors?

  - Who are our toughest competitors?

    - How do various competitors beat us out?[17]

  - What are our advantages over them?

- What will our industry be like five or ten years from now?

  - How are we going to handle new technology?

- What are you afraid of?

- What decision needs to be made today?

- Why isn't there . . . ?

- How quickly do we respond to complaints?

- What's the worst possible thing that could happen as a result of this risk taking?

- What will be the fallback of an idea or venture fails?

  - What can we learn if the attempt fails?

Questions That Work

The director of the world-famous Palo Alto Research Center, John Seely Brown, responded to the author's inquiry about risk taking with this set of questions to get employees thinking about change. Who better than a chief scientist at Xerox Corporation to give a powerful set of questions to think about the future and challenge people to reconsider the risks of not doing anything?

1. What strategic surprises do you expect to launch against your competitors this year?

2. What surprises might your competitors launch against you?

3. How might your biggest strength be used against you?

4. What happens when you take any trend to the extreme—e.g., bandwidth becomes infinite?

5. How would your teenager look at that?[18]

18/3 Taking Action

Assessment

If institutional strategy is ultimately the result of individual actions throughout the organization, no strategy will work unless people from across the organization are fully involved and invested. If you have already defined where you want to go (your ideal), questions determine how to get there (the action needed). Focused information is a spur to action, for it gives a sense of urgency about what you need to act on. This is why leaders who encourage questions and the exchange of information find that employees will rapidly react to both threats and opportunities without waiting for instructions. The use of questions to create an early warning system works best if, once the alarm is sounded, another set of questions helps the organization *respond*. Workers take action most effectively when they have some control and feel that their action makes a positive contribution. Andrew Zacharakis, a survey respondent, says that you should ask your staff, "If you saw a great opportunity, would you bring it to the company or pursue with your own entrepreneurial venture?" Zacharakis says if the person responds that she would pursue it on her own, you might want to hang on to her, since she likely has the drive and motivation necessary to succeed.[19]

Leaders use inquiry to not only inspire action but to discover the obstacles to action. Questions discover a lack of commitment, missing resources, a bureaucratic wall, or a lag in one department's response that breaks down communication and momentum. No one wants to fight his own organization. The author James Belasco suggests that you ask employees to write you a "dear boss" letter about what obstacles are in the way and what they are going to do to remove them.[20] Leaders know complete agreement is not necessary to act, but action often hinges on the knowledge that some organizational support will be provided. Leaders use questioning to help clear up confusion and determine the reasons for employees' high and low performance. Every manager knows high-performance employees inspire more action because their questions often trigger energy bursts among others. Leaders space out questions and challenges to work with the energy flow of the team they are leading. The danger always lies in asking too many questions and letting a Hamlet-like paralysis set in. Organizations that avoid this fate have leaders who create a plan that links strategy to tactics.

ASK YOUR COWORKERS:

- How do we turn ideas into action?

- What are the results we really want to have?

  - How do we create standards?

- You want to be number one; how are we going to reach that goal?

- What is the right environment?

- What is it that seems impossible to do today but that, if it could be done, would fundamentally change our business/organization?[21]

- What's relevant?

  - Are we competitive on this front?

- Is good performance rewarded not just with money but with emotional rewards?

- Do we have the time to tackle this new project?

- What do we have to do to develop the product or service to meet the anticipated needs of customers?[22]

- How can we attract the human and financial resources we need to pursue this opportunity?[23]

- What is it that really energizes you about the work that you perform, and therefore what do you need more of in this position?[24]

- What is getting in the way of our being successful?[25]

- When, how soon, will we do it?[26]

- What should we do next?

■ How are we growing ideas into innovations?[27]

■ Is this what we want?

■ Will this new effort lead to other opportunities?

Questions That Work

Mariann Jelinek, the Kraemer Professor of Business at the College of William and Mary, has researched innovation and organizational change. Her initial focus was high-technology companies, but "more recently I've turned to more established industries [because] virtually everyone's 'high tech' these days, and virtually everyone faces rapid and pervasive change." As she put it, no company wants its business or industry to be described as "mature," since this implies "obsolescence, rigidity, even bankruptcy." After studying such high-tech companies as Intel, National Semiconductor, Motorola, and Hewlett-Packard, she says managers who want to encourage innovation and action among employees should ask:

1 What are we doing that's in your view a complete waste of time, counterproductive, or useless?

2. What opportunities do you see that the company is missing?

3. What would we have to do to really exceed the customers' wildest expectations?

4. What am I personally doing that gets in the way of your success?

5. What can I personally do to help you be a hero on the job?[28]

18/4 Creating Knowledge

Assessment

The creation of knowledge is the result of asking and answering questions. Leaders must be champions of information access and adaptation. The new dynamic of the workplace, with its rapid teamwork and constant change, requires collaboration, which in turn depends on the free exchange of information. Leaders have to do more than just encourage the exchange; they have to push information into the workplace down to the levels where it can do the most good. Managers need to ask whether employees feel they have enough information about the organization and outside environment.

The management theorist Peter Senge has written about the danger of treating knowledge as an asset where "scarcity creates value."[29] This perceived value leads to hoarding in black binders, confidential memos, and reports. Growth of information without application is a slow but sometimes deadly form of corporate cancer. Too often a manager's information gathering is focused on immediate results and not the joy of discovery, the value of encouraging learning. Edward Miller, an instructor at the Poynter Institute, says one of his students, a newspaper editor, had an "aha" moment when he realized how much of management was about "teaching, not control."[30]

Successful organizations know that the process of creating knowledge is a close cousin of both creativity and quality. Creativity comes from the appreciation of something new and different. It also comes from destroying what you know and building anew, which is what constant positive questioning allows you to do. Quality often comes from finding new ideas, exploring the relationship between ideas, and adapting and refining ideas to improve performance.

It could be argued that leadership requires more creativity than problem-solving ability. Problem solving fixes what is broken; creativity discovers new opportunities. Which one is more important in setting the direction of an organization? Creativity is about learning and exploring, and those who learn and explore the most can embrace the most contradictory of statements. They know what they don't know.

ASK COWORKERS:

- What are our five best new opportunities?
- What's next?
  - What are we going to do next time?
  - What's the next big idea?
- Are curious people seeking out our company?[31]
- How do you get people to improvise?[32]

- How can we find fresh ideas inside the company?

- What have we done that was a wow?

- Do our customers have fun when dealing with us?

- What's good about this?

  - What's not perfect about it yet?

- How can we have fun doing it?

- What can we learn from this?[33]

- But what about . . . ?

- I wonder, do we . . . ?

- Can I share my view on this?

18/5 Teaching Leadership

Assessment

A top responsibility of any leader is to identify or teach a worthy successor. Managers who do not assume this responsibility abdicate one of the most important roles of leadership—finding, guiding, and training the next generation. An unspoken rule at some organizations is that to advance, you must be able to suggest a replacement able to carry on in your current position. Managers who want to advance should be able to answer the question "Who would replace you?" If no one comes to mind, the manager has not performed one key role as teacher. One of my bosses always said you should hire people who want your job; in effect, you should always be looking for your replacement.

A leader has many different ways to pass along the skills and attitudes the job demands. The most important way is leading by example and modeling important behavior, including the use of positive and consistent questioning. Inquiry emphasizes the importance of a leader's having a passion with a purpose. Positive questions focus on using strengths and managing weaknesses, reflect the need to anticipate and prepare for external forces, and welcome participation. A leader doesn't know all the answers but needs to know how to involve people. The most significant legacy a leader can have is to inspire employees at all levels to reach for their potential.

Mayor Ed Koch used to ask New Yorkers, "How am I doing?" and leaders should ask and teach others to ask the same. The leaders I work with teach others never to assume success and to always keep questioning. In many competitive businesses, the moment you think you've arrived is the point the momentum slows and the success rate slides. A leader's visibility—being seen as available for questions—can be one of the most important lessons she passes along. Leaders are never missing in action.

ASK YOUR EMPLOYEES:

■ Whom in your lifetime do you admire most as a leader?

   ■ Whom in this organization do you admire as a leader?

■ Who are the people here who have coached or mentored good leaders?[34]

■ Whom can you recommend that I recognize for their leadership?

■ How do we grow our own managers and leaders?

   ■ What experiences should new managers have to help them become a leader?

■ How would this company operate if you were the leader?

■ What is the big picture?

■ What do you want to see from me?

18/6 Creating a Vision

Assessment

The Book of Proverbs says, "When there is no vision, a people perish." An organizational crisis can be a violation of vision. It indicates that the leadership is falling short of the mark. A crisis can reveal leadership that does not know where it is going or has not communicated direction or destination. A true and lasting crisis can occur when the organization is not sure what it stands for. To prevent this, an organization should have an ongoing dialogue about what its group's vision or mission is. It is this conversation that generates the momentum to keep the organization going; it is the expression of the hope that things will continue to get better. Asking questions helps employees share this responsibility, involving everyone in defining and redefining priorities in an overwhelming world.

At the heart of every vision or mission of what an organization should be and do is a small set of the essential values. These are the values that transcend time and are the heart of meaningful traditions. The relationship between values and vision cannot be created on a spreadsheet. Positive questions help create a clear sense of what the organization should be; they clarify, emphasize, and stimulate existing values by starting discussions that articulate future action. A vision is more than a mission statement; it is a changeable and personally meaningful picture of the future. The secret of creating a powerful vision sometimes is not how many questions one asks but how many times one asks a limited number of questions. Individuals can ask themselves, "Who do I want to be tomorrow?" Leaders can repeatedly ask, "Who are we?" Asking questions about a shared vision can be humbling, for one of the greatest mistakes some leaders make is to mistake their authority for a vision. They give commands that often tell people what to do, but not why to do it.

A leader uses a larger vision to show everyone that the whole can be greater than the sum of its parts. Many employees do not understand the opportunity they have in an organization to reach and grow. The vision provides a guide to the unfolding of the individual's potential. A leader with vision walks in front and shows the way. His vision sets up a process of "becoming," rather than defining a moment in time. The vision has to be linked to the world, for the last thing a leader wants to be known for is being long on vision and too short on action.

By encouraging a dialogue about the organization's vision, a leader helps keep everyone involved in answering the question "What is the purpose of our organization?" This question can be explored further by asking, "What are the key elements of our vision of success?" One student of Professor Peter Drucker at the Claremont Graduate University described another question to start a discussion about a larger vision. He says Drucker would say that his first and favorite question to ask clients is, "What kind of business do you think you're in?"[35] A variation on this is a question their designer Jerry Hirshberg asked staff at a major newspaper to get them to rethink their vision of their business. He asked, "What would be lost if papers ceased to exist?"[36]

A vision is the first link in the chain that makes a great organization. The vision is linked to values, connected to goals, which all create the world the workers live in. Organizations that will survive are those with these characteristics—vision, values, and goals. Questioning speaks to all three. As one consultant once told me, the mission is today; a vision is tomorrow. It answers the big "Why bother?" question.

ASK YOUR COWORKERS:

- What's your vision for the company?[37]

  - What difference do you want to make here?[38]

  - What turns you on?[39]

    - I notice you light up when you talk about x—what's that about?[40]

- Is our vision clear?

  - What is the essential message?

  - What is it without which this institution would not be what it is?[41]

  - Why does this business exist?

  - What does the best mean?

- How do you develop a vision?

  - What are you committed to?[42]

  - What is possible in this situation?

- Does our vision get people excited?

  - How can you make this vision come alive?

  - Are we having fun yet?

- What are some high-visibility areas where you can try to demonstrate your vision?

  - What are three things you can do to demonstrate your vision?

  - What is your timetable for executing these items?

- Why are we doing this?[43]

  - Is what we are doing relevant to the vision we have?[44]

■ What outcome would you be really proud of at the end of this project?[45]

  ■ How do you want to be remembered?

    ■ How do you want our business to be seen?

■ What is the hot spot in our company?

  ■ How does it reflect our vision of what we want to be?

■ How are things going?

■ Can you restate our company mission in your own words?

■ What do you look forward to in the near future?

  ■ What would you like to learn tomorrow?

Questions That Work

Coming up with a vision answers the biggest questions of all: Why do we work? What do we really make? Whom do we want to sell it to? These are questions that go beyond "Do we make a profit?" Sometimes the answers require a soul-searching discussion; at other times they are based on down-to-earth practicalities. Even within organizations, there can be different visions, just as long as they all reach toward the same place. Roger Kaufman, who has written on "mega planning," says managers should ask questions that reverse the normal problem solution sequence. He suggests asking questions like the following:

1. If our organization is the solution, what's the problem?

2. If our operation is the solution, what's the problem?

3. If my pet or favored solution (e.g., benchmarking, training) is the solution, what's the problem?[46]

18/7 Sharing a Culture

Assessment

A culture can grow around a vision. Organizations have cultures, through which leaders specifically encourage certain traditions, stories, and even myths. An organization's culture weaves the leader's messages into stories that form the fabric of the company. People think, communicate, and remember stories. Positive stories can tell of people who saw the end results of their dedicated and consistent efforts. People can then question how these stories relate to their own future and to the advancement of their own careers. Some cultures have a bottom-dollar orientation. Their heroes are the ones who got the big account, who turned an extra big profit. Anyone who measures his worth strictly by the paycheck can find a home in those offices. Other organizations are the home of creative people or caretakers, where the salary is second to the psychic rewards of a job well done. Their heroes are the creators and givers who bring new ideas or comfort to others. Status in these workplaces comes not from seniority or size of office but from the size of the employees' ideas or hearts.

Cultures create and define organizational resilience, the quality that keeps people together through the inevitable tough times. Leaders concerned about their culture ask the question the writer John Hawkins once posed: "If everyone else is making decisions, what decisions will hold our organization together?"[47] Questioning can be a way to break down destructive internal competition that fractures a culture, encourage sharing of information that grows the culture, and create a way to keep social ties intact that passes on the culture. Leaders who neglect the power of organizational cultures can be out of touch with their employees. You have only to consider failed mergers to realize how corporate cultures can clash and collapse.

Leaders shape the culture with every question they ask. At one company I've studied, the primary question appears to be "How do we control our market?" At another, it is "How do we create a great product?" My sense is that the two companies are very different places to work and have completely different cultures. Dr. Mike Turner, a survey respondent, says creating a more meaningful culture is the way of the future: "As companies begin (at last!) to seek a wider definition of success than merely economic success, new criteria as to what it means to be successful are beginning to emerge." Turner says, "What is happening is that economic success is moving from being the FOCUS of the company's activities to being the FOUNDATION on which a more meaningful kind of success is built."[48]

ASK YOUR COWORKERS:

■ What do you think this corporate culture is?[49]

■ What do we most want?[50]

■ What are the topics of conversation when people are out in the parking lot?

■ Who are our heroes?

　■ How did they get to be heroes?

■ How are you going to get people to invest?

■ How are you going to give feedback?

　■ How often are you going to give feedback?

　■ How much will be positive?

■ How do we communicate?

　■ Are we clear and consistent in what we are telling people?

　■ What is the most important thing you can do to communicate our vision?

■ Can you sell me our product?

　■ Is that pitch true to what we believe in?

■ What happens when someone new comes on board?

　■ How can you convince me to join your part of the company?

■ How do you feel about the people around you?

■ What were the most recent big purchases?

　■ Why did you make them?

18/8 Creating an Ethical Workplace

Assessment

I hope the reader feels that the questions I have suggested throughout this book are ethical, fair to both parties, and positive. It could be argued that questions are ethically neutral, that the moral balance is tilted by the answer; however, inquiry indicates our state of mind and the decisions we are interested in making. Leaders set a moral tone with the questions they ask or do not ask.

Emerson once said, "An institution is the lengthened shadow of one man." What ethics does a driven and determined leader need to demonstrate? It all comes down to treating people with dignity. I once interviewed Michael Josephson, of the Josephson Institute for the Advancement of Ethics, and I still have notes, more than ten years later, on what we talked about: honesty, integrity, promise keeping, fidelity, fairness, caring for others, respect for others, responsible citizenship, pursuit of excellence, and accountability. Ethical questioning has much to do with these virtues. For, while we automatically know what we want to selfishly have happen, questions force us to consider the needs of others.

The need for ethical question asking is as great now as it ever was. We are in an ethical mess; science and technology are advancing ahead of any agreed-upon rules, and the digital divide is leading to the possible creation of a permanent underclass. Max Frisch defined the dilemma: "We can now do what we want, and the only question is what do we want? At the end of our progress we stand where Adam and Eve once stood; and all we are faced with now is the moral question."[51] Just as wearing a lab coat is no shield against this ethical dilemma, neither is sitting behind a corporate desk. It is the never-ending debate between what an individual and an organization *could* do and what it *should* do. The leader of a corporation can make decisions that influence the lives of not only thousands of employees but millions of consumers. The danger is an increasing compartmentalization of modern life can lead to tunnel vision, where many employees are focused only on their jobs. The moral person considers society as a whole. There is always the question of who is affected by your actions and how. Hopefully your family education or religion teaches you to ask, "What do I stand for?" rather than "What's in it for me?" The right questions challenge people to help everyone live better lives and protect against the strong temptation to mislead. Good questioning skills can sharpen your perception of the ethical dimensions of any situation; without them, you may not discover a moral dilemma until you have fallen deeply into it. Jeff De Cagna, a survey respondent, says questions on ethics and learning should be explicit, because if they are not, they may be missed.[52]

The changing nature of society has dissolved some of the "word is bond" nature of questioning and dealing. In smaller communities, people not only saw the person they were dealing with; they had to live with the consequences of any deception. Now the phone and the computer provide a faceless quality to many business situations. Another contribution to the ethical decay in business is the philosophy that being competitive requires having contempt for your opponent. It is difficult to question someone ethically if you are otherwise verbally dismissive of that person. The remote and sometimes abusive nature of business today often makes questioning more negative than positive.

You will know you are an ethical leader when others ask you for advice on difficult business matters. They may be checking their own moral compass against yours. It may also be that you are better skilled at asking the questions that will help others discover the essential ethical dilemma. Positive questions force us to be reflective, to discover what has meaning. The leader can ask not only "Are we doing things right?" but "Are we doing the right things?" This question challenges people's complacency. Asking such a legitimate and nontrapping question expresses confidence in the other's opinion and value as an individual. It is an expression of concern, and it shows respect for the right of others to choose freely for themselves. Without a personal philosophy, without a guiding set of ethics, work is just a place, the job is just a title, and the paycheck, nothing but an exchange of money for time.

ASK YOUR COWORKERS:

■ Does it feel right to you?

■ Is this action truly consistent with our organization's values of ethics, honesty, and integrity?[53]

■ Is this what we really want?

■ Will our idea work?

　■ How will it work?

■ Who benefits from this decision or action?

　■ Who ought to be the beneficiary?

　■ Who is harmed?

- How are the benefits and burdens distributed?
- Is the decision balanced?
- Does the act respect the rights of the individuals involved?
- How will this decision or action affect our credibility?
- What if this decision were public knowledge?
- How would you feel about explaining this to your children?
- What ought we do?
- Are we basing our actions and decisions on our core values?[54]
- Where are we now with this decision or action?
- Where do we want to be?
- What ethical issues will we need to consider to get there?
- Can we explain our policy?
- What would tomorrow's newspaper headline read?[55]
- Have we kept promises to our customers?

Questions That Work

When I was younger, this passage from *Profiles in Courage,* by then Senator John F. Kennedy, raised a series of questions about who we are at work and life:

> History asks, "Did the man have integrity?
>
> Did the man have unselfishness?
>
> Did the man have courage?
>
> Did the man have consistency?"[56]

Questions That Motivate

Are you willing to transform your own thinking, tell the truth and be in action to aspire to be the kind of person you really want to be?

John Tessier[57]

Chapter 18 Conclusion

Ideas into Action

This chapter on leadership questions ends with the matter of ethics. Ethical concerns are also the place to begin all questions. Philosophy and ethics are very much a matter of asking one question: "What is the good and correct life?" It is a question without one answer, for the asking of ethical questions is a never-ending task. With positive questions you define the priorities you bring to your daily decisions, the type of people you will associate with, and the purpose you will have in life. I believe each inquiry is a miniature study of character and circumstance. Positive questioning is a soft skill in a hard world, a talent to suggest, evoke, and explore what is yet to be done.

Leaders, who decide for others how to respond, how to change, and where to spend resources, can use questions to show concern for the wider community. Empathy is a quality found in the best leaders. They sense and share larger concerns and the dreams of others. They can, by creating a positive questioning culture, turn their people loose on the most important questions of work and life. The leader who does this will spur others to take responsibility for their actions and bring about a world of opportunity, success, and dignity.

Conclusion

I began this book with the aim of creating a questioning "manifesto." My intent was provocative, even revolutionary, but some warned the word "manifesto" suggested too political an approach. The thesis of *Questions That Work* is revolutionary compared with that of many other business books that approach the world with their series of "right answers." Too many writers argue a point, never opening the door to the reader's spirit of inquiry. The question set format of this book is also radical, but, the source of radical being *radix,* meaning root or source, is an approach that brings us back to the very starting point of thought. With passionate conviction I believe life is a series of questions, *for the very essence of the human condition is one of questioning.* Questions and answers are a part of all of us, a rhythm as old as the call and response of humanity's earliest music, music that reaches back to a time before language.

The introductory essays in *Questions That Work* argue that a well-asked question sets you apart from others by demonstrating the strength of your insight while downplaying your weakness in information. In a world where information is increasingly the currency and pulse of the marketplace, skillful questioning clearly communicates your ability to efficiently gather this valuable commodity. When done with intelligence and integrity, inquiry clearly contributes to business success and personal fulfillment. Positive questioning is the most practical of wisdoms. It is the architecture of possibility.

Positive questions are not only a business issue; they are a matter of consciousness. The questioning attitude is an essential to a life well lived. If you feel personally poor, no matter what your wealth, I suggest it is because you have not used positive questions to enrich your mind and your soul. A life without questions deadens the brain and blunts the wit. Questions give you a way to capture ideas and create an organized approach to the challenges you face each day. As you reach into yourself and out to others, you have to question your own beliefs, be aware of them, and evaluate them. Positive questioners recognize the value of discussion, dissent, and debate. Asking questions can be a humbling but rewarding experience, for continued curiosity is the foundation for strong relationships.

The need for a positive questioning attitude and culture has never been more urgent. In a time of instant information and a celebrity-saturated media, questions turn down the informational noise that can overwhelm and deafen us. The changing nature of work demands we learn new technologies, increase our pace of productivity, and cope with rising stress levels. We often find ourselves feeling as if we are working alone, isolated by the very communication devices and work-places that should encourage conversations. There is no more powerful way to recognize and respect those around us than to ask meaningful questions. By encouraging positive inquiry, you are agreeing to discuss what is right and fair.

Questioners who become leaders have unique responsibilities. Knowing the value of inquiry, they are morally obligated to use their strength to create new opportunities and to support others. They can create a questioning culture that addresses the need for community, for structure, and for meaning. Such a culture is not merely a question of what is but what can be. For as your questioning abilities dwindle, so do your options.

I leave you with a thought from English philosopher John Stuart Mill. It is a thought that stayed with me throughout the writing of *Questions That Work.*

> To question all things:—never to turn away from any difficulty;
> to accept no doctrine either from ourselves or from other people
> without a rigid scrutiny by negative criticism; letting no fallacy,
> or incoherence, or confusion of thought, step by unperceived;
> above all, to insist upon having the meaning of a word clearly
> understood before using it, and the meaning of a proposition
> before assenting to it;—these are the lessons we learn from
> ancient dialecticians.[1]

I hope you will contemplate and renew the value of questions in your life regularly and forever. To paraphrase W. B. Yeats, "Can we know the questioner from the question?" We become our questions.

A Closing Invitation

The more than one thousand questions in this book are based on wide-ranging personal experience, many years of research, and the generous sharing of questions by hundreds of people around the world. Many crucial questions are still missing. I encourage your suggested corrections, additions, and amplifications. This book, like all inquiries, is a work in progress and is sure to change. Your perspective will make the next round of questions on any of the many topics included here more focused and successful.

If you would like to suggest questions for future editions of this book, please visit: questionsthatwork.com.

Notes

Chapter 1

1 "The Science of Hope with Jonas Salk" (PBS Video), *A World of Ideas with Bill Moyers,* 1990.

2 Laurence J. Peter, *Peter's Quotations: Ideas for Our Time* (New York: Morrow, 1977), p. 333.

3 Charles Handy, *The Hungry Spirit beyond Capitalism: A Quest for Purpose in the Modern World* (New York: Broadway Books).

4 Gary Lockwood's reply to author query. Lockwood is a strategic business coach; he is also quoted in chapter 10.

5 Marilyn Hamilton, senior partner, Consulting Resource Group, Ltd., reply to author query.

6 Packard gave one other reason for his success; he said that, because the company started so small, he and Bill Hewlett did every job. Because of this firsthand experience, he says, they understood what their employees felt and needed. Interviewed by Brian Banmiller for "On the Money," KTVU, Oakland, CA, June 16, 1995.

7 Lewis D. Eigen and Jonathan P. Siegel, *The Manager's Book of Quotations* (New York: AMACOM, 1991).

8 Dale Carnegie, *How to Win Friends and Influence People* (New York: Simon and Schuster, 1964), p. 247.

9 Bruce Ganem, reply to author query.

10 Robert Grady, reply to author query.

11 Rey Carr, reply to author query. Carr has worked on how young people and adults can use questions as catalysts to develop relationships.

12 John Tessier, reply to author query.

13 Sam Albert, president, Sam Albert Associates, reply to author query.

14 Peter Senge, *The Fifth Discipline* (New York: Doubleday, 1990).

15 Robert Half International press release June 9, 1999.

16 Kenneth R. Hey and Peter D. Moore, *The Caterpillar Doesn't Know: How Personal Change Is Creating Organizational Change* (New York: Free Press, 1998).

17 Arie De Geus, *The Living Company: Habits for Survival in a Turbulent Business Environment* (Cambridge, Mass.: Harvard Business School Press, 1997), pp. 64–66.

18 Mike Montefusco, reply to author query. Montefusco is also quoted in chapters 11 and 13.

19 Mike Montefusco, reply to author query.

20 Margie Sweeny, reply to author query. She is also quoted in chapters 10, 11, 17, and 18. She is the CEO of TASL.com.

21 Jerry Hirshberg, *The Creative Priority: Putting Innovation to Work in Your Business* (New York: Harper Business, 1998).

22 Don Peppers and Martha Rogers, *The One-to-One Future: Building Relationships One Customer at a Time* (New York: Currency Doubleday, 1993), p. 336–337.

23 Mackie Morris, conversation with the author.

24 Pat Lencioni, reply to author query.

25 Diana Whitney, reply to author query. She is active with the Corporation for Positive Change and is an advocate of Appreciative Inquiry.

26 Kevin Kelly, *New Rules for the New Economy: 10 Radical Strategies for a Connected World* (New York: Viking, 1998), p. 88.

27 Roger Fisher and William Ury, *Getting to Yes: Negotiating Agreement without Giving In* (Boston: Houghton Mifflin, 1981), p. 117.

28 Peter Fahrenkamp, reply to author query. Fahrenkamp is a principal at Pax Consulting and is working with Ernest & Young on collaborative group facilitation.

Chapter 2

1 Quoted in Quinn Spitzer and Ron Evans, *Heads You Win: How the Best Companies Think* (New York: Simon and Schuster, 1997), p. 41.

2 Peter Drucker, *The Practice of Management* (New York: Harper Business), p. 351. This book is a classic (a term I rarely apply to a business book) well worth review today.

3 Gerald Butt, *The Spectator,* April 24, 1999, p. 22.

4 Helena Smith, "Down with Charles," *Prospect,* January 1999, p. 10.

5 Robert Helmreich, reply to author query. His research, while focused on airline pilots, has a wide range of applications in any situation where senior members interact with juniors. I was struck by the parallels to the situations found in newsroom control rooms where instant decisions have to be made.

6 John Tessier, reply to author query.

7 Douglas Stone, Bruce Patton, and Sheila Heen, *Difficult Conversations* (New York: Viking Penguin, 2000), from the book's press release.

8 Laurence J. Peter, *Peter's Quotations: Ideas for Our Time* (New York: Morrow, 1977), p. 468.

9 Guy Claxton, *Hare Brain, Tortoise Mind—How Intelligence Increases When You Think Less* (Hopewell, N.J.: Ecco Press, 1999), p. 6.

10 Alex Pattakos, reply to author query. He has worked on leadership development and strategic planning and is the author of *Intuition at Work: Pathways to Unlimited Possibilities.*

Chapter 3

1 Reply to author query. Jeff De Cagna thinks we learn best when we think of ourselves as explorers and he says "certainly one of the primary exploring 'tools' a learner has is the ability to ask challenging, provocative and generative questions." He is also quoted in chapters 13, and 18.

2 Ibid.

3 Michael Goodman, reply to author query. He is the author of seven books, including *Corporate Communications for Executives.*

4 Arnold Cooper, reply to author query. He received the International Award for Entrepreneurship and Small Business Research in 1997.

5 Michael Oneal, "Just What Is an Entrepreneur?" *Business Week/ Enterprise,* 1993, p. 105.

6 Peter Drucker, *People and Performance: The Best of Peter Drucker on Management* (New York: Harper's College Press, 1977).

7 Suzanne Vaughan, reply to author query. She is the president of Suzanne Vaughan & Associates.

8 Kathleen O'Toole, "Researchers Explore Knowledge Networks in Firms and Economies," *Stanford News* press release, August 11, 1999.

9 This includes such schools as Dartmouth College and the University of Pennsylvania's Wharton School of Business.

10 Mossimo Gianulli, interviewed by the author and Jodi Stewart for "On the Money," KTVU, October 21, 1994.

11 Pat Lencioni, reply to author query.

12 "A Liberal Education," T. H. Huxley, *Burke's Speech on Conciliation with America,* edited by Howard Bement (Chicago: Laurel Book Company, 1930), p. 6

13 Tom Peters, *Liberation Management—Necessary Disorganization for the Nanosecond Nineties* (New York: Knopf, 1992).

Chapter 4

1 Tom Peters, *Thriving on Chaos* (New York: Random House, 1995), p. 438.

2 Paul Theroux, "Portrait," *Prospect,* February 1999, p. 43.

3 Charles Handy, *The Hungry Spirit beyond Capitalism: A Quest for Purpose in the Modern World* (New York: Broadway Books, 1999), pp. 65–66.

4 James Robinson, "Conference Tackles Issue of Youth Citizenship," *Stanford News* press release, June 29, 1999.

5 A. Stephanie Stanor, "A Study of the Relationship between Teaching Techniques and Students' Achievement on High Cognitive Level Question-Asking Skills," Ph.D. dissertation, University of Chicago, 1981, p. 102.

6 Ibid., p. 38.

7 Dennis Rivers, reply to author query.

8 "Creating a New Corporation," *U.S. News & World Report,* May 8, 2000, p. 42.

9 Robert Mondavi, interviewed by Brian Banmiller for "On the Money," KTVU, November 7, 1995. If you had to pick a business to have as a lifelong passion, wine and food is not a bad one to pick. Mondavi said he chose the business not to make money but to live his life and enjoy it with his children. How many of us get that from our job?

Chapter 5

1 Quoted in Mary Bray Wheeler (general ed.), *The Basic Meeting Manual* (Nashville: Nelson, 1986), p. 317.

2 Stephen Stuntz, reply to author query.

3 David Shaw, Media Critic Scripps Howard Foundation, 35th Annual Ted Scripps Memorial Lecture, University of Nevada, Reno Reynolds School of Journalism, March 24, 1999, p. 16.

4 Robert Knowlton, reply to author query. He says one trainer, Michael Grinder, taught him about the power of asking for permission.

5 Arnold Wytenburg, reply to author query. He is a consultant to both the private and the government sectors.

6 Dale Carnegie, *How to Win Friends and Influence People* (New York: Simon and Schuster, 1964), p. 186.

7 Mick Yates, reply to author query. Yates has worked in Europe, the United States, and Asia. He has an interest in Asia studies and leadership development. He is quoted also in chapters 10, 11, and 13.

8 "America's Q&A Man," *Newsweek,* June 15, 1987, p. 50.

9 Thomas Faragher, reply to author query.

10 Mike Turner, reply to author query.

11 Bruce Woolpert, reply to author query. His company has been recognized as an example of progressive management.

12 Mick Yates, reply to author query.

Chapter 6

1 Jay Ferneborg, reply to author query. Ferneborg studied interpersonal communications at USC, where he learned that "communication" occurs on many levels [and] it can often be very predictable and manipulated to move in certain directions. Ferneborg is with a retained executive search firm.

2 Ibid.

3 Ibid.

4 Ibid.

5 Ibid.

6 Gerry Sexton, reply to author query. He is writing a book called *The Forty Fabulous Hours,* to help people redefine their work.

Chapter 7

1 Dan Thompson, reply to author query.

2 Amy Taylor, reply to author query. She is a business manager at the University of Delaware.

Chapter 8

1 Ron Popeil, interviewed by the author for a story for "On the Money," KTVU, November 17, 1995. He told me that his other secret to success is that he is on 500 to 600 TV stations at a time so he can make money.

2 David Palmer, reply to author query. Palmer took a class from the management theorist Peter Drucker at Claremont Graduate University, where Palmer says he first heard a question Drucker asked clients and that I included in chapter 18.

3 Bruce Woolpert, reply to author query.

4 Walter Dean, reply to author query. Dean is the associate director of the Pew Center for Civic Journalism. The center works with journalists to help them better connect with their readers or audiences to try to help those citizens become reengaged in the community.

5 Jay Arthur, reply to author query. Arthur has perhaps the most unique title of all those I surveyed. He calls himself a "corporate shaman," but lest you think this not applicable to the workplace, he says his consulting with Baby Bell helped reduce its billing expenses by $39 million per year. He is quoted also in chapters 9 and 18.

6 Ibid.

7 Pat Lencioni.

8 Jay Arthur.

9 Ibid.

10 Michael Grabham, reply to author query. His title on his business card is "lifelong learner." His company is First2learn.com.

11 Jay Arthur.

12 Jonna Contacos, reply to author query.

13 Ruth Owades, interviewed for "On the Money," KTVU, April 29, 1994.

14 Mark S. A. Smith, reply to author query.

15 Dale Carnegie, *How to Win Friends and Influence People* (New York: Simon and Schuster, 1964), p. 246.

16 Michael Lee, reply to author query. He is also the author of three books on working with people from other cultures, one of which is *Multicultural Tendencies*.

17 Ibid.

18 G. Richard Shell, *Bargaining for Advantage* (New York: Viking, 1999), pp. 144–145.

19 Mark McCormack, *What They Don't Teach You at Harvard Business School* (Toronto: Bantam, 1984), p. 133.

20 Seth Godin, reply to author query. Godin is the author of *Permission Marketing,* Simon and Schuster, 1999.

21 Charles Goeldner, reply to author query.

Chapter 9

1 Debra Giampoli, reply to author query. She is quoted also in chapters 10, 13, and 18.

2 Maurice Kanbar, interviewed by the author for "On the Money," KTVU, October 7, 1994. Kanbar showed another characteristic of a questioning attitude. He challenged the assumption that vodka was something made in Russia. He told me he had great faith that America can produce the best vodka in the world.

3 Jacques Barzun, "The Paradoxes of Creativity," *American Scholar* 58 (1989): 350, quoted by Alan G. Robinson and Sam Stern, *Corporate Creativity: How Innovation and Improvement Actually Happen* (San Francisco: Berrett-Koehler, 1998), p. 193.

4 Robert Buckman, reply to author query.

5 John Bourne, reply to author query.

6 Graham Raulinson, reply to author query. Rawlinson has been involved in helping people solve learning and behavior problems for thirteen years.

7 Dale Parish, reply to author query.

8 Perry Gruber, reply to author query. He is a press officer with Bonneville Power Administration.

9 Richard Sojka, reply to author query.

10 Paul Plsek, reply to author query. He is also quoted in chapters 10 and 18.

11 Ibid.

12 Graham Rawlinson, reply to author query.

13 Alex D'Anci, reply to author query.

14 Ibid.

15 Anne Robinson, reply to author query. Robinson uses the title "Creativity Connoisseur" and at age 86 still is active in the training and development field.

16 Bob Phillips, reply to author query.

17 Anne Robinson, reply to author query.

18 Madeleine Homan, reply to author query.

19 Dan Gillmor, "Inspired Minds Make All the Difference," *San Jose Mercury News,* August 15, 1999, p. 7E.

20 Paul Plsek, reply to author query.

21 Alex D'Anci, reply to author query.

22 Kristine Piazza Belser, reply to author query.

23 Barbara Waugh, reply to author query.

24 Rebecca Neff, reply to author query. She is the director of creative solutions at the SAS Institute, Inc.

25 Curtis Swisher, reply to author query.

26 Janelle Barlow, reply to author query.

27 Ibid.

28 Jay Arthur, reply to author query. He is also quoted in chapters 8 and 18.

29 Ibid.

30 Ibid.

31 Cathy de Seton, reply to author query.

32 Alain Rostain, reply to author query. Rostain runs Creative Advantage, a company that is based on his belief that improvisational theater techniques can help organizations.

33 Ruth Ann Hattori, reply to author query.

34 Dr. Edward Rockey, reply to author query. He is a professor of Behavioral Science at Pepperdine University.

35 Ellen Domb, reply to author query. Domb describes the *TRIZ Journal* as "the only English language publication on TRIZ, the 'Theory of Inventive Problem Solving.'"

36 David Kelley, interviewed by the author for "On the Money," KTVU, May 2, 1995. He says that the interface for many products is too difficult; products should be obvious in how you use them.

37 Arthur VanGundy, reply to author query.

38 Alex D'Anci, reply to author query.

39 Ibid.

40 Bruce Ganem, reply to author query.

41 Fred DaMert, interviewed for "On the Money," KTVU, March 28, 1994.

42 Quoted in Alan G. Robinson and Sam Stern, *Corporate Creativity: How Innovation and Improvement Actually Happen* (San Francisco: Berrett-Koehler, 1998), p. 49.

43 Alan G. Robinson and Sam Stern, *Corporate Creativity: How Innovation and Improvement Actually Happen* (San Francisco: Berrett-Koehler, 1998), pp. 11–12.

44 William Hodges, reply to author query. Hodges also writes a newspaper column on the importance of having a positive attitude.

45 Sue Scott, interviewed by the author for "On the Money," KTVU, March 22, 1994.

Chapter 10

1 Edward Miller, "Managing for Performance," Poynter Institute for Media Studies, Oakland, California, May 1999.

2 Louise Rehling, reply to author query. Rehling is an Associate Professor at the College of Humanities at San Francisco State University.

3 Debra Giampoli, reply to author query. She is the director of consumer promotions for the New Meals Division of Kraft Foods. She is quoted also in chapters 9, 13, and 18.

4 Mark Rice, reply to author query. Rice is the director for technological entrepreneurship at RPI's Lally School of Management and Technology. He is also quoted in chapter 18.

5 Ibid.

6 Ibid.

7 Ibid.

8 John Trebes, reply to author query. Trebes was involved in the U.S. space program, from the Mercury program to the space shuttle, and is the president of Future Scan Consultants.

9 Ibid. Trebes says he was asked to do this and found it a memorable experience.

10 Jim Benham, interviewed by Brian Banmiller for "Banmiller on Business," KTVU, December 17, 1992.

11 Mark Sanborn, reply to author query. He is the president of Sanborn & Associates, Inc. He is also quoted in chapter 18.

12 Ron MacNeil, reply to author query.

13 Mike Bull, reply to author query. Bull is a senior project manager with IBM in Canada. He is quoted also in chapter 11.

14 Ibid.

15 Debra Giampoli, reply to author query.

16 Mick Yates, reply to author query. He is also quoted in chapters 5, 11, and 13.

17 Margie Sweeny, reply to author query. She is also quoted in chapters 1, 11, 17, and 18.

18 Grant Todd, reply to author query. Todd's company is The Prevail Organization, a consulting firm that focuses on the role of knowledge as it relates to leadership. He is quoted also in chapter 13.

19 Gary Lockwood, reply to author query. He is also quoted in chapter 1.

20 Paul Plsek, reply to author query. He is also quoted in chapters 9 and 18.

21 David Cohen, interviewed by Brian Banmiller for "On the Money," KTVU, June 14, 1993.

22 Bill Boyd, reply to author query. Boyd is one of the members of the Leadership and Management Faculty at the Poynter Institute. He was one of my instructors for a program in leadership. Dr. Boyd teaches and consults on leadership, group dynamics, and organizational change.

Chapter 11

1 Herb Kelleher, interviewed by Brian Banmiller for "On the Money," KTVU, December 2, 1994. Of all the business executives I have met, he struck me as the one who had learned the value of asking questions of everyone. He was constantly asking people how they were doing and in a friendly, focused fashion. I also saw people ask him how he was doing and call him by his first name. That's not something I imagine happens to most CEOs.

2 Charles Schwab, interviewed by Sharon Owsley for "Banmiller on Business," KTVU, February 26, 1993.

3 James Collins and Jerry Porras, *Built to Last* (New York: Harper Business, 1994), p. 193.

4 George Paajanen, "Why the Wrong People Get Hired," *Executive Excellence,* June 1998, p. 18.

5 Jim Naughton, reply to author query. He has had a distinguished career as a journalist, including reporting from the White House and serving as executive editor of the *Philadelphia Inquirer.*

6 Fred Zehnder, former KTVU news director. Many of the questions in this group come from a set he used to interview reporters for KTVU. In using them, I would explain to candidates that the questions were standard and did not imply anything beyond our wish to gather information. Some assumed they were finalists from the tone of these questions.

7 Margie Sweeny, reply to author query.

8 Bill Hart, reply to author query. He is also quoted in chapter 2.

9 Albert Yu, *Creating the Digital Future* (New York: Free Press), p. 109.

10 Max DePree, *Leadership is an Art* (East Lansing: Michigan State University Press, 1987), p. 127.

11 Gary Omura, reply to author query.

12 Geoffrey Fountain, reply to author query.

13 Paula Becker, reply to author query. She is also quoted in chapter 17.

14 Bill Hart, reply to author query.

15 Ibid.

16 Dick Barnett, reply to author query. He says he specializes in working with successful organizations that are stuck. Barnett credits some of the inspiration for these three questions to the author Fernando Flores.

17 Mike Montefusco, reply to author query. He is also quoted in chapters 1 and 13.

18 Edward Miller, "Managing for Performance: Getting Started," Poynter Institute for Media Studies, Oakland, California, May 1999.

19 Paul Hampel, reply to author query.

20 Jonna Contacos, reply to author query.

21 Ibid.

22 Bill Hart, reply to author query.

23 Mary Hessler Key, reply to author query. She is president of Mary Key & Associates and past executive director of Inc. Magazine's Eagles CEO program.

24 Jonna Contacos, reply to author query.

25 Bill Boyd, reply to author query.

26 Claudia Deutsch, "Competitors Can Teach You a Lot, but the Lessons Can Hurt," *New York Times,* July 18, 1999, business section, p. 4. Continental Airlines asked this question of its employees.

27 Margie Sweeny, reply to author query.

28 Edward Miller, "Managing for Performance: Getting Started," Poynter Institute for Media Studies, Oakland, California, May 1999.

29 Michael Grabham, reply to author query.

30 Mick Yates, reply to author query. He is quoted also in chapters 5, 10, and 13.

31 Pat Lencioni, reply to author query.

32 Mike Bull, reply to author query. He is quoted also in chapter 10.

33 Gary Noseworthy, reply to author query.

34 Ibid.

35 Mary Cusack, reply to author query. Cusack has the unique title of Supreme Commander of a consulting firm named Joy Quest, which has worked with companies as diverse as The Body Shop and Kaiser Permanente.

36 Mike Turner, reply to author query.

Chapter 12

1 Lucetta Marty, reply to author query. She is the director of The Creativity Tank.

2 Peller Marion, interviewed by the author for "On the Money," KTVU, April 19, 1994.

3 Dr. Parthenia Franks, reply to author query. She is a speech pathologist and college professor. She is quoted also in chapter 15.

4 Bert Decker, reply to author query. Decker, whom I've called on to comment on political debates, talks about some of these ideas in his book *You've Got to Be Believed to Be Heard,* St. Martin's Press 1993. Decker is quoted also in chapter 15.

5 Barbara Waugh, reply to author query.

Chapter 13

1 Christopher Fildes, "City and Suburban," *Spectator,* October 3, 1998, p. 34.

2 Audrey Rice Oliver, interviewed for "On the Money," KTVU, March 11, 1994.

3 Quoted by Gayle Pergamit and Chris Peterson in *Leaping the Abyss* (Palo Alto, CA: knOwhere Press, 1997), p. 223.

4 Ian C. Haynes, reply to author query.

5 Paul Chaffee, reply to author query.

6 Dr. Serge Bouwens, reply to author query. He has been involved in company reorganization, information strategy, and Intranet applications.

7 Barbara Waugh, "The Self-Organizing Transformation of Hewlett-Packard Laboratories," Web site www.hpl.hp.com.

8 Grant Todd, reply to author query. Grant is also quoted in chapter 10.

9 Bruce Elkin, reply to author query.

10 Dr. Jim Botkin, reply to author query. He is based in Cambridge, Massachusetts.

11 Fred Martin, reply to author query.

12 Mike Montefusco, reply to author query. He is also quoted in chapters 1 and 11.

13 Barbara McRae, reply to author query. She is quoted also in chapter 17.

14 Bob Phillips, reply to author query.

15 Mary Lippitt, reply to author query.

16 Amy Taylor, reply to author query.

17 Debra Giampoli, reply to author query. She is quoted also in chapters 9, 10, and 18.

18 Darrell Mann, reply to author query.

19 Christopher Fildes, "City and Suburban," *Spectator,* November 28, 1998, p. 32.

20 Jonathan Littman, "Software's New Icon," *Upside,* September 1999, p. 96.

21 Perry Pascarella, "Winning Trust," *Executive Excellence,* June 1998, p. 19.

22 Jeff DeCagna, reply to author query. He is also quoted in chapters 3 and 18.

23 Ibid.

24 Mick Yates, reply to author query. He is also quoted in chapters 5, 10, and 11.

25 Rita Rizzo, reply to author query. Rizzo does training and consulting with leadership teams in the United States and in the United Kingdom.

26 Peter Reding, reply to author query. He is also quoted in chapter 17.

27 T. J. Rogers, interviewed by Brian Banmiller for "On the Money" September 13, 1993.

Chapter 14

1 Dr. Maynard Brusman, interviewed by the author for "On the Money," KTVU, January 23, 1996. He cautioned that corporate cutbacks have a long-lasting impact on the company. Productivity can drop because, if nothing else, the remaining employees are looking for work in case they too get fired.

2 Frances Quittel, interviewed by the author for "On the Money," KTVU, May 23, 1995. In 1995, she described the employment situation as being "out of control" for while the economy was doing fine, companies continued to lay off employees.

3 Mary Hessler Key, reply to author query. She is quoted also in chapter 11.

Chapter 15

1 Sylvia Mills, reply to author query. She is a licensed psychologist.

2 Marian Huttenstine, reply to author query. She is a professor at Mississippi State University.

3 Ibid.

4 Ibid.

5 Dr. Richard Rathe, reply to author query. He based some of his discussion on the BATHE technique in Marian R. Stuart and Joseph A. Lieberman III, *The Fifteen Minute Hour* (Westport, CT: Greenwood, Inc., 1993). He teaches a course in basic clinical skills to first-year medical students and sees patients one day a week.

6 Irving Lee, *Harvard Business Review*, January–February 1954, p. 284.

7 Peter Senge, *The Fifth Discipline* (New York: Doubleday, 1990), p. 199.

8 Ann Rosenthal, reply to author query. She told me she has always been in the information acquisition business and still is, as a scholar.

9 Parthenia Franks, reply to author query. She is also quoted in chapter 12.

10 Ibid.

11 Paul Krivonos, reply to author query. He is professor and chair of the Department of Communication Studies, California State University at Northridge.

12 Bert Decker, reply to author query. Decker is quoted also in chapter 12.

13 Dana May Casperson, reply to author query. Casperson is the author of *Power Etiquette* (New York: AMACOM, 1999).

14 Barbara Walters, *How to Talk with Practically Anybody about Practically Anything* (Garden City, N.Y.: Doubleday, 1970), p. xiv.

15 Dana May Casperson, reply to author query.

16 Quinn Spitzer and Ron Evans, *Heads You Win: How the Best Companies Think* (New York: Simon and Schuster, 1997) p. 118.

17 Mike Turner, reply to author query.

Chapter 16

1 George Zimmer, interviewed by "On the Money," KTVU, April 19, 1995.

2 David Kelley, interviewed by the author for "On the Money," KTVU, July 7, 1995. He says many inventors are so paranoid that they suffocate their idea by refusing to show it to people. He would try to convince people to find a company that would benefit from the product idea and disclose it to them in some way.

3 Kathryn McKee, reply to author query.

4 Bradley Ogden, interviewed by the author for "On the Money," KTVU, October 6, 1995. He told me he was working from eight in the morning until midnight.

Chapter 17

1 Dr. Mike Turner, reply to author query.

2 Jennifer Rousseau Sedlock, reply to author query.

3 Rey Carr, reply to author query. He is quoted also in chapters 1 and 3.

4 Barbara McRae, reply to author query. She is quoted also in chapter 13.

5 Peter Fahrenkamp, reply to author query. He is also quoted in chapter 1.

6 Peter Reding, reply to author query. He is also quoted in chapter 13.

7 Peter Fahrenkamp, reply to author query.

8 Ibid.

9 Barbara McRae, reply to author query.

10 Peter Reding, reply to author query.

11 Madeleine Homan, reply to author query.

12 John Nagy, reply to author query.

13 Paula Becker, reply to author query. She is a business communication coach who worked on a merger of two Fortune 50 companies. She said the challenge was to find the fear employees were feeling and defuse it through open communication. Becker is quoted also in chapter 11.

14 Ibid.

15 Madeleine Homan, reply to author query.

16 John Tessier, reply to author query.

17 John Nagy, reply to author query.

18 Barbara McRae, reply to author query.

19 Madeleine Homan, reply to author query.

20 Paula Becker, reply to author query.

21 John Nagy, reply to author query.

22 Margie Sweeny, reply to author query. She is also quoted in chapters 1, 10, and 18.

23 Margie Sweeny, reply to author query.

24 Curtis Sittenfeld, "The Most Creative Man in Silicon Valley," *Fast Company,* June 2000, p. 286.

Chapter 18

1 Jeff DeCagna, reply to author query. He is also quoted in chapters 3 and 13.

2 Mark Sanborn, reply to author query. He is quoted also in chapter 10.

3 Edward Miller, "Managing for Performance: Seven Steps to High Performance," Poynter Institute for Media Studies, p. 4.

4 Peter Drucker, *Managing for Results* (New York: Harper and Row, 1964), p. 178.

5 Warren Bennis, "Speed and Complexity," *Executive Excellence,* June 1998, p. 4.

6 Margie Sweeny, reply to author query. She is also quoted in chapters 1, 10, 11, 17, and 18.

7 Jay Arthur, reply to author query. He is based in Denver and is currently working on a book entitled *Take Control of Your Mind and Your Life: Nine Steps to Mental Mastery.*

8 Quinn Spitzer and Ron Evans, *Heads You Win: How the Best Companies Think* (New York: Simon and Schuster, 1997), p. 245.

9 Jay Arthur, reply to author query.

10 Paul Plsek, reply to author query. He is also quoted in chapters 9 and 10.

11 Gary Noseworthy, reply to author query.

12 Richard Sojka, reply to author query.

13 Henry Kissinger, "The Long Shadow of Vietnam," *Newsweek,* May 1, 2000, p. 47.

14 Quinn Spitzer and Ron Evans, *Heads You Win: How the Best Companies Think* (New York: Simon and Schuster, 1997), p. 245.

15 Max DePree, *Leadership Is an Art* (East Lansing: Michigan State University Press, 1987), p. 112.

16 Terry Pearce, reply to author query. He is the author of *Leading Out Loud* (San Francisco: Jossey-Bass 1995) and has consulted with Charles Schwab and Co.

17 Max DePree, *Leadership Is an Art* (East Lansing: Michigan State University Press, 1987), p. 112.

18 John Seely Brown, reply to author query.

19 Andrew Zacharakis, reply to author query.

20 James Belasco, *Teaching the Elephant to Dance* (New York: Crown, 1990), p. 147.

21 Niki Kunene, reply to author query. She quotes Joe Barker as saying something like this.

22 Mark Rice, reply to author query. He is also quoted in chapter 10.

23 Ibid.

24 Kathleen Hagfors, reply to author query.

25 Ibid.

26 Bill Gellermann, reply to author query. He is a registered organization development consultant and the coauthor of a book tentatively titled *Embracing Business Chaos,* which looks at how organizations must learn "to manage and create change in order to survive and thrive."

27 Alex D'Anci, reply to author query.

28 Mariann Jelinek, reply to author query. Her most recent book was *The Innovation Marathon,* Jossey-Bass 1993. She is working with the National Science Foundation, where she has the title of Program Director, Innovation and Organizational Change.

29 Peter Senge, "Sharing Knowledge," *Executive Excellence,* June 1998, p. 11.

30 Edward Miller, conversation with the author. Mr. Miller has been quoted in chapters 10 and 11. He certainly demonstrates the power of questions in his work as a member of the Leadership and Management Faculty at the Poynter Institute. His career has spanned work at the International Edition of the *New York Herald Tribune* and a stint as publisher of the Allentown *Morning Call.*

31 Tom Peters, *The Tom Peters Seminar* (New York: Vintage Books, 1994).

32 Warren Bennis, "Speed and Complexity," *Executive Excellence,* June 1998, p. 4.

33 Jeff De Cagna, reply to author query.

34 Warren Bennis, "Speed and Complexity," *Executive Excellence,* June 1998, p. 3.

35 David Palmer, reply to author query. He is also quoted in chapter 8.

36 Adam Bryant, "Want a More Aerodynamic Op-Ed Page?" *Newsweek,* August 16, 1999, p. 42.

37 Andrew Zacharakis, reply to author query.

38 Barbara Waugh, reply to author query. A Hewlett-Packard veteran, she is involved in what is called the "World's Best Industrial Research Laboratory."

39 Ibid.

40 Ibid.

41 Max DePree, *Leadership Is an Art* (East Lansing: Michigan State University Press, 1987), p. 17.

42 Susanne Alexander, reply to author query. She is a journalist and writing consultant.

43 Jeff De Cagna, reply to author query.

44 Kathleen Hagfors, reply to author query.

45 Debra Giampoli, reply to author query. She is also quoted in chapters 9, 10, and 13.

46 Roger Kaufman, reply to author query.

47 John Hawkins, "Influence and the Challenge of Trust," *Executive Excellence,* June 1998, p. 16.

48 Mike Turner, reply to author query.

49 Max DePree, *Leadership Is an Art* (East Lansing: Michigan State University Press, 1987), p. 112.

50 Bruce Elkin, reply to author query.

51 Charles Handy, *The Hungry Spirit: Beyond Capitalism: A Quest for Purpose in the Modern World* (New York: Broadway Books), pp. 103, 65–66.

52 Jeff DeCagna, reply to author query.

53 Ibid.

54 Kathleen Hagfors, reply to author query.

55 Gary Opper, quoting Weston Mayor Harry Rosen, "Thinking Ethically," *Equity,* Summer 1999, p. 15.

56 John F. Kennedy, *Profiles in Courage* (New York: Pocket Books, 1960), p. 178.

57 John Tessier, reply to author query.

Conclusion

1 John Stuart Mill, Inaugural Address as Rector, University of St. Andrew, February 1, 1867.

Index